The
Political Economy
of
RACISM

RAYMOND S. FRANKLIN
SOLOMON RESNIK

DEDICATION: To M.B.F. and B.K.

Preface

This book explores the nature of contemporary racism against black Americans in the broader context of general economic and political problems. Our basic assumption is that the specifics of the black malaise cannot be understood unless they are viewed as an outgrowth of general and basic forces in American society, some of which are independent of the particular factors that characterize the black community. It is the interplay between the general forces of American society and the specific forces within the black community which needs to be understood in dynamic terms—not one or the other separately. The book thus juxtaposes both the economic and political forces of American society with the forces that are operating to shape and define the specific nature of the black condition. This leads us to discuss areas such as the historic legacy of racism, the economics of discrimination, the black ghetto, class-race-ethnic divisions, various manifestations of black nationalism in relation to the American political system, broad economic policy considerations, and strategies for change.

In putting together these varied components of the race question, we hope to cast light on the whole system in relation to its major casualty—approximately 25 million black Americans.

Acknowledgments
The authors would like to note their appreciation for assistance rendered by Jane Cagen, Albert Fried, Jennifer Hunt, Robert Lekachman, Howard Sherman, William K. Tabb, Ilja Wachs, Alan Wolfe, and Michael Wreszin.
We would also like to thank the Research Foundation of the City University of New York for its financial assistance in the year 1970–1971. Finally, we wish to indicate our particular appreciation to Fred Goldman, Barbara Kaplan, and Doris Wallace.

Contents

CHAPTER 1

Problems, Issues, and Paradoxes

The ways in which black Americans have been characterized have changed radically since 1954. As a result of the civil rights movement, Southern economic boycotts, and the riots and disruptions of the 1960s, reflections about black history and interpretations of the current state of black-white inequality have been upset.

Historians, for example, have been forced to reexamine the position that blacks "accepted" their humiliating position in the early periods of American history. They no longer find it possible to accept Commager and Morrison's account (written in 1942) that "the majority of slaves were adequately fed, well-cared for and apparently happy. . . . Although brought to America by force, the incurably optimistic Negro soon became attached to the country and devoted to his white folk."[1]

The elimination of such mythical judgments about black history has not brought equanimity to historians.

[1]H. S. Commager, and S. E. Morrison, *Growth of the American Republic* (2nd rev. ed.). New York: Oxford University Press, 1942, p. 537.

The debate among and between black and white historians remains unsettled as to the extent of black accommodation to white-determined circumstances. They neither agree on the extent to which blacks pursued revolutionary changes and employed revolutionary tactics on the one hand, nor on the relative importance of nationalism and separatism versus integration and civil rights, on the other. The clarification of these differences is not simply academic. Much of the reasoning employed to analyze the present state of the black condition alludes to the nature of the black past and the black legacy. But to use the legacy of the past—which itself is often misinterpreted or misunderstood—in order to explain the present nature of black-white relations is at best ambiguous and at worst useless.

Another major problem for analysis lies in the apparent paradox noted by Nathan Glazer: "Something very strange is happening in the American racial crisis. On the one hand, the concrete situation of Negro Americans is rapidly improving. . . . On the other hand, as the Negro's situation improves, his political attitudes are becoming more extreme."[2] The two oft-repeated explanations of this apparent paradox, as Glazer points out, are the theory of rising expectations and the idea that improvement begets a "desire for change because people begin to feel stronger and more potent."[3] Although Glazer acknowledges that there is some truth to these explanations, in the final analysis he rejects them. He suggests instead that "somehow" black militancy has its own momentum, feeds on itself, and possibly has no connection with reality. Embodied in the word "somehow" is Glazer's lack of understanding of why black political militancy has manifested itself in its present form.[4]

The experience of the 1960s has not only sent some well-established social scientists into a state of nervous bewilderment about black militancy, but has also led to some contradictory explanations of the black population's lagging socioeconomic status in relation to that of whites. In his introduction to the Kerner Commission's report on civil disorders, for example, Tom Wicker of the *New York Times,* has written: "What white Americans have never fully understood—but what the Negro can never forget—is that white society is deeply implicated in the ghetto.

[2]N. Glazer, "The Negro's Stake in America's Future," *New York Times Magazine*, September 22, 1968, p. 30.

[3]N. Glazer, p. 31.

[4]For a discussion of Glazer's reasoning, see Chapter 9 of this book.

White institutions created it, white institutions maintain it, and white society condones it."[5] In a similar vein James Boggs, a revolutionary black militant from Detroit, states:

> *Racism is the systematized oppression by one race of another. In other words, the various forms of oppression within every sphere of social relations—economic exploitation, military subjugation, political subordination, cultural devaluation, psychological violence, sexual degradation, verbal abuse, etc.—together make up a whole interacting and developing process which operate[s] so normally and naturally and [is] so much a part of the existing institutions of the society that the individuals involved are barely conscious of their operation.*[6]

Since such views about the pervasiveness of racism and oppression are commonly held, the appearance of opposite generalizations—that is, ongoing oppression explains very little of the relatively inferior status of black Americans—are unexpected. Yet some social scientists, of varied ideological bents, are of the latter persuasion. One of the most articulate is Edward C. Banfield, a conservative political scientist whose position is well known and who has had significant influence in academic and government quarters:

> *If, overnight, Negroes turned white most of them would go on living under much the same handicaps for a longer time to come. The great majority of New Whites would continue working at the same jobs, living in the same neighborhoods, and sending their children to the same schools. . . . Today the Negro's main disadvantage is . . . that he is the most recent unskilled, and hence relatively low-income immigrant to reach the city from a backward rural area. . . . Almost everything said about the problems of the Negro tends to exaggerate the purely racial aspects*

[5]T. Wicker, "Introduction," *Report of the National Advisory Commission on Civil Disorders*. New York: Bantam Books, 1968, p. vii.

[6]J. Boggs, *Racism and the Class Struggle: Further Pages from a Black Worker's Notebook*. New York: Monthly Review Press, 1970, pp. 147–148.

> *of the situation. . . . The importance of racial factors is exagger-*
> *ated implicitly by any statement that fails–as almost all do–to*
> *take account of the many nonracial factors such as income, class,*
> *education, and place of origin. . . . The continuing causes of the*
> *Negro's problems . . . very often have little or nothing to do with*
> *race.*[7]

If income disparities are readily explained by nonracial black-white differences such as level of education, skill, family background, place of origin, how are these "explanatory" differences explained? Banfield does not inform us. He ultimately rests his case by implying that some kind of native endowment of blacks is the cause of their inferior status.

Between the positions that racism explains everything and that it explains nothing, there is a middle, eclectic view that seeks to "explain" which portion of the black-white socioeconomic status differences can be attributed to racial discrimination and which to "objective" variables, such as differences in education, age, or place of origin. This view often leads to a total preoccupation with the measurement of black-white economic differences as these are "caused" by variables which can easily be abstracted from a larger social and political context. However, it is precisely the omission of the larger context that makes many studies of race relations and race conflict irrelevant. What are absent in all such interpretations of racial disparities are the specific relationships between class and race that have combined to determine the general status position of blacks. It is ironic that the position articulated by Edward C. Banfield, who believes strongly in the verities of the private market, should be similar in some respects to that expounded by some Marxists whose views of racism are explained purely in class terms. The latter position holds that blacks are simply the poorest of the most propertyless segment of the working class, and therefore their exploitation is less related to blackness than to their lowly economic position vis-à-vis other workers specifically, and the business class in general. The fact that a conservative and a Marxist might come together, though from very different ideological starting points, does not debase the class view of race relations, but should on the contrary, serve as reason for reconsidering it.

---

[7]E. C. Banfield, *The Unheavenly City: The Nature and Future of Our Urban Crisis.* Boston: Little, Brown & Company, 1970, pp. 68–70, 73. Emphasis original.

Our analysis begins with the nature of the *social relations* in the marketplace, involving the specific relationships between black and white workers, black workers and consumers, and black workers and those who own and control the productive apparatus that drives the economy. The marketplace itself, however, is seen as engulfed by the larger society, with its own history and legacy. While we need to know how class-race relations operate in the marketplace in order to determine the character of nonmarket institutions, such as government agencies, political parties, educational practices, and private voluntary associations, it is also necessary to know how the nonmarket institutions react to affect the marketplace.

The interplay between market and nonmarket forces takes place on various levels. A critical one in our analysis is that of the metropolitan area—a structure stratified along class and race lines and containing a melange of political bureaucracies. For a variety of reasons, the dynamics of black-white relations have developed within the context of this structure. The nucleus of the metropolitan area is the central city, the fate of which will be profoundly affected by the black ghetto inside it. The success or failure of government policies with respect to cities generally and blacks specifically depends on how the dynamics of the ghetto are interpreted.

The magnitude and persistence of the black-white urban crisis, however, does not lend itself to a solution that can be divorced from consideration of the whole national economy and political system. Any implementation of a serious black salvation scheme requires the kind and amount of resources that essentially entail a challenge to the entrenched power elites and their interpretation of national interests and priorities. National and local priorities are forged in the political arena from which blacks have so far been excluded. But if blacks emerge as a new political power, they should have a profound effect on the major political parties—especially on the Democratic Party whose southern wing is based on the disenfranchisement of the black population. In addition, traditional local political machines should then be severely tested as blacks become politically conscious majorities in all major central cities.

Any crisis that the American society faces in the near future will be exacerbated by the race problem. Conversely, no serious examination of the race question can be undertaken without considering the broader contours of the American system. A conflict often emerges between the broader American needs as determined by the power structure, and the specific black needs expounded by black spokesmen. For this reason our view leads us to consider some aspects of the American society that normally fall outside the purview of an analysis of race relations proper, for example, the nature of America's pluralistic system, the changing face of America's political structure and governmental operations, and the nature of America's ruling establishment. The same kind of reasoning is also needed when we evaluate the viability of black strategies and goals. We must ask: Do black demands mesh with or complement other forces operating to change the social system? And if black demands and political activities do not mesh with the larger requirements of the system as determined by the authorities, how will the system choose to resist or obstruct them?

For these and related reasons this book is concerned with political economy, that is, with the way specific black-white market relations are transmitted to the general relations that affect the black population's position in the whole system, and with the barriers facing the black struggle to achieve economic and political equality.

CHAPTER 2

The Legacy of Racism

The main objective of this chapter is to challenge the idea, asserted only too often, that aspects of the black legacy perpetuate the present state of the black population's inferior status. We are concerned here with explaining the relationship between the past and the present.

Racism and discriminatory behavior in the United States derive from the development of the slave economy. Kenneth Stampp points out that "Negro and white servants of the 17th century seemed to be remarkably unconcerned about their visible physical differences," but as "slaves in southern agriculture became a deliberate choice (among several alternatives) made by men who sought greater returns than they could obtain from their own labor alone, . . . the distaste for Negroes became an appurtenance of slavery."[1] Other well-known historians have argued along similar lines.[2]

[1]K. Stampp, *The Peculiar Institution*. New York: Vintage Books, 1956, pp. 21–22.

[2]E. Williams, *Capitalism and Slavery*. Chapel Hill: University of North Carolina Press, 1944. A distinction between latent and manifest racism is needed here. There is little doubt that latent racism existed before slavery. Its manifest character, however, emerged alongside the development of slave institutions.

White Supremacy—Black Inferiority

The outcome of the American slave system is the legacy of white supremacy. White supremacy is rooted in the development of a slave system in which extreme paternalism and brute force were combined to maintain the discipline necessary to plantation labor and its derivative social system. The social characteristics of the master class, the slave owners, were described by one authority in the following terms:

> *the slaveholder's nature involved a simultaneous sense of dependence and independence; his strength, graciousness, and gentility; his impulsiveness, violence, and unsteadiness. The sense of independence and habit of command developed his poise, grace, and dignity, but the less obvious sense of dependence on a despised other made him violently intolerant of anyone and anything threatening to expose the full nature of his relationship to his slave.*[3]

The supremacist legacy of the master-slave relationship—as it diffused throughout the capitalist system, with its accent on self-reliance, fear of unemployment and poverty, and lust for gain—gave the lowliest white worker a sense of superiority arising from the existence of a contemptible pariah class below him.

The other side of the white-supremacy legacy enforced by paternalism and the machinery of violence is the legacy of black inferiority: repressed feelings leading to role-playing and duplicity in dealing with white masters and finally to outbursts of violence. One, but by no means the only, part of the black legacy was the set of prescriptions to be followed by the "good" slave as designated by the master. The master class sought to shape the black man's mentality by:

1. discouraging his exercise of will and judgment in relation to demands made by the master;
2. seeking to instill a sense of inferiority of self and fear of the master's power;

[3]E. D. Genovese, *The Political Economy of Slavery*. New York: Vintage Books, 1967, p. 33.

3. forcing the acceptance of the master's judgment of what constituted good conduct and sense;
4. encouraging the habit of helplessness and dependence.[4]

In addition to the white-supremacy and black-inferiority legacies, the more general historic assertion that permeates black culture, rhetoric, and actions is the call for freedom, equality, and justice. In music, dance, speech, politics, and acts of sabotage, blacks have expressed their quest to escape from the state of servitude and inferiority which has characterized their condition from the earliest periods of slavery to the present.

The legacies of white supremacy and black inferiority, and the periodic efforts to escape from both, make up the complicated threads which constitute black history as well as many aspects of the contemporary black condition.

From what we have suggested above, the effects of the legacy of the black population on the structure of the black family, black male-female relations, attitudes toward work, education, leisure, and social struggle for change are complex. It is commonly argued that some aspects of the black legacy perpetuate the present condition of blacks. An illustration of this mode of reasoning is the following statement: "black adaptations over generations have in many cases become 'functionally' autonomous. They are, for many, now a preferred way of life; an appropriate life style that includes 'bunking in,' welfare chiseling, borrowing from working women, or women on relief, etc."[5]

In our view it is incorrect to overemphasize the role of the black legacy in the determination and maintenance of the present state of the black population's relatively inferior economic, social, and political position in the American social order. The operational relevance of a legacy is either increased or diminished by the nature of present conditions. The power of the past in determining the present is related to

[4]See M. L. King, Jr., *Where Do We Go From Here: Chaos or Community?* New York: Harper & Row, 1967, p. 39. While there may be blacks who would deny the operational relevance of these slave atavisms for the present—and we do not wish to overclaim their applicability—it is interesting to note that many prescriptions for a "good" black-power militant simply accent the opposite qualities prescribed for a "good" slave, for example, independence, cultivation of one's own standards, black superiority. This point is further developed in Chapter 8.

[5]H. L. Sheppard, "Poverty and the Negro," in B. B. Seligman (ed.), *Poverty as a Public Issue*. New York: Free Press, 1965, p. 124.

how substantively different the present is from the roots of the original conditions that gave birth to the legacy. Discrimination by whites and adaptations to it by blacks have, of course, changed over the years. Nevertheless, de facto parity in American society is far from realized. Blacks are grossly underrepresented in politics, lag considerably behind whites in education, and own much less property and earn much less income than their white counterparts.[6] Consequently, blacks still feel a sense of powerlessness and a sense of being subordinated by a dominant group. The persistence of these inequalities is what vitalizes or sustains the atavisms of the past, although they are more modern in their manifestation. In essence, atavisms do not merely propel themselves independent of the ongoing stimuli. They occur and recur under different guises because they are still "needed" for purposes of "surviving" in the present environment.

As an example, let us consider the way blacks choose the neighborhood in which to live as a consequence of the perpetuation of de facto residential segregation. As numerous studies have repeatedly shown, residential segregation is a result of a concatenation of forces in which an array of property interests and governmental policies converge with racist attitudes.[7] Residential segregation leads to the exclusion not only of low-income propertyless blacks, but also of those middle-class blacks who wish to live in houses and neighborhoods commensurate with their income. Residential segregation can occur because racist sentiments predispose white Americans to believe (1) that all blacks are alike, and (2) that if you let a few blacks into your neighborhood, many others will follow, thereby producing a decline in property values and a general deterioration of the neighborhood. The interesting fact about such reasoning is that it implicitly views the black population in terms of an *assumed* set of lower-class characteristics, which are then applied to all blacks, including those who are not members of the black lower class and who have all the objective class characteristics of the whites who practice the exclusion. It follows that many middle-class blacks experience "pure" discrimination, that is, discrimination unrelated to any characteristic other than that of race.[8]

---

[6]The actual magnitudes involved in these areas are presented and discussed in Chapter 4.
[7]For a more detailed discussion of residential segregation, see Chapter 5.
[8]See R. S. Franklin, *Relative Economic Status of the Negro Male: An Econometric Study.*

Given the forces at work to produce residential segregation, how does a politically weaker and economically poorer or black population respond to these forces? It has been suggested that blacks may actually *choose* to be segregated, that is, they may *choose* to live close together.[9] Residential segregation, in other words, may not necessarily reflect the supremacy impulses of a white dominating society, but, rather, the role of a black legacy in which "living with your own kind" is voluntary.

To talk about black choice in this context is absurd. Of course, some, even many, blacks may choose the security, or protection, or familiarity of a ghetto in favor of the insults, burning crosses, and social harassment that can accompany a relatively small, detested minority in an all-white neighborhood. There is no reason to believe, however, that blacks of all income levels will continue to seek one another out in a larger context of equality and freedom. The test of such a possibility will be possible only *after* blacks have achieved general parity for a *sustained* period. If blacks should then choose to associate with blacks, it would be of little social consequence and would warrant no public notice. Segregation, in other words, is not a social problem when it is voluntary. The racist meaning of segregation in the American context derives from the fact that it is forced. Forced segregation not only sets in motion historically conditioned black adaptations, but allows whites the luxury of indulging in their historically determined white supremacist sentiments and fears, unchallenged by concrete experience. It is relatively easy to attribute any number of "evil" or subhuman characteristics to black persons if black persons are never encountered in multidimensional relations. Forced black segregation leading to degrees of social and psychological separation between the races is the *sine qua non* of white supremacist fantasies, not to mention what it does to the black man's fantasies about the white world.

Similarly, job discrimination against blacks affects the occupational "choices" of blacks as well as "proving" to many whites what they are

Unpublished dissertation, University of California, Berkeley, 1966, Chapter 5. Franklin shows a significant statistical relationship between the over-representation of lower-class blacks in metropolitan areas and income discrimination against middle-class blacks that cannot be explained by such factors as black-white differences in education, age, and occupation.

[9] E. C. Banfield, *The Unheavenly City: The Nature and Future of Our Urban Crisis.* Boston: Little, Brown & Company, 1970, p. 86.

predisposed to believe about the black man's place in the occupational structure. It is often pointed out, for example, that the black community lacks a sufficient supply of black entrepreneurs, allegedly a factor in the stunted growth of black capitalism or black enterprise. It has been argued that black entrepreneurship has been regarded by the religious and communal legacy that permeates aspects of black cultural values: "Black people have the weakest commercial tradition of any people in the United States. For historical reasons . . . and from their African communal tradition, they have been little attracted to trade, shopkeeping, buying and selling, or employing labor for the purpose of exploitation."[10]

This anticommercial legacy, the argument runs, leads talented black males to avoid "choosing" risk-taking jobs or taking advantage of risk-taking opportunities; their "choice" tends to be in the direction of the secure and less remunerative vocations. In other words, black choices reveal a "taste" or "preference" for security that is related to the operation of the black legacy. However, in examining why blacks do not gamble more for bigger gains in their occupational choices, it is necessary to note that black chances of success are not only lower than white chances, but that black failure tends to involve a greater loss than white failure. A black man who does not succeed with one occupational choice may not simply drop down to the next notch on the occupational ladder, as may be the case for his white counterpart.[11] The cost of being wrong, in other words, is greater for blacks than for whites. Again, the adaptive decisions of blacks, while related to their historically determined values, are not made without the ongoing objective factors that make the black legacy a *necessary defense* against the system's unequal distribution of hardships.

[10]E. Ofari, *The Myth of Black Capitalism*. New York: Monthly Review Press, 1970, p. 10.

[11]The problem was observed many years ago by Frederick Douglass when he pointed out that:

> Prejudice against the free colored people in the United States has shown itself nowhere so invincible as among mechanics. The farmer and the professional man cherish no feeling so bitter as that cherished by these. The latter would starve us out of the country entirely. At this moment I can more easily get my son into a lawyer's office to study law than I can into a blacksmith's shop to blow the bellows and to wield the sledge-hammer. Denied the means of learning useful trades, we are pressed into the narrowest limits to obtain a livelihood.

F. Douglass, "A Letter to Harriet Beecher Stowe." In A. C. Littleton and M. W. Burger (eds.), *Black Viewpoints*. New York: Mentor Books, 1971, p. 28.

In regard to black political leadership, it has been suggested that the role of the professional black politician working within the boundaries of a white-dominated political party displays a duplicity not unlike that of the black plantation driver whose job was:

> *to minimize the friction by mediating between the Big House and the slave quarters. On the one hand he was the master's man; he obeyed orders, inflicted punishments, and stood for authority and discipline. On the other hand, he could and did tell the master that the overseer was too harsh, too irregular; that he was incapable of holding the respect of the hands. . . . The driver was the slave's voice in the Big House as he was the master's voice in the quarters.*[12]

Since the driver was neither a clear representative of his own slave constituency nor an unmistakable ally of the master who appointed him to carry out his orders, he was in a perennial state of compromise. How he translated his orders from white masters to keep his black slave constituency in its place, that is, productive and docile, and how he translated the complaints of the slaves to the masters in order to maintain rapport with his slave constituency, was a position which inherently made it almost impossible for a driver to avoid duplicity as a way of life. More likely than not, the driver's social relations, determined by his role in the plantation, probably led to a preoccupation with maintaining his own position at the expense of effectively representing his slave constituents.

The black politician—often dependent upon the white-dominated political party for his job—is in a position parallel to that of the driver. The professional black reformist politician must acquire reforms for his constituency from an alien power constellation, in which he represents a minority that is neither able to get sufficient power in its own terms nor able to be assimilated into the dominant white system. At the same time, he must translate to his black constituency the political limits set by the white political chieftains for whom he works. All too often he finds himself caught in positions that are neither acceptable to his white controllers nor palatable to his black constituents. His rhetoric and his actions

[12]E. D. Genovese, "American Slaves and Their History," *New York Review of Books,* 1970, **15** (10), p. 42.

become grossly unrelated; at an early stage he learns the necessity for duplicity if he is to survive as a politician; his own salvation sooner or later rises above all other considerations.

Conclusion

The legacy of white supremacy, as well as the legacy underlying the modes of black adaptations to a white-dominated society, are independent neither of each other nor of the present circumstances which define black-white relations. The white and black legacies—so frequently alluded to as independent streams of history—will not disappear until the present circumstances of inequality cease to operate in ways that parallel the slave and related conditions which gave birth to them.

CHAPTER 3

The Structure of Discrimination

Continuing discrimination against blacks constitutes a formidable social stockade which prevents them from achieving the basic amenities of whites. The purpose of this chapter is to develop a theoretical framework that can be used to identify and interpret the processes of discrimination and the nature of black-white differences in income, occupation, education, social mobility, and political power. These differences are, of course, the main source of black grievances and the basis of black-white conflict. They shape many of the policies and programs that are concerned with black-white disparities.

Discrimination Defined

Gary Becker, in his important book on the economics of discrimination, seeks to make discrimination a relatively simple extension of the general process that characterizes the way people go about the daily business of making choices:

> *Discrimination and prejudice are not usually said to occur when someone prefers looking at a glamorous Hollywood actress rather than at some other woman; yet they are said to occur when he prefers living next to whites rather than next to Negroes. At best calling just one of these actions "discrimination" requires making subtle and rather secondary distinctions.*[1]

Since making choices is an inevitable part of life and since the nature of any choice involves the exclusion of something else, discriminatory behavior against blacks is here reduced to the trivial problems faced daily by every consumer. Apple-eaters discriminate against oranges and orange growers; orange-eaters discriminate against apples and apple growers. This type of choice model can, of course, be extended to all decision makers in the economy. Its essential weakness when used to explain the nature of discrimination against blacks is that it ignores the context in which choices are being made and, therefore, cannot explain why choices by whites with respect to blacks are not random.

Becker errs because his analysis ignores the distribution of power and the use of a double standard. Discrimination in the context of American society, given its racist heritage, involves antipathetic distinctions that are made systematically (in contrast to randomly-made distinctions) by a dominant white majority to the disadvantage of a subordinate black minority. These distinctions differ from the larger number of distinctions that people make in the normal course of exercising choice in that they involve the systematic use of a double standard by the dominant group. Whites reject blacks for reasons that are different from those they use when they reject other whites. The combination of both dominant-subordinate patterns and a double standard explains the perpetuation of the black population's inferior position in general and its market position in particular.

The systematic use of a double standard manifests itself in gross and subtle ways. For example, with respect to the grosser kinds of discrimination, jobs made available by whites to whites may be very different from those made available to blacks.[2] On the more subtle side, ill-

---

[1]G. Becker, *The Economics of Discrimination.* Chicago: University of Chicago Press, 1957, p. 5.

[2]It should be noted that this kind of discrimination implicitly assumes the unequal distribution of power, since blacks are rarely in the position to decide whether to employ or not to employ whites.

mannered whites may be designated by their own kind as uncouth, while such manners displayed by blacks might be designated as animal-like. Uncouth behavior is still viewed as human; animal-like behavior has different connotations: it places one outside the human species.

Discrimination against blacks in the marketplace, especially in the factor market where blacks sell their services, is different from discrimination against blacks that involves cultural slurs used to describe attributes associated with being black. The reasons why white residents exclude blacks from their neighborhoods may be different from why skilled, blue-collar, white workers exclude blacks from their unions. Nevertheless, though the domains are different in which double standards are employed and enforced, they do not exist without affecting each other. Black workers experiencing segregation in housing that relegates them to "rat-infested, overcrowded, personally hazardous, and miserably serviced environments"[3] cannot easily turn around to join the outside world and deliver high performance at jobs, even if those jobs have some promise. The interrelationship between work, productivity, and other societal practices must be recognized and cannot be readily separated as economists are prone to do. More will be developed on this matter at a later juncture. Our main point now is to underscore how discrimination manifests itself in the context of dominant-subordinate relations that are justified in terms of a double standard.

Mechanisms of Discrimination

There are four types of mechanisms which operate to enforce or maintain discrimination that we will discuss in some detail:

1. covenants, statutes and practices, enforced by the apparatus of the state;
2. social preferences of the community that can impinge upon the freedom of individuals in the dominant group who refuse or wish not to discriminate against blacks. This can be accomplished by group ostracism or boycotting of particular businesses that choose to affront the social preferences of the majority, or by outright acts of violence;

[3]T. Vietorisz and B. Harrison, *The Economic Development of Harlem.* New York, Praeger, 1970, p. 59.

3. stereotypes derived from the culture and other sources that operate to produce generalizations about black character, work habits, and abilities. This leads to exclusion practices by certain industries and from certain jobs;
4. market circumstances that make discrimination economically profitable to particular groups whose personal prejudices toward blacks may, in fact, be nominal. For example, trade unions might exclude blacks to maintain higher wages for their white members, or businessmen might find discrimination profitable and therefore "invest" time in or donate money to "hate-black" organizations.

Legal Statutes and Overt Political Discrimination

Discrimination by law is an impersonal process that removes the burden of choice from the individual. Discrimination of this kind, in essence, becomes formalized in the institutional structure of the society. Violating the law by not discriminating involves a confrontation with the powers of the State which, of course, makes the cost or penalty of deviating from institutionalized discrimination much greater than if informal enforcement devices prevailed.

Although there are presently no communities in which discrimination is legalized to the extent suggested, one major difference between southern and nonsouthern states is that the former have inherited the legacy of legalized discrimination, that is: "white segregationists still control the government and economy of the South; they dominate the political apparatus, police force, factories, and plantations, although this control is no longer absolute and unchallenged."[4] As a result, the state's enforcement agencies and judicial systems in the South operate as if discrimination were legal. This is clearly illustrated, for example, in the many rape charges and convictions found in southern courts:

> The rape penalty of death among southern and border states is not an accident. The death penalty for rape is a tool of the racists and bigots—and its purpose is to impose punishment upon Negroes where methods of the lynch mob and Klu Klux Klan

[4]M. Leiman, *Capitalism, Socialism and the Negro*. Binghamton, N.Y.: New Left Forum, January-February, 1968, p. 22.

have failed or fallen into disrepute. . . . Statistics show that the death penalty is almost exclusively reserved for black men–and then, usually only if the victim is white. . . . A study by the NAACP Legal Defense and Educational Fund a few years ago showed that the 20 death penalty cases in Alabama involved 19 black defendants. All of the victims were white. No sentence of death was imposed in Louisiana during 20 years except upon a Negro convicted of raping a white victim. No available factor other than race satisfactorily accounts for this disproportion.[5]

One of the outcomes of this quasi-legal discrimination is that the black population's economic position is more closely related to formal discriminatory practices in the social and political spheres of society in southern areas than in northern ones. For example, white political dominance and control of the agencies of state and local governments have led to significant differences in per capita expenditure on education for blacks relative to whites. This has led, in turn, to an educational deficiency among black workers, a critical labor-force characteristic affecting black employment opportunities in the private sector. In this context, employers operating in the economic sphere—in contrast to the politicians operating in the political sphere—do not need to discriminate against blacks. The economic process has already operated to put blacks in their place. White employers merely need to apply the standard economic criterion of productivity to determine employment, income, and job mobility. White capitalists can proceed in a "free" market to hire blacks for those jobs for which they are most qualified without reference to color. Employers can "honestly" say that their only concern in their market decision is work ability.[6] On such a basis blacks are allocated to lower-paying jobs or less desirable industries than whites.

[5]*Southern Patriot*, February, 1971, p. 7. It should be pointed out that the NAACP study was only concerned with actual sentencing; it was not concerned with the possibilities of frameups or with the extent to which "rape" was properly defined in the convictions of blacks.

[6]Employers might also say that as political animals they believe strongly in white supremacy, but as rational, economic animals they only hire on the basis of productivity. This mode of reasoning is not unlike the standard economic theorizing that argues problems away by taking the political, social, and cultural environment as given, thereby implicitly assuming that the noneconomic environment is independent of the economic one.

Conforming to Social Preferences

Every individual is to one degree or another "caught" in the mainstream of a social system and must pay a price or suffer losses for deviating from the social discipline emanating from the structure of power. Discrimination, therefore, may not be a result of a personal opinion of the individual exercising the discrimination. It may simply reflect the individual's conjecture about the social preferences of the community or group. A person may choose to conform to the social preferences of the system in order to avoid the losses or punishments associated with not conforming. This can happen without any legal sanctions. A restaurant owner may refuse to serve blacks, or an airline company may refuse to employ black stewardesses because it is believed that not doing so will adversely affect the business income of the seller's services or products. Such reasoning was explicitly used for example, by Dr. Alvine, the owner of the Robin Dee Day Camp, in his testimony before the New Jersey Supreme Court. While admitting that he refused admittance to black children on grounds of race, he adamantly denied that he was prejudiced. Dr. Alvine simply stated that "admission of Negroes would injure my business."[7]

Let us examine, in another instance, how the social preferences of employers in the labor market may operate to induce discrimination by considering the hypothetical case of a single employer who decides to lay off black workers before white ones during the seasonal slowdown in business activity. The firm is a small textile factory, employing twenty semi-skilled workers, ten of whom are black. The black and white workers are perfect substitutes, and seniority rules do not exist because the firm employs nonunion workers. Seasonal fluctuation in the business requires only ten workers eight months of the year; four months of the year this employer's labor needs are reduced by 50 percent. How may he decide which workers to lay off? The answer is quite simple: if he is rational and seeks to minimize his labor turnover costs, he will lay off his ten black workers on the assumption that they will be unlikely to get permanent or better jobs elsewhere because of the discriminatory practices of other employers. The costs of retraining newly-employed workers at the end

---

[7]Reported in the *New York Times*, May 18, 1965, p. 4. The part of the testimony involving the possibility that Dr. Alvine's business would be ruined was, incidentally, not disputed by the Civil Rights Commission, thus suggesting that the Commission agreed with Dr. Alvine's rationale.

of the lay-off period have been avoided. The preferences of other employers thus affect the rational cost decisions of an individual employer—even, perhaps, if they are counter to his personal sense of justice.

The above examples illustrate how, given the objective of maximizing returns or minimizing costs, or using some other mode of rational economic calculation, discrimination ceases to be simply a function of individual racist attitudes. Each individual becomes trapped in a system that requires him to *act* like a racist simply to avoid the negative consequences of being color blind in his decisions. In essence, the act of discrimination may be quite independent of a person's "heart-felt" personal views.

Stereotyping Blacks

Discrimination here arises from the fact that the dominant group has fixed generalizations or holds stereotyped ideas about the Negro's work effort, productivity, sense of responsibility, or general personality.[8]

Discrimination that results from stereotyping may be one of the important factors that leads employers to underestimate the Negro's actual or potential worth, thus affecting the Negro's job, promotional opportunities, and income. Stereotyping may also operate to determine the white employee's willingness to work with blacks on equal terms. Stereotyped views about the Negro's life-style certainly affect the fears that have run through white residential neighborhoods when confronted with the entry of black families whose income position is similar to that of the average white resident.

Profitability of Discrimination

There is a strong predilection in American society to sanction the role of group interest. The idea that each group should look out for its own

[8]The fact that stereotypes play a role in the employer's decisions to hire or promote blacks is revealed in numerous studies of management on this question. See P. H. Norgren, A. N. Webster, R. D. Borgeson, and M. B. Pattern, *A Study of Management Practices*. New York: Industrial Relations Counselors Inc., 1959, p. 55; J. J. Morrow, "American Negroes, a Wasted Resource," *Harvard Business Review,* January–February, 1957, p. 69; L. T. Hawley, "Negro Employment in the Birmingham Metropolitan Area, Case Study No. 3," in *Selected Studies in Negro Employment in the South,* National Planning Association, Committee of the South, Report No. 6, February 1955, p. 270.

interests, in terms both of defending itself against its competitors and of gaining at the expense of its competitors, is a natural extension of the market economy and laissez-faire state. As a matter of principle and ethics, it is argued that the social good is served when each individual pursues his own, narrowly defined self-interest. It is not, therefore, a very radical proposition to suggest that groups will discriminate against blacks when it is in their group interest to do so. While there may be differences about whether the operation of vested-interest actions determine the circumstances or follow them, it is clear that such actions facilitate maintenance of the circumstances that keep blacks vulnerable to exploitation and discrimination. In any event, it has been pointed out that the following interest groups have economic exigencies which benefit from discrimination and lead to the perpetuation of a black subproletariat:

> 1. *Employers benefit from divisions in the labor force which enable them to play one group off against another, thus weakening all. Historically, for example, no small amount of Negro migration was in direct response to the recruiting of strikebreakers.*
> 2. *Owners of ghetto real estate are able to overcrowd and overcharge.*
> 3. *Middle and upper income groups benefit from having at their disposal a large supply of cheap domestic labor.*
> 4. *Many small marginal businesses, especially in the service trades, can operate profitably only if cheap labor is available to them.*
> 5. *White workers benefit by being protected from Negro competition for the more desirable and higher paying jobs. Hence the customary . . . exclusion of Negroes from apprentice programs, the refusal of many unions to admit Negroes, and so on.*[9]

While the rationale of some of these interest groups is self-evident, a few additional comments are warranted. It has been argued by a market-oriented writer that discrimination among workers themselves operates

[9]P. Baran and P. Sweezy, *Monopoly Capital.* New York: Monthly Review Press, 1966, pp. 263–264.

to discourage blacks and whites from joining in common union causes, and therefore may function to affect employers' profits by lowering the total wage bill. Morris Silver, the author of this argument concludes:

> *Far from being indifferent to the existence of discriminatory attitudes on the part of workers, the capitalist gains from them and may find it profitable to invest in their creation. Needless to say, such investment would perpetuate and reinforce discrimination and the social problems associated with it.*[10]

The weakness of the argument of putting the case of business interests in such a general form is that it obliterates the subtle discriminatory differences between big, capital-intensive operations and small, labor-intensive ones.[11] Nevertheless, there is a sense in which both big and small businesses need some kind of dual or partially-segregated labor market in order to maintain a supply of labor for those jobs which white labor will not readily accept. In other words, blacks are conceived as a reserve labor pool that must be forced by circumstances to perform tasks that whites tend to resist. This view was expressed by a superintendent of a Kentucky plough factory: "Negroes do work white men won't do, such as common labor; heavy, hot, and dirty work; pouring crucibles; work in the grinding room; and so on. Negroes are employed because they are cheaper. . . . The Negro does a different grade of work and makes about 10 cents an hour less."[12] Lest this be thought of as a southern

[10]M. Silver, "Employee Tastes for Discrimination, Wages and Profits," *Review of Social Economy*, 1968, **26**(2), p. 185. Emphasis original.

[11]This point was articulated at a meeting sponsored by the National Industrial Conference Board in 1968. The meeting was concerned with exploring ways and problems associated with changing the occupational status of minority manpower (euphemism for black and Spanish-speaking workers). A number of businessmen, especially those representing small businesses, privately, if not always publicly, acknowledged the fact that uplifting the skills of black workers and increasing minimum wages would be harmful to many small and middle-sized enterprises. Implicit in their view was their desire to stimulate blacks to work at the going wage rather than to upgrade them by investing in skill formation. Several people pointed out that a large number of labor-intensive small business firms would simply lose their labor supply if in fact the manpower goals of the numerous programs succeeded in upgrading the skills of minority workers. They argued that the profit margins of small businesses simply did not permit the absorption of the costs entailed in upgrading black labor.

[12]S. D. Spero and A. L. Harris, *The Black Worker*. New York: Atheneum, 1968, p. 169.

view, it should be noted that a similar, albeit more patronizing, attitude was expressed by foremen at a northern steel mill: "Blacks are well fitted for . . . hot work, and we keep them because we appreciate this ability in them."[13]

An extension of this line of reasoning suggests that black capitalists, especially small-scale black capitalists, have narrow economic interests similar to those of small-scale white capitalists, and therefore are not opposed to the kinds of discrimination that generate cheap labor. There is some validity to this argument. However, the views of black capitalists are far more complex. Since the black capitalist operates primarily in segregated markets, he is more keenly aware of the fact that low black wages also mean limited demand for the services and products that he might sell. His economic interests, therefore, are not as narrowly defined as are those of his white counterpart.[14]

Sources of Discrimination

Discrimination by Consumers

Some aspects of consumer discrimination are extremely difficult to identify, since it is often the employer who acts as a proxy for what he interprets to be general consumer preferences. The employer does this because he is concerned with profit, not with forging a good society or changing consumer values. To exemplify this, we will examine several work situations in which the consumer is assumed to be the only source of discrimination in the market, and in which the employer and employees are neutral with respect to the color composition of the work force.

1. Your Home TV Service Co. XYZ
Company XYZ is a TV repair service company that employs only white TV repair men. It operates in a large metropolitan area in which about 15 percent of the population is black. The company employs ten white TV repair men. The main feature of this particular company is that it

---

[13]Quoted by H. M. Baron, "The Demand for Black Labor: Historical Notes on the Political Economy of Racism," *Radical America,* 1971, **5**(2), p. 23.

[14]See the discussion of black capitalism, Chapter 11.

specializes in home-repair TV servicing. The company operates in a white neighborhood and only occasionally repairs a set in a home occupied by a black family. Although the company hires only white TV servicemen, the owner of the company is free of any racial biases (even making an annual contribution to the NAACP). His employment policies are determined by his customers. He assumes that his customers connect the actual quality of the service which they are purchasing from Company XYZ with the particular person who provides the service. Technically, the customer in this example purchases only the service—the repair of a TV set. But since consumers in this market are anything but experts they also purchase the "intrinsic" qualities of the person supplying the service, which may have little connection to the actual service being performed. Extending this assumption that the owner of Company XYZ makes about his customers, he further assumes that his white customers have an aversion to blacks entering their homes, and especially an aversion to a relationship in the supplying of the services that reverses the dominant-subordinate relationships that whites assume when they "deal" with blacks. While whites, for example, may prefer white window washers, at least they "deal" with black window washers in the terms that are consistent with white expectations and conditioning (that is, in terms in which whites direct, order, "boss," or tell the black service worker what to do or how to do it). This requires a context in which the white person can pass immediate judgment about whether the job has been done well. A TV repair man essentially reverses this dominant-subordinate role. He becomes, in relation to the consumer, the technical expert whose diagnosis and decision must more or less be accepted on faith. White consumers are not readily seduced into a black-white relation in which the dominant-subordinate pattern is reversed or simply changed to a level of equality. Because of these considerations, our white employer does not employ black TV repair workers, since to do so may cost him money in the form of a decline in demand for his company's services. As a consequence of this decision, job opportunities are not available for blacks in this service industry, unless, of course, it proceeds on a segregated basis.

Lest this be considered an isolated example, it is worth noting other examples of "pure" consumer-determined discrimination. Brokerage firms do not hire black brokers to give àdvice to white clients. Black lawyers, doctors, and dentists do not have white clients or patients. In all these cases, consumption of the service is confused or connected with preconceived, personal characteristics of the suppliers of the service. Since blackness is imbued with negative personal attitudes in our society, putting suppliers of services in dominant positions vis-à-vis white consumers may lead to a decrease in customers, and consequently may lead to the rejection of black suppliers in various occupational lines that deal primarily with white consumers.[15]

2. L & O Department Store

Our second case involves a department store in a large metropolitan area that employs more than a token number of black sales persons. Moreover, the employment pattern appears to be on an integrated basis, that is, some counters or store sections are manned by blacks, others by whites, and still others by blacks and whites jointly. The customers of the L & O Department Store are primarily white, although there is a representative number of black buyers. Upon close inspection one finds, appearances to the contrary, that black employees are not randomly distributed throughout the store. Although there are particular selling jobs that both blacks and whites perform, there are also selling jobs that are reserved solely for whites. What determines this relatively subtle job-caste arrangement is related, as with the TV repair company case, to the dominant-subordinate relation that is technically defined by the nature of the commodity being sold. Blacks are found at those sales counters where the consumer requires little advice, guidance, or information from the seller. Blacks thus tend to sell those commodities or provide those services where they act mainly as instruments in the collection of money after the consumer has made an "autonomously" determined decision to buy. The sales person simply conforms to the decisions of the consumer; the dominant-subordinate relationship remains intact.

On the other hand, the purchase of electric appliances or other durable goods, which needs to be explained to the consumer in order to facilitate a decision to buy, requires sales personnel who can maintain a dialogue with the potential consumer and interpret his needs. In these kinds of jobs, sales persons tend to be white. Thus, the employment

[15]It should be noted that a change in the racial composition of a particular company's customers may lead the owner to change his employment policies and develop some kind of quota system. A limited number of blacks might be hired to serve the black portion of the company's market.

practices of this department store, ostensibly unbiased, result in the racially determined placement of personnel within the store. This process operates to limit the job opportunities of blacks, especially those involving greater responsibility and pay. Over time, it adversely affects the acquisition by blacks of higher skills vis-à-vis the work experience itself.

3. *T-X Business Machine Company*

This is a large office equipment supply company that sells and leases everything from big computers to mini-bugging devices and employs blacks in higher-paying occupations only. The company's hiring policy, perhaps contrary to expectations, exhibits a willingness to hire some black salesmen at the higher-paying computer-selling job while not employing blacks for the lower-paying typewriter-selling job. The clue to the understanding of the company's decision, as in the previous cases, is understanding who buys computers and who buys typewriters. The computer is bought or leased for use by a technical expert. Buyers for companies that use computers spend thousands of dollars on a single item, and have experts do their buying. As an expert, the buyer is only concerned with the specifications of the product as it can be observed or explained by another technical expert, in our case, a black salesman. The expert does not confuse the commodity with the person who is selling it; that is by definition what an expert buyer is. Therefore, the T-X Business Machine Company does not resist hiring qualified black computer salesmen.

In the case of typewriters, the consumer ceases to be an expert. While typewriters are ostensibly purchased by companies, white female secretaries often make the decision. Selling typewriters often involves a give-and-take relation between the salesman and the secretary. Appearance, presence, rapport, might be considered important attributes of a typewriter salesman as he explains the virtues of a particular piece of equipment. In any event, the relation in this transaction is one of equality. While the salesman wishes to please his customer, he also is assumed to have superior technical knowledge about the commodity being sold. The secretary is capable of confusing a black salesman with the commodity being purchased, especially if white salesmen are competing with black ones. This possibility leads the T-X Business Machine Company to hire white typewriter salesmen exclusively.

In all the above examples occupational barriers operate to limit black job opportunities. The source of the discrimination is the consumer;

the form of the discrimination manifests itself in racial differences in occupational distribution. The mechanism involves a social perception of the black worker that is not exercised in judging the white worker. The companies in the examples vary significantly in size and by industry classification, but the choices that were "forced" upon the company by the market are the same.

Discrimination by Workers

Employee discrimination can take the form of collective or individual action. Collective action is most blatantly manifested in the construction industry where workers, through their union, function collectively to exclude blacks from entry. When the union controls entry into the industry, collective action can limit the supply of workers, and therefore affect the wage bargain with the employers. Controlling the supply side is accomplished through apprenticeship rules and nepotism. The more potentially competitive the excluded group, the greater the exclusion propensities of the dominant.[16]

Within the work place of a large firm, discrimination becomes more subtle than when a union overtly practices exclusion. The view of a personnel manager who operates from the apex of a large, impersonal bureaucracy is probably socially neutral with respect to the color composition of his labor force. But, it should be noted, there is no neutrality with respect to the collective performance of the enterprise's labor force. A manager sees his employees as a unit that must work in harmony if work standards and daily routines are to proceed smoothly. For this reason, even the employer of a large, nationally established business might come to develop race rules for job allocation and promotion that are related not to his own views, but to those that conform to the preferences of his employees. This is clearly seen in the case of the automobile industry, whose management, while preaching nondiscrimination, readily adjusts its policies to the local-market racial biases of its employees. Roy Wilkins, in his testimony at a congressional hearing, pointed out that:

---

[16]See R. W. Hodge and P. Hodge, "Occupational Assimilation as a Competitive Process," *The American Journal of Sociology*, 1965, **71**(3), pp. 249–253.

Although the automobile industry has a nationwide policy of non-discrimination, employment opportunities for minority workers differed from city to city:

In Detroit, Negroes constituted a substantial portion, that is from 20 to 30 percent, of the total workforce in the automobile industry. Although their representation in nontraditional jobs was slight, all companies employed them in all classifications other than management positions, and one company employed Negroes in administrative and management jobs as well.

But in Baltimore, each of the companies employed Negroes only in production work and not above the semiskilled level as assemblers, repairmen, inspector, and material handlers.

On the other hand, in Atlanta, the two automobile assembly plants contacted employed no Negroes in assembly operations. Except for one driver of an inside power truck, all Negro employees observed were engaged in janitorial work–sweeping, mopping, carrying away trash.

This means that even where an industry has a nondiscrimination policy, its nationwide actual operations may differ as is illustrated by Detroit, Baltimore, and Atlanta in the industry.[17]

"Enlightened" employers, like those who manage the automobile industry, adjust to the preferences of their nonsupervisory employees in order to insure interemployee harmony between the races. They do this by relegating blacks to the occupational lines that are subordinate to the occupations assigned to white workers, and by segregating the workforce between plants or within plants. In general, whatever the particular form of adjustment, the employer, reflecting the preferences of his employees and not wishing to disrupt the harmony of his labor force, avoids putting blacks in positions in which they supervise whites and/or where they work in close proximity to whites on jobs that require interemployee equality. Blacks can, of course, supervise blacks, in which case

[17]R. Wilkins, Equal Employment Opportunity. Hearings before the Subcommittee on Employment and Manpower of the Committee on Labor and Public Welfare, United States Senate, 88th Congress, 1st Session, on S.77.3, S.1210, S.1211, and S.1937, July 24, 25, 26, 29, 31, August 2 and 20, 1963, p. 197.

upgrading is along segregated lines. But this promotional route does not tend to upset the expected dominant-subordinate relations on the job. The fact that the employer must consider job lines and routines when he has an "integrated" labor force leads him, in order to keep his labor force working in harmony, to exclude blacks from more skilled jobs, since more skilled jobs often require more authority over others or implicitly more equality in on-the-job work relationships.

Let us take, as an example, two industries with the same number of semiskilled positions. In the first, the semiskilled positions exist in a technical context dominated by machines involving minimal human interaction. In the second, the context is one in which cooperative human interaction is required on equal terms in the production process. The employer in the more impersonal, technically driven industry, whatever his personal racial attitudes may be, would not have to consider the racial biases of the machines which are operated by blacks. But this is obviously not the case for the second employer, who manages a firm that requires a great deal of cooperative human interaction. Even if the latter employer is personally more "enlightened" on matters of race than the one in charge of the mechanized industry, he might be induced to hire fewer blacks in occupational lines involving interemployee cooperation because costs increase if interemployee relations on the job interfere with production.

Discrimination by Employers

We have already discussed some aspects of employer discrimination in relation to its profitability. We have also alluded to the fact that employers, as well as employees and consumers, may have stereotyped views about the black worker's habits, and therefore exclude black workers from employment, deny black workers promotional opportunities, or require higher levels of education for blacks relative to whites for any particular job. Finally, we have identified reasons why employers might tend not to employ blacks even if this does not represent the employer's personal "taste for discrimination."

One aspect of employer discrimination that we have not examined, which is rarely touched upon in the literature, but is known to be fairly widespread in large manufacturing industries, is the ongoing discrimination against black workers by plant foremen. Foremen represent management on the lowest level of the managerial hierarchy and have considerable control over intraplant occupational mobility. The foreman is often the first person to know of a new opening and is often in charge of actually upgrading an in-plant worker. Thus, all public pronouncements about compliance with equal opportunity laws to the contrary, top management of middle-sized and large firms does not control the decisions affecting nonsupervisory employees. Rather, many labor-allocation decisions are made by foremen.

There have been no systematic studies of foremen as a group, but our impressions (gathered from numerous business executives) are that many a foreman has sabotaged a company's efforts, however modest, to implement improved job and promotional opportunities for blacks already tenured, or recently employed.[18] Foremen have direct personal contact with the factory hands. As a group, they come very close to sharing all the racial prejudices of the white, lower-middle class, skilled, blue-collar workers. Like them, they tend to have contempt for the class of unskilled and semiskilled workers below them, who must be regulated and continuously provoked to work. Foremen also tend to resent the upper echelons of management whose members are forever instructing them with white-paper orders on how to manage the "field hands." The foreman's position is ridden with tension, which he readily displaces on blacks. Foremen have been known not only to ride "blacky's back" to the point of job discouragement, but to exclude blacks completely from consideration for promotion or dissemination of information about opportunities to improve their skills in the plant. In general, in their unofficial personnel role, foremen practice a quasi-nepotism. They recommend relatives, friends, or relatives of friends for promotion or other kinds of advantageous job moves within the plant. Since foremen are almost always white, even where considerable numbers of blacks are employed, blacks have minimal connection to this avenue for job improvement. Even when union equity rules apply equally to both races, and black and white workers are simultaneously eligible for promotion or for an advantageous job change, many such opportunities are often made available at the foreman's discretion and blacks are frequently bypassed or excluded from them.

---

[18]Derived from conversations at a meeting of specialists and business executives sponsored by the National Industrial Conference Board, June 1968. The meeting was concerned with the education, training and employment of the disadvantaged.

Conclusions and Implications

1. In our analysis of discrimination, we have identified and described various processes that operate to perpetuate the black population's inferior socioeconomic position. These are quasi-legal and political, individual adaptations to community social preferences, stereotyping, and the operation of vested economic interests. While these processes originate from different spheres, the market in some cases, the political in others, they interact and reinforce each other. These processes, moreover, impinge upon the individual in ways that "force" him to discriminate. Sometimes the force of circumstances is directly related to racist sentiments and sometimes it is combined with other matters (for example, property values, profit seeking, desire for good schools) which make up the individual's vested or broader domain of interests. That is to say, the individual is often locked into the necessity of discriminating even when it does not involve an expression of his personal "tastes." This, of course, is one of the most important dimensions of the argument that we live in a racist *system*. In some cases, the system allows the individual the luxury of rationalizing or justifying his acts of discrimination in self-righteous terms. Witness the following statement of a slumlord who, when accused of exploiting blacks, retorted: "Who else but me would take care of the whores, pimps, winos, addicts, hoodlums, queers—the dregs of humanity that nobody wants. It's a lousy zoo and I take care of some of the animals—but that's more than the federal government."[19]

2. While it is possible in conceptual terms to identify three distinct sources of discrimination—the consumer, the employee, and the employer—it needs to be emphasized that the *employer* is most often the active decision maker. He is the one who interprets or complies unilaterally with the other sources of discrimination because of his overriding preoccupation with profit. The profit motive makes business cautious and conservative. Profit is the employer's main rationalization for his passive attitudes toward social justice. And, lest it be forgotten, employers themselves have vested economic interests in discrimination; they are not immune to stereotyping and they have been known to support social and political hate groups in order to contain the "natives."

3. It should be evident that to the extent that the various processes

---

[19]A. Schuchter, *White Power/Black Freedom*. Boston: Beacon Press, 1968, p. 100.

affecting discrimination are interrelated, and to the extent that the sources of discrimination (consumer, employee, and employer) converge within the larger context of any particular industry or community, discrimination barriers are more severe and therefore more difficult to overcome. The managers of large automobile factories are less likely to be concerned with discrimination emanating from consumers than are the managers of TV repair companies. The reason was put accurately, if crudely, by a West Coast personnel officer talking to a black youth:

> *No one cares if a factory worker speaks crudely, scratches himself in the wrong places or is physically unattractive; if he can read signs like DANGER: NO SMOKING and if he keeps his part of the assembly moving, little else matters. In many service jobs, on the other hand, it is essential that the service worker "make a good impression" on the middle-class people he serves. If . . . racial . . . characteristics render him unattractive in their eyes, he is for that reason unemployable. The problem is not that he is unskilled but that he is* aesthetically *objectionable—he spoils the decor, so to speak.*[20]

If the product is distinctly separate from the worker, then the consumer, whatever his prejudices, ceases to become a consideration to the employer. With the consumer out of the picture, the employer considers only his own interests and views, and those of his employees. Large, bureaucratic management tends to be relatively impersonal when it relates to hiring procedures of nonsupervisory workers; it tends to focus most of its attention in interemployee harmony. On this basis, the employer's decisions to hire and promote blacks are cautiously shaped so as not to upset the dominant-subordinate work relations between the races. If blacks rise to positions of authority, their authority is over other blacks. They do not occupy positions in which they exercise authority over whites.

[20]E. C. Banfield, *The Unheavenly City: The Nature and Future of Our Urban Crisis*. Boston: Little, Brown & Company, 1970, p. 284. It should be pointed out that the service industry (for example, finance, trade, insurance) in which "aesthetics" count is becoming increasingly more important relative to the goods industry. (See V. R. Fuchs, "The Growing Importance of the Service Industries." National Bureau of Economic Research, Occasional Paper 96. New York: National Bureau of Economic Research, 1965).

This phenomenon limits the number of skilled jobs available to blacks. Put the other way around, this means that blacks find themselves overrepresented in the less skilled jobs that are imbued with less authority, and they also have less opportunity for job improvement.

If an industry is capital-intensive, or has the kind of machine work, skilled or semiskilled, which does not require much employee cooperation, management might more readily be pressured into promotional policies that maintain racial parity or ignore race altogether. The management of industries characterized by a different technological arrangement, ones that require employee cooperation on equal terms, will be less likely to succumb to pressures for equal job opportunities.

4. The outcome of the numerous mechanisms and sources of discrimination, and the extent of their convergence, is crystallized in black-white socioeconomic differences, for example:

(a) income or wage differences for identical jobs;
(b) unemployment differences due to differences in hiring and firing practices by employers, and/or to differences in industry distribution;
(c) differences in educational requirements for identical jobs, such that blacks are required to have higher levels of educational achievement than whites for identical jobs;
(d) differences in career ladders as a result of the fact that higher-ranking jobs are less available to blacks than to whites;
(e) differences in educational achievement due to the variations in educational facilities that are made available to blacks relative to whites;
(f) differences in the amount of social freedom to move, travel, participate in political activity, and live in residential locations of one's own choosing.

Most of these outcomes reduce themselves to the crowding of blacks in particular industries and occupations, or in social spheres that limit the opportunities or experiences of blacks in relation to whites.[21] Blacks, as a result, become highly competitive with one another, and therefore excessively powerless and exploitable with respect to the labor and product markets (the most important being in real estate).

[21]For the development of the implications of occupational overcrowding on black-white income differences, see B. R. Bergmann, "The Effect on White Incomes of Discrimination in Employment," *Journal of Political Economy,* 1971, **79** (2), pp. 294–313.

This overrepresentation in particular occupations, industries, and neighborhoods not only has economic consequences, but generates the social image with which blacks are viewed and which is applied to all blacks. If blacks are overrepresented among muggers in relation to their number in the total population, the dominant white society extends this fact into a belief that not merely are all muggers black, but that all blacks may be muggers. This is one reason why innocent blacks become the target of many irrational white fears that are assumed to be rational primarily because the society is racist. Prophecies, as we have learned from the sociologists, are often self-fulfilling. Similarily, objective black-white differences are both an effect and a cause of racism and discrimination. For these and related reasons, estimates of the extent of these differences are important and necessary to the understanding of black-white relations; they will be pursued in the following chapter.

CHAPTER 4

Black-White
Economic Differences

The simplest overall measure of status differences between the black and white populations is income. Put in a one-dimensional form, individual or family real-income differences represent differences in command over goods and services, and therefore in physical standards of well-being. Sustained differences in income suggest more general phenomena which are not often thought about when income data alone are arrayed in a column. In the broadest possible terms, sustained income differences indicate differences in life chances defined by the standards that prevail in a particular society. Life chances include a bundle of "goods," for example, health care, education, longevity, information about employment opportunities, the acquisition or purchase of knowledge not available through general education, and superior social contacts. The substantive implications of income differences in terms of life chances were stated by John F. Kennedy in 1963:

The Negro baby born in America today—regardless of the section or state in which he is born—has about one half as much chance of completing high school as a white baby born in the same place on the same day—one third as much chance of completing college—one third as much chance of becoming a professional man—twice as much chance of becoming unemployed—about one seventh as much chance of earning ten thousand dollars per year—a life expectancy which is seven years less—and the prospects of earning only half as much.[1]

Income differences also suggest differences in social prestige, in the power to initiate change and manipulate the environment, and to forge one's own life-style. Income differences mean variations in ability to withstand unpredictable disturbances which emanate from the economic and social environment. Complex differences in the adaptations to unpredictable disturbances make up part of life's realities. Thus, the individual's reaction—more formally, his decision-making range of alternatives—is tempered by his current and expected future income. If there is a threshold for the inability to react to disturbances, a threshold for the inability to make the right decision, a threshold for despair, it is reached sooner at lower levels of income.

Median Income Differences

Table 4.1 presents the secular changes in the income position of black and white males from 1939 to 1969. Although this table is not a sophisticated numerical description of black-white income characteristics, it can be used to raise a number of extremely important questions. One is: Are blacks making progress? While this is a simple and direct question, no simple and direct answer is possible. If the answer were yes, then the explanation of black social and political unrest would be different than if the answer were no. This is because of the common connection that is made between economic betterment and the nature and intensity of social and political attitudes concerned with reform.

[1] J. F. Kennedy, Congressional Record, 88th Congress, 1st Session, February 28, 1963, pp. 3245–3246, in R. Bardolph (ed.), *The Civil Rights Record*. New York: Crowell-Collier-Macmillan, 1970, p. 353.

TABLE 4.1

Median Annual Income of White and Nonwhite Males
(1939–1969)

Year	1 White Males	2 Nonwhite Males*	3 White/Nonwhite Difference	4 Percent of Nonwhite to White†
1939	$1112	$ 460	$ 652	41
1945	2176	1158	1018	53
1946	2223	1367	856	61
1947	2357	1279	1078	54
1948	2510	1363	1147	54
1949	2471	1196	1275	48
1950	2982	1828	1154	61
1951	3101	1708	1393	51
1952	3255	1784	1471	55
1953	3396	1870	1526	55
1954	3359	1678	1681	50
1955	3542	1868	1674	53
1956	3827	2000	1827	52
1957	3910	2075	1835	53
1958	3976	1981	1995	50
1959	4208	1977	2231	47
1960	4297	2258	2039	53
1961	4432	2292	2140	52
1962	4460	2291	2369	49
1963	4816	2507	2209	52
1964	4936	2797	2139	57
1965	5290	2848	2443	54
1966	5592	3097	2495	55
1967	5862	3448	2414	59
1968	6267	3827	2440	61
1969	6765	3935	2830	55

*95 percent of this group are black.
†100 percent indicates perfect income equality; 0 percent indicates perfect inequality.

SOURCE: U.S. Bureau of the Census, *Current Population Reports—Consumer Income,* Series P-60, "Income of Families and Persons in the United States," annual issues.

It is argued that blacks are making progress but not at a sufficiently rapid rate. The need for more rapid progress, in this view, is often seen as essential if social and political peace are to be achieved. What constitutes a more rapid rate of progress and under what conditions it can be achieved are matters frequently left unspecified. On the one hand, the view that a more rapid rate of progress is essential for social peace is often expounded by the enlightened members of the ruling establishment. The rhetoric of the establishment is that we are making progress, that faster progress is certainly desirable, and that programs are being developed and moneys spent for such a purpose. But, so the line of reasoning continues, *time* is needed. On the other hand, blacks, whose relative share is perennially viewed as grossly unequal, inevitably see the established rate of progress as insufficient. Progress relegated to maintaining social peace by those who possess power limits the purview of what constitutes the proper or desired rate of improvement. To those who are relegated to the bottom layers of the society, progress is never fast enough. In light of these differing positions on whether blacks are making economic progress and at a sufficient rate, it is necessary to examine the problem further.

Income Levels, Gaps, and Ratios

It has been pointed out that the per-capita income of blacks in Mississippi is higher than the average income of two-thirds of the world's population. While we do not contest this statistic, it is nevertheless meaningless when intent of such observations is to demonstrate that "blacks are not so badly off" or that "blacks have no reason to complain as much as they do." Obviously black unrest and the progress of black income are not related to income levels in other countries; therefore, absolute levels of income cannot be used to examine the dynamics underlying black-white tensions.

A cursory examination of the changes in black income levels over time (see Table 4.1) shows that black male median income has risen steadily in the period from 1939 to 1969, from $460 to $3935, or more than 800 percent. While this rise is inflated because the levels are in current rather than constant dollars, it is nevertheless true that in absolute terms black living levels have risen. The black population is better educated, better housed, better fed, and lives longer today than thirty years ago. Is this progress? What does this climb illustrate?

It is a kind of progress that the economic historian, looking backward, might employ to show that blacks moved along with the general increases in the productivity and urbanization of the economy which occurred over that period of time. The rate at which absolute levels of income change, however, is not, by itself, too useful if one wishes to explain the tempo and quality of black protest. For the latter purpose, we must look at columns 3 and 4 in Table 4.1, which takes us into the discussion of the black population's relative position vis-à-vis the white population. An inspection of column 3 indicates that the absolute income gap between black and white males has increased steadily from 1939 to 1969. Is that an indication that the Negro's position is worsening, or that relative progress has not occurred? While a precise answer to this question is not possible, the widening gap cannot be superciliously dismissed, as was the case when Nathan Glazer argued:

> Some who insist that the Negro's economic situation is getting worse point to the rising absolute gap and ignore the fact that the percentage gap is diminishing. According to their logic, if at some future time median white incomes are $10,000 and median nonwhite incomes are $8,000, one might conclude that Negroes are worse off than they were when whites made $5,000 and they made $3,250.[2]

Although widening income gaps at high-income levels are not consequential, those at low-income levels are extremely important, that is, a $5000 gap among individuals earning $15,000 or more is less significant than a $2000 gap among individuals close to or at poverty levels. In 1960 it was estimated for example, that

> almost 10 1/2 million multi-person families with annual incomes under $4000, and almost 4 million unattached individuals with annual incomes under $2000—approximately 38 million Americans—lived in poverty. In deprivation, above poverty but short of minimum requirements for a modestly comfortable level of living, there were almost 10 1/3 million families with incomes from

[2]N. Glazer, "The Negro's Stake in America's Future," *New York Times Magazine,* September 22, 1968, p. 31. Emphasis original.

*$4000 to just under $6000, and more than 2 million unattached
individuals with incomes from $2000 to just under $3000—more
than 39 million Americans.*[3]

Given these income levels separating those who have adequate living
standards from those who do not, it turns out that in 1960 there were
about twice as many nonwhite families living in poverty or deprivation
as there were white families.[4] More recent poverty statistics reveal that
the poverty population increased in 1970, reversing a ten-year trend.
Defining poverty at $3968 for a family of four, it was estimated that 25.5
million people were poor, that about 33 percent of them were black,
and that the average Negro family's income was about $1300 below
the poverty line. If the definition of poverty income were increased to
$4960, that is, by one-fourth, poverty among Negroes would increase
from 33 percent to 44 percent.[5]

Whether these income levels are adequate designations for measur-
ing poverty or deprivation is not our concern. There is no doubt that
some degree of arbitrariness exists in the designation of the income
cut-off point which divides those who live in poverty from those who
escape it. But this line of reasoning can be overstated, and not infrequently
it leads to the idea that poverty exists in the mind of the social scientist
rather than amongst those who are, in fact, poor.[6] There is a great deal

[3]"Poverty and Deprivation in the United States," New York Conference on Economic Progress, April 1962, pp. 2–3.

[4]"Poverty and Deprivation in the United States," p. 55.

[5]U.S. Bureau of the Census, Current Population Reports, Consumer Income Series P–60,
No. 77.

[6]The concept of poverty, or the idea of a socially necessary minimum standard of living,
is no more arbitrary than many concepts in the social sciences that are often not viewed
as arbitrary. While it may not be a simple matter to define the minimum bundle of goods
and services that a family or individual at various stages in life needs in order to function
in a viable way, it can be done in reasonably objective terms. The whole discussion about
absolute and relative levels of poverty as it relates to where to draw the cut-off point is
sophomoric. Poverty as a concept and as a reality has obviously changed; nevertheless,
its meaning has relevance either in some historic context or within a context of a specific
system in which rewards, punishments, and the distribution of income and wealth are specified.
Within the confines of a given system with objective requirements for viability (for example,
a necessary amount of food, clothing, shelter, leisure, entertainment, knowledge about opportunities), what constitutes poverty or deprivation can be objectified to determine the numbers
of the population whose circumstances prevent them from performing and living socially
productive lives.

of political motivation to the debate about where to draw the poverty line; not infrequently the purpose is to decrease the numbers classified as poverty-stricken. Given an objective definition of what constitutes a necessary and viable standard of living, the income-gap indicator is a relevant measure of progress between two groups. This is especially true if a large proportion of one of the groups is at, or close to, the poverty level. A closing of the income gap by 50 percent would affect the living standards and life-styles of millions of blacks.

Perhaps of more interest is the black-white income ratio, column 4 in Table 4.1. The black-white income ratio has been graphed in Figure 4.1 and indicates the relative income status of black males from 1939 to 1969. In a very real sense, the meaning of the black population's income position is not pegged to past levels or some absolute sense of poverty or deprivation, but to how blacks perceive their income status relative to the white population. An examination of Figure 4.1 reveals that the black population's relative position made a significant advance between 1939 and 1946; thereafter, however, there was little relative progress, that is, nonwhite male income as a percent of white male income fluctuated around 53 percent average without any discernible trend. In essence, the black male's relative income position has been stagnant for the past 20 years. This is significant for at least two reasons: (1) during this period blacks made dramatic political and legal efforts and applied considerable social pressures in various spheres of American society to improve their relative position; and (2) black expectations or visions-of-the-possible accelerated or expanded beyond what was warranted by the nature of the social realities confronting blacks.

Another point depicted on Figure 4.1 is the marked improvement made by blacks from 1939 to 1946 due to World War II and its accompanying extreme labor shortage. Unemployment rates dropped to about 1 percent in the latter part of this period. Most of the progress occurred between 1942 and 1946. The general facts are well-known and can be briefly summarized:

> *Nationally, the demand for black labor was tremendous. In the Spring of 1942 it composed 2.5% to 3% of the war-production work force, . . . by the fall of 1944 this proportion had risen to 8.3%. These million and a half black war workers were concentrated in the areas of the most stringent labor shortage. . . . Train-*

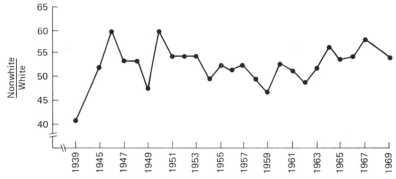

SOURCE: *Table 4.1, column 4.*

FIGURE 4.1 Nonwhite Median Male Income as a Percent of White Median Male Income, 1939–1969

ing programs for upgrading to skilled and semi-skilled jobs were opened up, at first in the North and later in the South. By 1943–44, 35% of pre-employment trainees in shipbuilding courses and 29% in aircraft were black. . . . The income of black workers increased twice as fast as that of whites. Occupationally blacks bettered their positions in all of the preferred occupations. The biggest improvement was brought by the migration from South to North. . . . However within both sections the relative proportion of blacks within skilled and semiskilled occupations grew. In clerical and lower-level professional work, labor shortages in the government bureaucracies created a necessity for a tremendous black upgrading into posts hitherto lily-white.[7]

Although the connection between major wars and black employment opportunities is frequently made, its real meaning is often obscured or omitted. The war experience destroyed the gradualist argument that was then and is presently emphasized to rationalize the slowness of black progress. The gradualist view asserts that progress is being and will be made, but *time* is needed to bring blacks from the rural South into the modern industrial sector; *time* is needed to train blacks, upgrade black skills, acculturate blacks to city life, and so on. What World War

[7]H. M. Baron, "Demand for Black Labor: Historical Notes on the Political Economy of Racism," *Radical America*, 1971, **5** (2), pp. 28–29.

ll proved is that this time-worn argument is politically motivated and serves as a rationalization for not creating the economic and social conditions necessary for full employment and for not ending discrimination. When the conditions prevailed and necessity called upon the ruling oligarchs to remove some of the racial barriers, millions of blacks moved into industry, were trained, and became a disciplined industrial army of labor in about three years. The reasons were uncomplicated and no manpower studies were required to examine the so-called pathology problem of the "hard-to-employ" black worker. There was an extensive demand for labor at all levels of skill, an outreach effort by American businessmen to bring blacks into industry, and a great determination by blacks to modify numerous racial barriers.[8]

Our society does not need time to "gradually" bring the black population up to parity with the white one; it needs the political and social determination to achieve parity necessitated by the exigencies of an extremely tight labor market. Although the 1950s and 1960s were reasonably prosperous by past standards and black agitation reached unprecedented levels, neither the economic conditions nor the levels of agitation were sufficient to mobilize the white establishment to the extent that it was mobilized by the market conditions that prevailed during World War II. It appears that the white establishment, given the system it manages, cannot create the war-market conditions necessary to bring down completely the barriers of discrimination in the shortest possible time.

Occupations

Sustained income differences are mainly due to differences in black-white distribution by occupation. By lumping together the many specific types of occupations into broad occupational groups, it is possible to observe the extent to which blacks are under-represented in higher-paying occupations and over-represented in lower-paying occupations. Table 4.2 shows the occupational distribution between blacks and whites, broken down by sex. The occupational groups have been ranked from 1 to 11 on

[8]On January 1, 1941, A. Phillip Randolph, President of the Brotherhood of Sleeping Car Porters, an all-black AF of L union, issued a call for a massive march on Washington to improve black opportunities in the war-related defense industries. The march was called off in exchange for Roosevelt's establishment of a Fair Employment Practice Committee.

the basis of the median incomes of each group that prevail for the nation as a whole.[9] The occupational group with a rank of 1 has the highest, and that with the rank of 11 the lowest median income. The broken line separates the occupations above and below the national median income. For males, four occupations were above, and seven below the median; for females, three occupations were above, and eight below the median.

As can readily be seen from Table 4.2, 54.4 percent of the white male experienced labor force was employed in four occupations ranked above the national median, while only 26.8 percent of the black male experienced labor force was so employed. At the bottom of the occupational ladder, 73.1 percent of the black male labor force was employed in the lower-ranked occupations, whereas only 45.5 percent of the white males were employed in these occupational categories. While the position of black females vis-à-vis their white counterparts was somewhat closer, 70.8 percent of the black female labor force was employed in the lower-ranked occupations compared to 47.0 percent for white females. In general, more than 1½ times more blacks than whites appeared in the lower-ranked occupations, or 1½ times fewer blacks than whites appeared in the higher-ranked occupations.

The over-representation of blacks in the lower-paying occupations is a critical reason for overall black-white income differences, but it is not the only one. Black incomes are not equal to those of whites for identical occupational groups. For example, black professionals earn less than their white counterparts. There are three major reasons for these intraoccupational divergences.

First, a general occupational group, for example, professional and kindred workers, is a composite of many suboccupations ranging from higher-income neurosurgeons to lower-income social workers, teachers, and store-front preachers. As might be expected, blacks are over-represented in the lower-income professions, and under-represented in the higher-income professions. Second, blacks get less income than whites for identical occupations. This is, in part, due to direct discrimination, and, in part, to the segregation of markets (blacks being forced

[9]The median incomes used to rank occupations are for year-round full-time workers. Source: Income in 1969 of families and persons in the United States, U.S. Bureau of the Census, Current Population Reports, Series P-60, No. 75, Washington, D.C.: U.S. Government Printing Office, 1970. Table 50.

TABLE 4.2

Occupations of Males and Females with Work Experience,
by Race and Longest Job, 1969

Rank		Percent Distribution	
		White	Negro and Other Races*
	OCCUPATIONS: Males		
1	Professional, technical and kindred workers	14.1	4.5
2	Managers, officials and proprietors, except farm	14.0	7.0
3	Sales workers	6.0	1.5
4	Craftsmen, foremen and kindred workers	20.3	13.8
	Total (1-4)	54.4	26.8
5	Clerical and kindred workers	7.2	7.9
6	Operatives and kindred workers	19.0	26.7
7	Service workers, except private household	6.2	12.7
8	Laborers, except farm and mine	7.1	19.0
9	Farmers and farm managers	3.6	1.4
10	Farm laborers and foremen	2.3	5.1
11	Private household workers	.1	.3
	Total (5-11)	45.5	73.1
	OCCUPATIONS: Females		
1	Professional, technical, and kindred workers	14.3	9.2
2	Managers, officials and proprietors, except farm	4.1	1.5
3	Clerical and kindred workers	34.6	18.4
	Total (1-3)	53.0	29.1
4	Craftsmen, foremen and kindred workers	1.1	.7
5	Operatives and kindred workers	15.0	17.9
6	Laborers, except farm and mine	.5	.9
7	Sales workers	8.1	3.3
8	Service workers, except private household	15.7	25.8

Table 4.2 (Continued)

9	Farmers and farm managers	.4	.2
10	Private household workers	4.1	18.1
11	Farm laborers and foremen	2.1	3.9
	Total (4-11)	47.0	70.8

*Negro equals 95 percent of the total.

SOURCE: Work Experience of the Population, Special Labor Force Report 127, Table 5-A; U.S. Department of Labor, Bureau of Labor Statistics, 1971.

to operate in lower-income areas). With regard to the segregation effect, black professionals must compete with their white counterparts for lower-income black consumers, but they are not in a position to compete for higher-income white consumers. A black lawyer, for example, has only black clients, but a white lawyer has access to both white and black clients. This asymmetry on the demand side for the black lawyer's services means that he operates in a restricted market. The restricted market is due to the general pattern of exploitation and discrimination directed toward the black population and the specific discrimination applied against the black lawyer by white consumers. Finally, for each occupational group, blacks experience higher unemployment rates and a longer duration of unemployment.

Education

One important reason for the differences in occupational distribution between blacks and whites is related to differences in educational achievement. Table 4.3 shows the labor-force status of the population by color, sex, and years of school completed for the year 1969.

As Table 4.3 clearly indicates, fewer blacks finish high school, and thus fewer blacks enter and finish college. Black women in the labor force appear to have more schooling than black men but they still lag behind their white female counterparts.

Compounding the gap in formal educational achievement, as measured by years of schooling completed, is a quality gap. While it is difficult to observe and measure educational quality directly, it cannot

TABLE 4.3

Labor-Force Status of the Population by Color, Sex and
Years of School Completed, 1969

		Percent Distribution			
		Male		Female	
Years of Schooling		White	Negro and Other races	White	Negro and Other races
Elementary	0–8 years	19.3	35.1	13.2	26.3
High school	1–3 years	17.4	24.7	16.2	24.7
	4 years	35.4	25.6	46.9	31.9
College	1 or more years	27.8	14.6	23.7	17.1

SOURCE: "Educational Attainment of Workers," March 1969, 1970, *Special Labor Force Report 125*, U.S. Department of Labor, Bureau of Labor Statistics, 1970.

be ignored. Blacks attend inferior (physical plant) schools that are staffed by inferior (administrative and teaching) personnel, in relation to whites. Public expenditure per pupil differs among school districts along racial lines (white districts being favored).[10] In general, "sound" teaching, "sound" curriculum, and "sound" learning environments are primarily a white experience.[11]

Educational achievement for identical grades differs between the races. What proportion of this difference is due to factors outside the quality differences of school per se (for example, home environment and cultural deprivation) and what proportion is related to differences in the quality of the school impact for whatever reasons, is not possible to know with much precision. Table 4.4 shows that reading achievement for like grades differs for black and white students, and the reading gap widens with age.

Since occupational opportunities and occupational choices, independent of job discrimination against blacks, are reasonably associated with job mobility, it is often alleged that the crux of the problem of the

[10]J. E. Coons, W. H. Clune, 3d., and S. D. Sugarman, *Private Wealth and Public Education*. Cambridge, Mass.: Belknap Press of Harvard University, 1970.

[11]For a discussion of the impact of differences in the quality of educational resources for blacks and whites, see S. S. Bowles, "Towards Equality of Educational Opportunity," *Harvard Educational Review*, 1968, 38 (1).

TABLE 4.4

Mean Achievement Levels in National Standardized Tests of Reading and Other School Subjects, by Race, 1965

Grade in School	Negro	White	Difference
Sixth	4.4	6.8	−2.4
Ninth	7.0	9.9	−2.9
Twelfth	9.2	12.7	−3.5

SOURCE: Computed from the 1965 survey on "Equality of Educational Opportunity," directed by James S. Coleman for the United States Department of Health, Education, and Welfare. See N. D. Glenn and C. M. Bonjean (eds.), *Blacks in the United States.* San Francisco: Chandler Publishing Co., 1969, p. 50.

black population's relatively inferior economic status rests on the matter of educational differences. Blacks accumulate smaller "stocks" of marketable knowledge than whites, and therefore are differentially priced and differentially allocated by occupation and by industry. However, as will be discussed in the following section, the matter cannot simply rest with differences in educational achievement.

Education and Lifetime Earnings

When one examines the relationship between black-white differences in education and black-white differences in earnings, there is a good deal of variation in black-white earnings that is not explained by the educational differences, even when quality differences are added to the differences in formal levels of achievement. This is shown in Table 4.5, which relates lifetime earnings, education, and race.

The following major points are illustrated:

1. The pattern for the South and non-South is essentially the same, except that relative differences in lifetime earnings are greater in the South.
2. The level of lifetime earnings rises for both whites and blacks as educational levels rise; therefore education pays in terms of improving absolute levels of well-being over a lifetime.

TABLE 4.5

Estimated Lifetime Earnings for Males, by Years of School Completed, Region and Race

Years of School Completed	United States			North and West			South		
	White	Nonwhite	Percent of Nonwhite to White	White	Nonwhite	Percent of Nonwhite to White	White	Nonwhite	Percent of Nonwhite to White
Elementary School:									
less than 8 years	157,000	95,000	61	175,000	135,000	77	133,000	77,000	58
8 years	191,000	123,000	64	198,000	144,000	73	167,000	96,000	57
High School:									
1–3 years	221,000	132,000	60	229,000	152,000	66	197,000	102,000	52
4 years	253,000	151,000	60	257,000	168,000	65	240,000	115,000	48
College:									
1–3 years	301,000	162,000	54	305,000	179,000	59	241,000	127,000	44
4 years	395,000	185,000	47	403,000	209,000	52	369,000	154,000	42
5 years or more	466,000	246,000	53	470,000	269,000	57	455,000	213,000	47

SOURCE: Bureau of the Census, *Income Distribution in the United States*, by Herman P. Miller (A 1960 Census Monograph). Washington, D.C., U.S. Government Printing Office, 1966.

3. The relative differences between the races (that is, nonwhite earnings as a percent of white earnings) become greater as educational levels rise. This suggests the possibilities that (a) discrimination against blacks becomes greater for occupations that require more education, or (b) educational achievement and occupational aspirations differ between the races, or (c) both (a) and (b). Point (b) is no less discriminatory than point (a), since blacks adjust their aspirations to market conditions in which discrimination occurs.

4. A considerable magnitude of the lifetime earning differences between black and white males cannot be explained by differences in education, even when quality differences are considered along with formal educational similarities. This point underscores the place of discrimination in the present discussion.

The lifetime earning differences in Table 4.5 show that a nonwhite male with four years of college will earn $185,000, an amount which is less than the lifetime earnings of white males with only eight years of education. One can readily argue that a black man's college degree is not equal to a white man's college degree, especially if blacks have inferior high school experience or are educated, as many are, in inferior black southern colleges. Equal levels of formal educational achievement are not to be interpreted as equal real levels of achievement. However, one cannot argue or even entertain the possibility that eight years of education for whites is equivalent to four years of college for blacks. Therefore, there is a significant income gap between the races even when compensation is made for quality differences in schooling. If one generously assumes that four years of college for blacks is equivalent to a white high school diploma, blacks with four years of college should earn $253,000 and not the $185,000 shown. There is a $68,000 gap which cannot be explained by educational differences alone. While the unexplained gap is smaller in the North and West than in the South, the pattern is the same. Education pays in absolute terms; in relative terms—those that affect the black population's position vis-à-vis whites—education explains less of the income differences than is generally assumed.[12]

[12]Studies have shown that differences in years of schooling, standardized for race, region, sex, and age, explain approximately one-third or less of the differences in earnings between individuals. If blacks gain less than whites for added years of schooling, and if, after a point, staying in school for blacks actually leads to a reduction of expected lifetime earnings compared

While we have shown that income differences are related to discrimination, we have not shown estimates of what proportion of the income differences are related to the different spheres in which discrimination occurs. Otis Dudley Duncan has made one of the best studies of these relationships.[13] Duncan studied a sample of white and black men, twenty-five to sixty-four years old with nonfarm backgrounds. He sought answers to two general questions: (1) What proportion of the economic status differences between black and white males can be accounted for in terms of social characteristics inherited from the past (for example, father's education and occupation, family structure)? and (2) What proportion of the economic status differences is explained by ongoing discrimination against blacks? The economic status difference is reflected in an income gap of $3730 between the two races. Just over one-quarter, or $1010, of the gap could be explained by inherited family characteristics, or what economists sometimes refer to as objective variables (in contrast to variables associated with discrimination). Thus, $2780, or about three-quarters, of the income gap was found to be related to ongoing discrimination in the income, occupation, and education spheres. The measurement of the extent of discrimination associated with each sphere is as follows:

Income discrimination	$1,430[14]
Occupation discrimination	830
Educational discrimination	520
Total discrimination	2,780

Wealth Accumulation Differences

The final, and perhaps most important, difference in status between the races is revealed by the relative size of black wealth accumulation. The stock of owned wealth is vital "in assessing economic status . . . [since]

---

to what could be earned by work experience, it becomes economically rational for blacks to discontinue their education sooner than whites. For this reason salvation by way of education can operate effectively only with an overhaul of the society in which the education is taking place.

[13]O. D. Duncan, "Inheritance of Poverty or Inheritance of Race?" in D. P. Moynihan (ed.), *On Understanding Poverty: Perspectives from the Social Sciences*. New York: Basic Books, 1969. Reported in J. F. Kain (ed.), *Race and Poverty*. Englewood Cliffs, N.J.: Prentice-Hall, 1969, pp. 13–15.

[14]That is, of the total income gap, $1430 is determined by wage and salary differences which cannot be explained by occupation, education, and objective family characteristics.

many economic decisions . . . depend on wealth accumulation."[15] Table 4.6 presents the differences in net wealth accumulation between black and white families by income class for 1967, the only year for which such data are available.[16]

Table 4.6 shows the following: (1) For any observed income level, black families have significantly less wealth than white families. On the average, black families have slightly less than one-fifth of the wealth of white families. (2) The lower level of wealth for any given income level is probably related to lifetime earning differences between white and black families (see Table 4.5). As we have shown, these differences reflect considerable discrimination. (3) Observed income differences, given the even greater black-white differences in wealth accumulation, are inadequate for the purpose of explaining long-run, general black-white status differences.[17] (4) Since wealth accumulation differences do not

TABLE 4.6

Total Net Wealth of White and Black Families, by Income Class
(mean amounts in dollars)

Income Class*	Net Wealth		Ratio of Black to White Wealth
	White	Black	
$ 0–2,499	$ 10,681	$ 2,148	20.1
2,500–4,999	13,932	2,239	16.1
5,000–7,499	13,954	4,240	30.4
7,500–9,999	16,441	6,021	36.6
10,000–14,999	24,304	8,694	35.8
15,000–19,999	43,413	20,533	47.3
20,000 & over	101,009	30,195	29.9
All units	20,153	3,779	18.8

*Evaluated at mean income within each income class.

[15]H. S. Terrel, "Wealth Accumulation of Black and White Families: The Empirical Evidence," *Journal of Finance* (Proceedings), May 1971, p. 363.

[16]*Ibid.* H. S. Terrel, p. 363.

[17]It is pointed out by Henry S. Terrel that observed income data between black and white families are inadequate . . . "since black family income: (1) supports more people, (2) is not augmented to the same degree by returns to owner-occupied housing, (3) is earned by the efforts of more people, and (4) is spent on goods and services costing higher prices. It was estimated that the observed ratio of black to white mean family income of 63.9 for urban families in 1968 should have been reduced by roughly ten percentage points."—H. S. Terrel, "Wealth Accumulation of Black and White Families: The Empirical Evidence," *Journal of Finance* (Proceedings), May 1971, p. 365.

change significantly, short of *drastic* changes in the structure of society, black-white differences in economic status cannot be expected to change measurably in the future unless, of course, there are structural changes in the economy that affect the capacity of blacks to accumulate wealth at a much faster rate.

There are many other descriptive facets that define black-white socioeconomic differences, for example, black-white differences in distribution by industry; differences in unemployment rates; differences in health, neighborhood, and housing conditions. Some aspects of these differences will be examined in subsequent chapters in the context of particular problems. Many of these dimensions derive from black-white differences in income, occupation, and education, as explored in the present chapter.

Conclusions and Implications

What we have developed conceptually in the previous chapter, and have demonstrated in the present one, is that discrimination is a dynamic process, which operates in different spheres and takes different forms that cannot be isolated from each other. Differences in wages for like jobs affect the performance of blacks on the job, a factor that is often used by employers to justify differential pay or treatment on the job. Thus, the various kinds of discrimination affect the post-school work experience of blacks, a factor that has been used by human capital economists to "explain" why blacks whose education is no different from that of whites earn less.[18] Differences in expected lifetime earnings, standardized for education, lead blacks to "invest" less time and effort in their own education; and thus blacks are seen as "contributing" to their own educational deficiencies.

In a society in which property ownership and power are twin cohorts, the relatively large number of propertyless blacks places them in a position in which they are more vulnerable than whites to impersonal technological forces, exploitation, and intense competition. Differences in vulnerability

[18]See J. Mincer, "The Distribution of Labor Incomes: A Survey with Special Reference to the Human Capital Approach," *Journal of Economic Literature,* 1970, **8** (1), pp. 1–25.

also exist because blacks are over-represented in lower-ranked occupations. Whites' image of the black population is derived from the black population's over-representation in the less skilled, lower-ranked occupations, which has been a result of systematic discrimination by all segments of the white population. Thus, white society has established the circumstances that nourish and perpetuate an inferior style of life for the black majority. This, in turn, feeds the white stereotypes that are the lens through which whites view even those blacks who manage to climb into the middle class. Thus, the whole black population, regardless of its own intraclass differences, is looked upon by whites as one inferior status group. In this way the class analysis leads to one of status, with race providing the critical link. The whole configuration breeds the conditions that enable whites to escape the personal moral anguish, if there be any, of their particular actions. The established dominant-subordinate pattern of white-black relations and the double standard employed to rationalize the black population's subordinate position are maintained.

In summation, racism and discrimination must be viewed as part of a whole system. The authors reject the approach, so common among mainstream economists and social scientists, that seeks to isolate specific factors for separate consideration and proceeds to develop *ad hoc* policy measures to fit each particular problem. The various processes that affect the relative status of the black population, in the words of Michael Reich, are not:

> *simply additive, but mutually reinforcing. Often, a decrease in one narrow form of discrimination is accompanied by an increase in another. Since all aspects of racism interact, an analysis of racism should incorporate all of its aspects in a unified manner.* [19]

Beyond this interactionist view, the black position must be seen in the institutional context which links its particular conditions to those shaping the general society. This consideration takes us into the metropolitan area, the black ghetto, and some of the larger forces affecting the American economy.

---

[19] M. Reich, "The Economics of Racism," in D. M. Gordon (ed.), *Problems in Political Economy: an Urban Perspective.* Boston, Mass.: D. C. Heath and Company, 1971, p. 109.

CHAPTER 5

The Social Surface
of the Metropolitan Area

The volatile nature of black-white relations cannot be completely grasped by the inspection of income, occupational and educational differences, important as such differences are. The black population's relations with the white population have acquired contemporary meaning in a specific institutional and spatial context, that is, in the politics and economics of the metropolitan area, an area consisting mainly of a central city and surrounding suburban communities.[1]

Urbanization

The urbanization of the black population occurred along with and in response to the larger industrial forces propelling the urbanization of the whole society. Table 5.1 shows

[1]We recognize that there are large numbers of blacks who still reside in rural areas. Insofar as they are part of the crisis with which we are concerned, it is their migration to urban areas and not simply their existence on the farm that is relevant for our purpose.

TABLE 5.1

Percent Distribution of Population by Location,
Inside and Outside Metropolitan Areas, 1950, 1960, and 1969

	Negro			White		
	1950	1960	1969	1950	1960	1969
Metropolitan areas	56	65	70	60	63	64
Central cities	43	52	55	34	30	26
Suburbs	13	13	15	26	33	38
Outside metropolitan areas	44	35	30	40	37	36

SOURCE: "The Social and Economic Status of Negroes in the United States, 1969," BLS Report No.375, Current Population Reports, Series P-23, No.29. U.S. Department of Commerce, Bureau of the Census.

the urbanization trends that have occurred in the post-World War II period 1950 to 1969. The percentage of blacks living in metropolitan areas increased from 56 percent in 1950 to 70 percent in 1969. A population breakdown by region and city size reveals that black-population movement has occurred not only from rural to nonrural areas, but from southern cities to large nonsouthern ones.[2] Consequently, racism and its correlative problems have ceased to be geographically localized, and black anguish and protests cannot be readily contained or sealed off.

Intra-metropolitan Stratification

Of more importance than this general interregional migratory pattern, however, is the one that has developed within the metropolitan area itself. As the movement of blacks into the cities has increased, whites have tended to move out. As shown in Table 5.1, the black population in the central cities increased by 12 percent between 1950 and 1969 while the white population declined by 8 percent. It takes no great predictive insight to suggest that it will not be long before many of our major central cities will have black majorities. Slowly, but inevitably, the metropolitanization of American society has taken a distinct form, essentially

[2]"The Social and Economic Status of Negroes in the United States, 1969," BLS Report No. 375, Current Population Reports, Series P-23, No. 29, U.S. Department of Commerce, Bureau of the Census, pp. 4, 9.

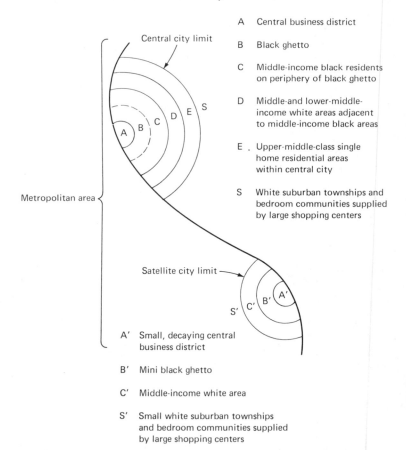

A   Central business district

B   Black ghetto

C   Middle-income black residents on periphery of black ghetto

D   Middle-and lower-middle-income white areas adjacent to middle-income black areas

E . Upper-middle-class single home residential areas within central city

S   White suburban townships and bedroom communities supplied by large shopping centers

A'   Small, decaying central business district

B'   Mini black ghetto

C'   Middle-income white area

S'   Small white suburban townships and bedroom communities supplied by large shopping centers

FIGURE 5.1   Schematic Profile of Metropolitan Area: Central City, Suburbia, and Satellite City

delineated along race and class lines. A simplified graphic illustration of the profile that has emerged is shown in Figure 5.1.

The schema represents a reasonably accurate picture of America's urban terrain and the black population's spatial location within it, although there is deviation from this pattern because of the diversity of topographical and economic development.[3]

[3]New York, Boston, and San Francisco are examples of partial exceptions because of their geographic and economic peculiarities.

Residential Segregation

In addition to this larger picture, in which blacks are located in central cities surrounded by white suburban rings, there are the details of black-white residential divisions associated with significant income differences. A comprehensive study of residential segregation made by Karl and Alma Taeuber, covering the period from 1940 to 1960 and using census statistics for city blocks, enabled the Taeubers to calculate segregation indexes for a very large number of American urban centers.[4] The segregation indexes have a hypothetical range of 0 to 100. A zero value indicates no segregation; a value of 100 indicates complete segregation. A given index for a particular city, for example 75, indicates the proportion of the black population that must move to white neighborhoods in order to achieve complete desegregation.

In 1960, the values for 207 American cities "ranged from 60.4 in San Jose, California, to 98.1 in Fort Lauderdale, Florida. Half of the cities had segregation indexes above 87.8, and only eight cities had values below 70. Thus, in all but eight of the 207 cities for which indexes were computed, at least 70 percent of the Negroes would have to move" to white neighborhoods to accomplish residential desegregation.[5]

Residential segregation is one of the main institutional barriers affecting the supply of adequate dwellings for the black population in the central cities.[6] This deficiency, in turn, critically affects the *rate* at which blacks find adequate housing, that is, housing of sufficient size and at rents and of a quality comparable to that of whites in similar circumstances.[7] Black-white differences in housing are due not only to differences in income, which determines what can be afforded; they are also the result of "discriminatory treatment in the housing market, so that the purchasing power of the dollar spent by nonwhites is less than that of the dollar spent by whites. [This means that for every income

[4]K. Taeuber and A. Taeuber, *Negroes in Cities: Residential Segregation and Neighborhood Change.* Chicago: The Aldine Publishing Co., 1965.

[5]J. F. Kain. "Introduction," in J. F. Kain (ed.), *Race and Poverty.* Englewood Cliffs, N.J.: Prentice-Hall, 1969, pp. 21–22.

[6]See C. Rapkin, "Price Discrimination against Negroes in the Rental Housing Market," in J. F. Kain (ed.), p. 113.

[7]For an elementary but sound discussion of the housing problem within a welfare-liberal, mixed enterprise framework, see D. Netzer, *Economics and Urban Problems.* New York: Basic Books, 1970, pp. 72–108.

class] the median rent-income ratio of Negro renters is higher than that of whites."[8]

Behind price discrimination is the institutional wall of segregation determined by larger forces operating throughout the whole metropolitan area. This institutional wall, made up of governmental policies, consumers, real estate brokers, landlords, banks, insurance companies, savings and loan associations, and other financial intermediaries, prohibits blacks from acquiring, at sufficiently rapid rates, the older stock of dwellings in the gray areas of the central cities, even though many blacks could afford to rent or buy such dwellings.[9]

Segregation, at the highest levels of government, was formerly maintained by the housing policies of the Federal Housing Administration. In the words of the late Charles Abrams, a nationally recognized authority on housing: "From 1935 to 1950 discrimination against Negroes was a condition of federal assistance. More than 11 million homes were built during this period, and this federal policy did more to entrench housing bias in American neighborhoods than any court could undo by a ruling."[10] The FHA did this by requiring racial covenants before insuring mortgages issued through financial intermediaries such as savings and loan associations. In fact, such racial covenants were justified in terms of "sound" planning practices, for example, the guarantee that neighborhoods would be kept homogeneous. The Veterans Administration continued this practice by providing assistance in getting home mortgages to millions of white families seeking private dwellings in suburban areas, and thereby accelerating the flight from the central cities.[11] This boiled down, in part, to subsidizing the segregated preferences of whites seeking to maintain distance from black neighborhoods.

It would be incorrect to deduce from this that the federal government is solely responsible for residential segregation since it is not an indepen-

[8]C. Rapkin, pp. 113–114.

[9]Gray areas are those transitional neighborhoods consisting of older houses and apartments occupied by lower-middle-class whites and perhaps a few middle-income blacks.

[10]C. Abrams, "The Housing Problem and the Negro," in T. Parsons and K. B. Clark (eds.), *The Negro American*. Boston: Houghton Mifflin Company, 1966, p. 517.

[11]While other government agencies (for example, the Model Cities programs under the auspices of the Department of Housing and Urban Development) have supplied funds for "low-cost" housing, they have not done so in order to break up segregated residential patterns, but mainly to increase the supply of dwelling units within existing residential patterns. The achievements in this more limited direction have been woefully inadequate as a result of underfinancing.

dent force in these matters. The agencies of the state in a private-enterprise system must work through the private financial markets. The government is dependent on these markets for the success of its policies. Therefore, it cannot axiomatically institute policies on behalf of some abstract notion of general welfare that would upset the money-making sources of these financial institutions without incurring their organized wrath. The financial interest groups are intimately allied with real estate brokers who practice racial discrimination in buying and selling. Brokers divide cities into zones in which black belts are designated. These zones are determined on the basis of trends in property values, income, and race. Such influential factors as making mortgage capital available, block busting (scaring whites to sell at below-market prices and inducing blacks to buy at above market prices), and related matters originate in financial and real estate offices. The net results are simple: blacks cannot obtain loans "in the older . . . areas where [they] are not yet present or are just entering."[12] As one broker put the matter: "A lot of insurance companies won't loan [to Negroes] . . . let alone in this area. You see maps on the wall, shaded areas. They'll strike some areas out completely. Yet, that is writing off an area. . . . Hardly any insurance companies will loan to colored."[13]

Put somewhat differently, it is relatively easy for brokers to maintain segregated patterns, since low-income areas that "need" containment overlap with large concentrations of blacks within metropolitan areas. This enables real estate brokers to discuss neighborhood segregation in terms of homogeneity and property values without necessarily mentioning race.[14] But their concealed racism is punctured when high-income black professionals seek entry into carefully protected areas. Loans become difficult to acquire and real estate brokers become uncooperative, if not directly hostile. Thus, individual blacks, even when they can afford entry into a white neighborhood, are obstructed by the collusive practices of financial institutions and real-estate interests.

Municipal governments, often reflecting the exigencies of the dominant property interests of local areas, gerrymander districts, establishing

[12]R. Helper, *Racial Policies and Practices of Real Estate Brokers*. Minneapolis: University of Minnesota Press, 1969, p. 166.

[13]R. Helper, p. 167.

[14]Actually, most real estate brokers are reasonably frank about their racial practices and do not, as a rule, hide behind public relations rationalizations.

zoning codes and related regulations so as not to upset prematurely the spatial equilibrium established by the racially tempered market which guards the property values of whites.

Neighborhood improvement associations, reflecting the racial attitudes of their residents, actively lobby for the kinds of restrictive covenants (for example, land-lot size requirements) that serve to maintain segregation. When the "normal" kinds of pressure-group politics fail, they have been known to undertake vigilante actions against those blacks who seek to break out of the segregated zones. The whole matter was succinctly summarized by J. F. Kain who pointed out that the enforcement of housing segregation is:

> both legal and extra-legal; racial covenants; racial zoning; violence or threats of violence; preemptive purchase; various petty harassments; implicit or explicit collusion by realtors, banks, mortgage lenders and other lending agencies, and in the not-so-distant past, FHA and other federal agencies. [15]

The discriminatory policies in the housing market that are responsible for the residential patterns within the central city are not only a result of the individual's personal attitudes toward blacks, however negative such attitudes may be. Consumers are concerned with property values, and financial agencies base their behavior "primarily on the idea of risk and the safety of the investment."[16] The system of particular interests requires discriminatory calculations quite independent of personal racial sentiments. These calculations induce the deterioration of black neighborhoods and thereby influence white sentiments toward blacks. The processes that operate to reinforce the black population's subordinate position verify the *a priori* racist predispositions of whites. The black population's inferior housing is thus maintained by the self-fulfilling prophecies of whites who create the realities that "validate" their racist attitudes.

---

[15]J. F. Kain, "Housing Segregation, Negro Employment, and Metropolitan Decentralization," *Quarterly Journal of Economics,* February 1968, pp. 176–177. Cited by P. Labrie, "Black Central Cities: Dispersal or Rebuilding," *The Review of Black Political Economy,* 1970, **1** (2), pp. 6–7.

[16]R. Helper, p. 167.

Lower-Middle-Class Gray Areas

Surrounding the densely populated black portions of the central city are lower-middle-class whites, many of whom are clustered in terms of ethnic identity. An examination of the social statistics of these white families reveals that a significant portion are older, on the average, than the corresponding black families, and without children or have children who fall into the category of young adults.[17] Age and income levels prevent many whites in the gray areas of the central city from having the kind of residential mobility characteristic of younger or more wealthy families. This relatively immobile white group constitutes an important component of the white backlash in every major city.[18]

However heterogeneous this group may be with respect to many matters outside the race question, it feels directly threatened by the compressed black community that is forever seeking new areas in which to live. The middle-class whites residing in the gray areas tend to see their salvation in terms of keeping the blacks from confiscating "their" neighborhoods, "their" public parks, "their" public schools, and "their" city funds that go to support blacks existing on welfare payments.

While the demographic, income, and occupational data about the white lower middle class, whose members live in the central city, point to some of the quantitative dimensions of our observations and argument, the actual voices of this group illustrate the qualities of their antiblack defensive justification, which appears perfectly reasonable to those defending "their" city territory. It is a justification which need not, though it often does, take on overt antiblack tones. Impressions gathered by a reporter returning to his native Slovak community in Cleveland are worth quoting at some length, because they illustrate in gut terms the reactions of a relatively *moderate* white ethnic group to black efforts to find adequate residential communities in which to live.

Stated the aging Father Michael Jasko:

> We had 2,000 families and 8,000 souls [some years ago]. . . .
> Now it's 1,000 families and 3,000 souls, and most of them are

---

[17]*Selected Area Reports, Standard Metropolitan Statistical Areas.* Final Report PC (3) 10. Washington, D.C.: U.S. Government Printing Office, 1963.

[18]For an excellent article concerning the backlash question, see D. Danzig, "Rightists, Racists, and Separatists: A White Power Block in the Making," *Commentary*, August 1954, **38**, 32.

> *pensioners. We stopped the Canteen* [*a weekly dance for teenagers*] *10 years ago and hoped to reopen it, but never did. We made $45,000 in a big year at the bazaar; last year we got $24,000. Novenas and other night-time services have been stopped. The old ladies of the church were getting beaten and robbed on their way to early mass, so we stopped those. Now the first mass is at 7 o'clock, except in the summer when we have the 5:30.*[19]

The widow of a neighborhood gas station attendant who was killed in a robbery lamented: "To many people around here, Joe was a fixture, the honest business man who made it by hard work. We all knew the neighborhood was changing, but then this. . . . I think of leaving the neighborhood now, but where would I go? Everything I know is here. I just want those killers found and I want them to get their due."[20]

The editor of the Slovak neighborhood newspaper, a self-described "superhawk and ultra-conservative" concluded after a long conversation:

> *In everything I've told you, I've not once mentioned race. It isn't race; it's law and order. We Slovaks are too trusting, too honest, too open. There was never trouble here just because blacks moved in. In Murray Hill, the Italians told the blacks they would kill any who dared to move in. In Sowinski Park, the Polish pointed shotguns at them. This is not our way of life but look at what we are reaping now.*[21]

From Bill Blissman, bachelor and owner of a corner grocery store:

> *Things were bad before Mayor Stokes, a black, was elected, but since his election, the situation in the neighborhood has quickly become untenable. Stokes is responsible for encouraging blacks to come up from the South and get on Cleveland's welfare and crime rolls. Stokes has allowed a new permissiveness. The*

[19] P. Wilks, "As the Blacks Move In, the Ethnics Move Out," *New York Times Magazine,* January 24, 1971, p. 10.

[20] P. Wilks, p. 10.

[21] P. Wilks, p. 11.

blacks are cocky because one of their own is downtown. . . .
In Cleveland, in the old neighborhood, it is largely Stokes' fault.[22]

Finally, a neighborhood ethnic militia has arisen in the name of the Buckeye Neighborhood Nationalities Civic Association. One of the organization's founders reported on the planned operations of the group:

This is our battle plan. We want to have each house with a code number so that our police can get to any house in minutes. The city police won't cover us, so we are willing to give ourselves. . . . I know people are calling us vigilantes. . . . Anything blacks say against us is out of ignorance. This neighborhood should be preserved as a national historic monument to mark the contribution of the nationalities. Monuments are WASP or black, nothing for us. We don't want our neighborhood liberated as a slum. And we don't want blacks in our group; we are for the preservation of the nationality way of life.[23]

While these impressions are derived from Cleveland and represent the reflections of only one ethnic group, we believe that all the major central cities have their white lower middle class with attitudes that range from a benign sense of self-preservation against "outsiders" to preparation for paramilitary confrontation.[24]

[22]P. Wilks, p. 11.

[23]P. Wilks, p. 57.

[24]An Irish worker from Brooklyn articulated the lower-middle-class view in somewhat more analytical terms:

Economics, I think is the biggest strain because, in this area, a man's whole idea of an investment in the economy of the United States is the house he owns. He invests $9000 in 1950, it's worth $21,000 in 1969. He's really knocking them dead in the economy, right?. . . . But when he feels threatened, this money, this investment that he's made, he's desperate. He says what the hell are they doing to me. This is where I put my money. I didn't put it in General Motors. I didn't . . . you know, they don't move Mits Bitsi Steel in alongside of Bethlehem Steel Company, did they? A man realizes this. At least they have tariff to protect Bethlehem or United States Steel, but here they just—they take my house and they threaten me with it. They say—you know—they're going to devaluate on him. I don't say that it's got any validity, this feeling. What I'm saying, is this is the way they feel. This is where their money went, and this is what they're trying to protect.

From "An End to Innocence," WCBS-TV Special Broadcast, Producer-Director Warren Wallace, September 17, 1969.

The composition of the gray areas surrounding the black ghetto has three general consequences. First, it affects the housing supply for blacks by preventing them from finding dwellings at a rate equal to black demand and, therefore, leads to higher rents for substandard housing units. Black slums have become the marketplace for slippery entrepreneurs and landlord sharks looking for quick profits (fast depreciation operations and preparation for the possibility of windfalls derived from urban renewal projects and/or expressway construction). Second, the composition of the gray areas has encouraged block-busting techniques of real estate sharks and money speculators who prey on the fears and insecurities of lower-middle-class home owners. Finally, it has poisoned the social and political atmosphere of the central city. Class and race factors have combined to establish a potential civil-war situation between workers that can only lead to chaos and further decay.

Beyond the lower-middle-class buffer zones of the central city resides a shrinking upper middle class (zone E in Figure 5.1) who live in privately-owned residences of reasonable quality. Many in this group are on the verge of leaving the central city to join the suburbanites (zone S in Figure 5.1) who are wealthier and younger than central-city whites. In age, white suburbanites come close to matching the blacks inhabiting the ghetto. As a result, white children live at considerable distances from black children of the same generation, a demographic fact that makes integrated schooling on a meaningful scale spatially difficult. In addition, the problem is accentuated by the extreme class differences between the white and black children.

Reproducing the profile of the large metropolitan areas are smaller satellite cities with smaller ghettos, smaller black populations, and smaller gray areas. As in the larger metropolitan areas, huge shopping-office-building complexes have developed outside the mini-satellite central cities. The downtown areas (zone A' in Figure 5.1) contain low-tax, small-scale, hardworking merchants who are foreclosing with bitter feelings about the changes in their fortunes, a fate which they more often than not attribute to the arrival of blacks. Blight and deterioration in these small black communities are accumulating in a context, like the larger central cities, where expenditures are insufficient to meet social needs.

Central City

Under the surface of the metropolitan profile are additional forces and problems that compound the strains between the black ghetto, the central city, and the suburban rings. The central city, while a diminishing part of the metropolitan area, is still its core. It provides the larger urban area with its meaning and direction. Like the brain of a large organism, its importance to the whole body is not measured by the fact that it is much smaller than the sum of the many parts that are related to it, but by its strategic function.

The central cities are experiencing a rapid deterioration of their social capital, especially the older northeastern ones. Housing and institutional facilities (for example, schools, roads, transit systems, hospitals, streets, water supply, sewage, terminals) are overworked or not properly maintained or constructed to meet the magnitude or the kinds of demands placed upon them. The deterioration of these facilities is largely related to the fact that local governments do not command sufficient resources to deal with the deterioration and the resulting problems. While the deterioration affects the whole community, it is disproportionately felt by the black population which tends to be trapped within the confines of the central cities.

Changes in the location and composition of American industry in the post-World War II period have added to the problems of the central cities. Large land requirements, improvements in highway transportation heavily subsidized by the federal government, and the desire on the part of the white population to move out of the central city have converged to produce high rates of unemployment among blacks in the ghettos of our central cities. The most lethal blow to employment is the flight of industry to the hinterland. But even to the extent that jobs are available to blacks in the suburbs, blacks lack the means of getting to them. The unemployed have become spatially "locked" into their unemployed state. Even if blacks had the transportation and market knowledge that would enable them to get to and find the growing job opportunities in the suburbs, it is not clear that they have the "qualifications" to fill jobs that are conveniently upgraded. Many jobs have phony education requirements that are unrelated to the actual routines of the available jobs.[25] Why business should persist in imposing such requirements is not clear, unless it has become the extralegal way of excluding blacks from job opportunities. This implies that jobs are less abundant than is commonly believed.[26] The black man's search for employment is thwarted under the guise

[25]I. E. Berg, *Education and Jobs: The Great Training Robbery.* New York: Praeger, 1970.
[26]If jobs were in fact unfilled, it is unlikely that business would persist with its education requirements for the purpose of screening blacks.

of "technological" unemployment (for example, the shift in the location of industries). Suburban-based businesses may be attempting to use the better educated "liberated" suburban housewives to meet their growing labor needs, a possibility that does not bode well for aspiring, job-seeking black males.

In general, the quality of the American urban environment has deteriorated. Pollution, congestion, and the declining aesthetic qualities of the urban area are intimately related to the ability of private enterprise to escape payment for the many negative spillovers to which they are the greatest contributors. Blacks, in their crowded, densely populated quarters of the central cities, more than any other group experience the effects of these negative spillovers.[27]

The Urban Malaise

Overseeing the conglomerate called the metropolitan area is a central city government and numerous smaller, fragmented municipal ones. These governments have become extremely defensive, inept, bureaucratic, and incapable of responding to the growing needs, changing circumstances, and new problems which confront the urban environment. The central city government is losing its tax base and developing increasingly disparate interest-group constituencies. Among these are militant blacks articulating needs derived from the exigencies of those living in the slums; more moderate blacks seeking neighborhood conditions and space commensurate to their actual economic status; white liberal middle-class professionals whose political rhetoric and life styles are grossly inconsistent; hard-hat lower-middle-class backlash reactionaries who see the issue of home ownership and residential integration in life-death terms; and finally, a host of business and property-value defenders whose primary interest is focused on the frozen capital in the central business districts. The latter interest group is the prime pusher for urban renewal and expressway construction into and out of the central city's downtown area. Added to all of this is the growing army of municipal employees which is pursuing straight trade union demands in areas not renowned for efficiency, for example, sanitation and hospital workers, police and fire-

[27]N. Hare, "Black Ecology," *The Black Scholar,* April 1970, pp. 2–8.

men, teachers, and clerical and technical employees. The central cities, along with their minicounterparts, can barely establish coherent priorities, let alone acquire the means to pursue effectively perceived targets.

Black-white relations in the marketplace are institutionally centered around a class-race stratification of our metropolitan areas. This is compounded by a more general set of problems characteristic of highly urbanized societies in which the private ownership of the means of production sets the tone and boundaries within which public policies are formulated and executed. The locus of these tensions has culminated in the inner city where the vast majority of the black population resides. What was taking place in the inner city motivated Charles E. Silberman to write in 1964:

> *Negroes of whatever class [are coming] to regard their separation from American life as permanent, and so consider themselves outside the constraints and allegiances of American society. The Negro district of every large city could come to constitute an American Casbah, with its own values and controls and implacable hatred of everything white, that would poison American life.* [28]

How far this process has gone is not, of course, readily measured. Its potential, however, necessitates a close inspection of the inner city, its industrial structure, demographic characteristics, and its relation to the larger edifices of the American social system.

[28]C. Silberman, *Crisis in Black and White.* New York: Random House, 1964, p. 15.

CHAPTER 6

The Ghetto: A Case
of Chronic Disequilibrium

Our primary rationale for examining the black ghetto as an entity stems from our belief that the critical problems facing the central cities emanate from the problems of the ghetto or inner city. The difficulties of the central cities, in turn, have accelerated metropolitanization across the entire nation. This rapid metropolitanization has compounded the difficulties of the central cities and those municipal leaders who man outdated political systems. Since it is blacks who predominate in the central cities, the urban crisis becomes closely linked to the black crisis.

Class Structure

When the black ghetto is described in toto, it takes on the appearance of a complete society encompassing a total range of socioeconomic classes. At the apex of the black class structure is a:

> s.nall *Negro upper class whose solid core is a group in the professions, along with [a significantly smaller number of] well-to-do business men who have had some higher education. . . . Within this group are individuals who maintain some type of contact—though seldom any social relations—with members of the local power elite.*[1]

At the other end of the class spectrum are the unorganized or "disorganized" members of the lower class,

> *functioning in an anomic situation where gambling, excessive drinking, the use of narcotics, and sexual promiscuity are prevalent forms of behavior, and violent interpersonal relations reflect an ethos of suspicion and resentment. . . . It is within this milieu that criminal and semi-criminal activities burgeon.*[2]

Between these class poles are the middle classes and the organized lower classes. The middle class covers a wide income and occupational range, from professionals to postal clerks.[3] The "organized" lower class consists of those semiskilled and unskilled workers, as well as perhaps welfare recipients, who have low (frequently below the poverty level) but reasonably predictable sources of income.

Characterizing the black ghetto in general terms is difficult, not only because of its complexity, but also because it is in a continuous state of flux. In the recent past, it might have been possible to describe the ghetto's heartland by conjuring up images of the "smell of barbecued ribs," the sound of "gut music," and on the streets the hustle and bustle of adults and children, slickly-dressed, swaggering teenage dropouts, and winos and drunks. The "spontaneity" of black men, women, and children moving about the ghetto avenues of commerce was interpreted by outsiders as representing a life-style that was "free" of the anxieties

[1]St. C. Drake, "The Ghettoization of Negro Life," in L. A. Ferman, J. L. Kombluh, and J. A. Miller (eds.), *Negroes and Jobs.* Ann Arbor: University of Michigan Press, 1968, p. 119.
[2]St. C. Drake, pp. 117–118.
[3]St. C. Drake, p. 120.

and occupational pressures of the white world.[4] Current impressionistic images of the ghetto accent the prevalence of derelict hordes menacing the streets and parks, homes and stores. "Whole neighborhoods have declined; others have been completely abandoned to junkie squatters," writes a black congressman from Harlem.[5] Whatever general overview one might get by observing the social surface of the ghetto, its underbelly is made up of unskilled workers, of high unemployment and underemployment, of individuals with low incomes and educational deficiencies, of "overcrowded rooms, . . . [in]adequate maintenance standards, and the too prevalent vermin and rats."[6]

Standing as intruders in the midst of congeries of black people are the police, the big merchant of durable household goods in "easy" terms, the pawnbroker, the social worker, and the teacher—all of whom are lumped together and conceptualized as "The Man."[7]

As much social distance as there might appear to be between the top and bottom layers of the black residents of the ghetto, the race issue links, if not unites, each and every ghetto resident. Upper-class blacks who mingle primarily with their own black peers and have only occasional contact with whites are forced to:

> *think of themselves as symbols of racial advancement as well as individuals, and they often provide basic leadership at local levels for organizations such as the N.A.A.C.P. and the Urban League. They must lend sympathetic support to the more militant . . . organizations . . . by financial contributions, if not action.*[8]

Middle-class blacks, even those most insulated from the bigger political and social questions of the day, must come face to face with them—if only in the search for "decent" schools for their children. Are "decent" segregated schools possible? It is in this area that the black middle class feels the victimization of being subordinated by white society

[4]St. C. Drake, p. 116.

[5]C. B. Rangel, "Do You Know Any 12-Year-Old Junkies?" *New York Times,* January 4, 1972, p. 33.

[6]St. C. Drake, p. 116.

[7]St. C. Drake, p. 116.

[8]St. C. Drake, p. 119.

and must register concern with social change as it relates to the race issue.[9]

Finally, there is the black worker with his menial job. In his fine book, *Tally's Corner,* Elliot Liebow tries to convince Tally, a black worker, not to be ashamed of the fact that he is a cement finisher, a specialty comparable to the doctor, lawyer, or teacher. Liebow says: "Nobody knows everything. One man is a doctor, so he talks about surgery. Another man is a teacher, so he talks about books. But doctors and teachers don't know anything about concrete. You're a cement finisher and that's your specialty." Tally replies: "Maybe so, but when was the last time you saw anybody standing around talking about concrete?"[10]

There are, of course, many other ways in which the issue of race emerges daily in black lives. There are daily cultural slurs, racial politics ranging from moderate to revolutionary, and finally, the general sense in which all blacks feel that they are surrounded and dominated by a world that is partially or wholly foreign and inaccessible. This leads to a feeling of involuntary isolation which cannot be overcome simply by personal determination or good works. Blacks feel that they are overwhelmed by the burden of circumstances which they cannot manipulate. This feeling of powerlessness, moreover, is shared to one degree or other by blacks of all classes.

To the black individual's sense of powerlessness must be added the lack of collective power derived from the fact that the black population is inadequately organized. Thus, the black ghetto is not really a complete society parallel to the white one, since it is a society in which there is a relatively small and essentially propertyless elite that must deal with a larger white elite that owns wealth and has power.

The descriptive details of ghetto life allow us to develop, for lack of a better term, ghetto models. These are simplifications by which the essential features can be isolated that give the black ghetto its main problems. They permit analysts to achieve coherence and develop consistent strategies of change. Deficiencies in models lie not so much in their failure to duplicate reality, as in their failure to include the critical variables that give the system its essential qualities. From a radical perspective,

[9]St. C. Drake, p. 120.

[10]E. Liebow, "Tally's Corner: Work Patterns of Negro Streetcorner Man," in L. A. Ferman, J. L. Kornbluh, and J. A. Miller (eds.), p. 429.

in which analysis is closely linked to advocacy of fundamental changes in the social order, an abstract model or category is not simply an aesthetic device. It is purposely designed to assist in the changes advocated, or in describing the nature of the barriers that must be broken down if the advocated changes are to occur. Inherent in the selection of a model is the presumption of "causes;" the "causes" identified will determine the recommended means to be used to eliminate the black population's relatively inferior status position. Let us assume, for example, that the main "fact" which distinguishes the ghetto from other social clusters is the pathology of the black family. Let us also assume that the family's disorganization adversely affects the whole fabric of Negro life; and, finally, that this disorganization is *not* significantly related to present manifestations of racism but has its own momentum independent of the larger forces impinging on the black ghetto. It is obvious that, on the basis of these assumptions, the policy measures recommended would be directed less towards changing the external institutions surrounding the ghetto and more towards counseling, education, and social and psychiatric therapy.[11]

In some models of the ghetto a certain weight is given to the external processes of discrimination, forced segregation, and exploitation; in some, the weight of the past is considered more important than that of the present. In others, while ongoing discrimination is fully acknowledged, it is not made an integral part of the model. In still others, the role of past discrimination is acknowledged, but it is assumed that the past is dead in terms of present black problems. The analysis of the ghetto which we develop below accents the role of ongoing discrimination and the overwhelming circumstances that limit the capacity of the black community to develop countervailing power.

Sector Analysis[12]

The critical focus for our purposes involves identifying the main sources of the black population's income—sources which constitute the weak

---

[11]L. A. Ferman, J. L. Kornbluh, and J. A. Miller, "Background Factors in Negro Inequality in Employment: Introduction," in L. A. Ferman, J. L. Kornbluh, and J. A. Miller (eds.), pp. 109–110.

[12]The sector analysis was developed by D. R. Fusfeld, "The Basic Economics of the Urban and Racial Crisis," *The Review of Black Political Economy*, 1970, **1** (1), p. 68. We have added one sector—the public sector—to Fusfeld's analysis.

economic foundation on which the black population's well-being rests. The weakness of this foundation, in turn, is the basis of the ghetto's chronic disequilibrium. Five sectors are relevant for the purposes at hand: public, high-wage capital-intensive, low-wage labor-intensive, irregular, and welfare.[13]

1. Public Sector

In 1969, 13.7 percent of the experienced black labor force was employed by the government (federal, state, and local); the percentage of whites employed in this sector was 17.0. If the percentage of blacks employed in educational services (primarily as public-school teachers) is added to government employment, the percentage for blacks is 26.0 compared to 28.1 percent for whites, a difference that appears modest compared to those in some of the other sectors.[14]

The single most important characteristic of the public sector is the nature of its labor-market structure. This has been defined by Phelps as:

> a set of "established practices" which are applied consistently in carrying out the various employment functions of recruitment, selection, assignment to jobs, wage payment, transfer, separation, and the like. Established practices are created by law, contract, custom, and managerial policy.[15]

Phelps goes on to denote unstructured and structured markets. The former is defined as one that:

> contains few, if any, established institutions by means of which people obtain market information, move into and out of jobs, qualify for advances in rank or pay, or identify themselves with

[13]While it is true that the occupational distribution of blacks is skewed to the lower-ranked occupations in each sector, whether a black worker is a clerk employed in a government bureaucracy or in a privately owned trucking warehouse makes a difference. The public market is structured very differently from the private market.

[14]These figures are derived from "Work Experience of the Population," Special Labor Force Report 127; U.S. Department of Labor, Bureau of Labor Statistics, 1971.

[15]O. W. Phelps, "A Structural Model of the U.S. Labor Market," *Industrial and Labor Relations Review,* 1957, **10** (3), p. 403.

> *any type of organization—either employer-sponsored or employee-sponsored—for the purposes of security or self-support.*[16]

On the other side of the market spectrum, there are three kinds of structured markets:

> [1] ... *market* [s] *for public employees, structured from entry to exit by legislation and administrative rules* ... [2] ... *nonunion labor market* [s] *in large firm* [s], *where* ... *primary institutions consist of the employer's personal practices* ... [3] ... *the labor market in which the major institutions* ... [consist of] *rights and privileges established by union work rules and the labor agreement.*[17]

Structured markets in the public sector are most organized with respect to entry requirements, promotion, job security, and retirement. To the extent that nondiscriminatory laws are enforced, blacks probably have more equal opportunities in the public than the private sector. While most of the jobs which blacks find in the public sector are low-paying (for example, postal clerks, social workers, teachers), they provide a great deal of occupational security, an important consideration in black occupational choice. Since job classifications are closely specified, income differences for similar or like jobs are practically nonexistent. Thus, in cities where the federal government is a big employer, relative income differences tend to be smaller than in cities where the government sector is less consequential.[18]

2. High-Wage Capital-Intensive Sector

In some cities, such as Cleveland and Akron in Ohio, and Detroit and Flint in Michigan, reasonably large numbers of blacks living in the ghetto

[16]O. W. Phelps, p. 406.

[17]O. W. Phelps, p. 407.

[18]See R. S. Franklin, *The Relative Economic Status of the Negro Male: An Econometric Study.* Unpublished doctoral dissertation, University of California, Berkeley, 1966.

are employed in the capital-intensive sector. This is a more technologically advanced sector, though often plagued with greater fluctuations in output and employment compared to the more modest ups and downs that characterize the national economy. The amount of capital per worker is higher, labor productivity is higher, and wages are higher than in other industrial sectors. This sector consists of industries in which "competition" is among the few giant corporations in each industry; thus, each particular industry's market relations are set by the noncompetitive practices of the largest firms in the industry. Workers in these industries generally belong to large, strong, industrial unions. The labor market here is structured, although to a lesser extent than in the public sector. In this context, the better-paid black workers who are classified as semiskilled operatives do, in fact, earn annual incomes almost comparable to whites who hold the more menial white-collar jobs.

As we have argued earlier, urban economies which are dominated by capital-intensive modes of production have large-scale enterprises guided by impersonal managers who have little need to form "coalitions" with consumers for the purpose of discrimination. Capital-intensive modes of production generally separate the product or service from the worker. Moreover, the technical conditions of production, such as big assembly plants or machines which are operated by one person and involve a repetitive process, tend to require a minimum of personal interaction on equal terms between workers or interaction in which blacks might have jobs vested with authority over whites. Therefore, the employer in capital-intensive operations has less reason to be concerned with the product-color connection made by the consumer, or with the breakdown of the dominant-subordinate work pattern that tends to operate as a barrier to the black worker's occupational mobility within the plant.

Blue-collar black workers have achieved modest occupational mobility and security in portions of the capital-intensive sector, but these gains have been mainly limited to semiskilled and low-level skilled positions. Moreover, it should be noted that productivity gains (output per manhours) in this sector have been most pronounced in recent years, with the result that blue-collar jobs are diminishing because more output is achieved with the same or fewer workers. It appears that the impersonal forces of technological progress are rapidly eroding the modest foundations of success achieved by blue-collar black workers.

3. Low-Wage Sector

Workers in the low-wage sector are recruited in primarily unstructured markets. Industries in this sector consist of many small, highly competitive firms. The firms employ transient labor that usually does not enjoy union support or statutory protective regulations. The jobs in this sector are varied and may be found in light manufacturing and service industries, or in retail and wholesale trade lines.

The technology in these industries is labor-intensive. Labor productivity and profits are low, and therefore business mortality rates and labor turnover rates tend to be relatively high. A large proportion of the jobs in this sector are dead-ends, that is, without possibilities for occupational advancement. The single most common characteristic of the industries in this sector is that "many full-time employees who work steadily in [them] earn less than a poverty-level income"[19] (see Table 6.1). The low-wage sector is the occupational home of a disproportionate number of black-ghetto residents: "Whereas Negro women make up one out of eight working women, they make up one out of six women in low-wage occupations. . . . For Negro men the situation is [worse]; whereas they compose but one-twelfth of the non-agricultural male workforce, they hold one out of four low-wage jobs."[20]

Thus, in this sector we have a consequential number of blacks working full time in industries and at occupations that render an insufficient living wage.

4. Irregular Sector

The occupations in the irregular sector are partly legal, though unconventional, partly extralegal, and partly illegal. They involve:

> *informal work patterns that are often invisible to outside observers; a network of occupational skills unique to ghetto life but which have little significance for jobs outside the ghetto; [and] acquisition of skills and competences by workers in non-traditional ways, making their use in the larger society difficult if not impossible.*[21]

[19]D. R. Fusfeld, p. 69.

[20]B. Bluestone, "Low-Wage Industries and the Working Poor," *Poverty and Human Resources Abstract,* 1968, **3** (2), p. 3.

[21]D. R. Fusfeld, p. 70.

TABLE 6.1

Selected Low-Wage Industries Employing Substantial Numbers
of Black Ghetto Workers (in 1966 dollar equivalents)

Industries	Year	Total Employment	Average Hourly Earning	Percent of the Workers Earning Less than $1.60 per Hour.
Nursing homes and related facilities	1965	172,737	1.19	86.3
Laundries and cleaning services	1966	397,715	1.44	72.5
Hospitals, excluding federal	1966	1,781,300	1.86	41.2
Work clothing	1964	57,669	1.43	72.8
Men's and boy's shirts	1964	96,935	1.45	70.4
Candy and other confectionery	1965	49,736	1.87	34.2
Limited price variety stores	1965	277,100	1.31	87.9
Eating and drinking places	1963	1,286,708	1.14	79.4
Hotels and motels	1963	416,289	1.17	76.1
Miscellaneous retail stores	1965	968,200	1.75	58.0
Retail food stores	1965	1,366,800	1.91	42.6
Department stores	1965	1,019,300	1.75	59.6

SOURCE: Industry Wage Surveys, Bureau of Labor Statistics, U.S. Department of Labor (1961–1966).

A sample of some of the occupational routines identified with this sector are:

The artist: Entertainers, humorists, painters, craftsmen.

The hustler: The supersalesman who often operates on both sides of the law. For example, the "casket salesman" who retrieves coffins from the local cemetery, refurbishes them, and offers them for sale.

The fixer: The expert who can repair cars, appliances, plumbing or electrical wiring.

The information broker: The individual who receives cash income

> *in exchange for information. Sometimes the information concerns the availability of stolen merchandise, sometimes job opportunities, sometimes the details of the welfare system. The product developer: Products such as rum-raisin ice cream, sweet potato pie and barbecued spareribs enjoy a large sale in some ghettos. They are also produced there by the ghetto residents.*[22]

The precise quantitative importance of the irregular sector is difficult to assess but impressionistic information suggests that it is large and an important supplement to the income of black-ghetto residents.[23]

Two major features that characterize the occupations found in the irregular sector warrant emphasis. The first is that many of these occupations are unique to the ghetto, and are therefore not transferable to the sectors outside the ghetto. The occupations also involve "skills" that cannot easily be formalized into training programs and are thus frozen to particular circumstances. The second major characteristic is their irregularity, their nonroutine nature, and the fact that they are performed without supervision or any need for punctuality, time-pacing, and so on. The job routines of this sector lack the standard social discipline associated with more "normal" jobs.[24]

5. Welfare Sector

This sector is defined by the fact that the income generated within it is not related to the performance of any productive service. Welfare pay-

---

[22]D. R. Fusfeld, p. 70.

[23]For some quantitative impressions and their implications, see D. B. Mitchel, "Black Economic Development and Income Drain," *The Review of Black Political Economy,* 1970, **1** (2), pp. 47–56.

[24]In somewhat more positive terms, this sector might be viewed as the reservoir of black entrepreneurial talent of which the black community is allegedly in short supply. There is no doubt that a great deal of entrepreneurial energy is expended in this sector. The black youth who begins hustling in drugs and stolen goods at an early age would win untold Junior Chamber of Commerce awards if he were selling *Life, Time,* or *Fortune.* Whether the entrepreneurial energies, which have been channeled into illegal activities, could be rechanneled into legal activities is unknown, since no systematic effort has been made in this direction.

ments related to public assistance are generally classified under Aid to Families with Dependent Children, Unemployment Insurance, Disability Programs, Assistance to those 65 Years and Over, General Assistance, and Assistance-in-Kind. The particular welfare instrument that is most relevant to our purposes is the one concerned with Aid to Families with Dependent Children (AFDC). The AFDC program, more than any other, has received the lion's share of the criticism from all sides of the political spectrum.

AFDC was originally conceived as a program for widowed mothers and their children, but it gradually became a program dependent less on the death of the family's main breadwinner and more on the socially-induced separation of the father from the family as the result of divorce, desertion, imprisonment, or simply legal absence.[25]

In the fiscal year 1970, $4.1 billion were channeled through the AFDC public assistance program to support a little over nine million persons. While half of the AFDC recipients are white, a very large proportion (approximately 45 percent) are black.[26] In view of the fact that blacks make up only 11 percent of the total population, the percentage of blacks receiving aid through the AFDC program is very substantial. It is not surprising, therefore, that criticism of the AFDC program has an explicit racist slant. Popular condemnation originates from the hard-working, tax-paying, lower-middle classes who believe that welfare money is squandered on undeserving people who are unwilling to work. More serious and specific criticisms emanate from a variety of sources with varied motivations, some decent and humane and others suspect. These criticisms are:

(1) Benefit levels are alleged to be much too low, with the possible exception of a few states and cities; (2) variations in benefit levels by state and locality are said to be arbitrary and to encourage undesirable mobility patterns among the poor; (3) welfare rules are alleged to discourage efforts at self-improvement by the poor and thus lead to a perpetuation of reliance on public

---

[25]"Income and Poverty," *Toward a Social Report,* U.S. Department of Health, Education, and Welfare, 1969, p. 49.

[26]Reported by H. J. Gans, "Three Ways to Solve the Welfare Problem," *New York Times Magazine,* March 7, 1971, p. 94.

support through several generations; and (4) AFDC is blamed for the disruption of . . . stability among . . . urban black families.[27]

If to all these specific criticisms, one were to add that the welfare-dispensing system is "inefficient in the sense that administrative costs are high relative to the benefits that go to the poor,"[28] one can only conclude that it is time for a fundamental change.

Can serious change be expected to come about in the near future, except, perhaps, in the area of administrative efficiency? The answer is probably negative. The present function of the welfare system is not to redistribute income, to rehabilitate the poor, or to provide family guidance or a decent standard of living for the less fortunate in our society. Its main function is to provide what minimum income is necessary to purchase a semblance of social peace from a class of people whom the economy is incapable of using in productive ways. The level of this minimum income, moreover, is limited by the income gap necessary to maintain work discipline among employed workers. Furthermore, according to Cloward and Piven, those who legislate the welfare sector understand its purposes. For these reasons, humane changes in the welfare system are unlikely.[29]

The observations made about the location of blacks and their sources of income in the various sectors discussed are not new. Viewed as a whole, they emphasize the relatively weak economic foundation on which the confined black-ghetto population rests: a welfare sector based on dependence; a low-wage sector consisting of dead-end jobs; a high-wage sector which is automating out of existence the very jobs that represented some marginal progress in the post-World War II period; an irregular sector made up of invisible, nontransferable skills; and finally, a secure low-paying public sector which, in some ways, represents the best and most promising path for black mobility as regards individuals who seek to operate within the existing system.

[27]M. K. Taussig, "Evaluation of Programs of Economic Intervention in the Income Maintenance Area," unpublished paper, prepared for the *Handbook of Evaluation Research,* 1970, pp. 23–24.

[28]M. K. Taussig, p. 24.

[29]See F. F. Piven and R. A. Cloward, *Regulating the Poor: The Functions of Public Welfare.* New York: Pantheon Books, 1971.

Poverty Trap and Chronic Disequilibrium

The demise of the post-World War II civil rights movement that "began" with the 1954 Supreme Court school desegregation decision reached its climax with the passage of the 1964 Civil Rights Act. Integration as a goal to be pursued by traditional reformist means (for example, pressure group politics, legal testing of discriminatory practices, and mass demonstrations involving the proper acquisition of legal permits and the like) ceased to become the only focus of black social energies. During the post-World War II period, a black power ideology derived from the belief that the black population will continue to reside in a permanent ghetto began to compete with the policies that fell under the rubric of integration. The characteristics of this permanent ghetto began to take on new meaning, which blacks related to the problems faced by "third world" nations. The new view of the ghetto was eloquently articulated by Kenneth Clark:

> [The dark ghetto involves] invisible walls ... erected by white society, by those who have power, both to confine those who have no power and to perpetuate their powerlessness. The dark ghettos [have] social, political, educational, and ... economic [dimensions.] Their inhabitants are subject peoples, victims of the greed, cruelty, insensitivity, guilt, and fear of their masters. The objective dimensions of the American urban ghettos are over-crowded and deteriorated housing, high infant mortality, crime and disease. The subjective dimensions are resentment, hostility, despair, apathy, self-depreciation, and its ironic companion, compensatory grandiose behavior. . . . The ghetto is ferment, paradox, conflict, and dilemma. . . . It is the surge toward assimilation, and it is alienation and withdrawal within the protective walls of the ghetto. The pathologies of the ghetto community perpetuate themselves through cumulative ugliness, deterioration, and isolation, and strengthen the Negro's sense of worthlessness, giving testimony to this impotence. Yet the ghetto is not totally isolated. The mass media—radio, television, moving pictures, magazines, and the press—penetrate, indeed, invade the ghetto in continuous and inevitable communication, largely one-way, and project the values and aspirations, the manners and the style of the larger white-dominated society. Those who are

> required to live in congested and rat-infested homes are aware
> that others are not so dehumanized. . . . Whatever accommoda-
> tions [black ghetto residents] must make to the negative realities
> which dominate their own lives, they know consciously or uncon-
> sciously that their fate is not the common fate of mankind. They
> tend to regard their predicament as a powerlessness which all
> Negroes share.[30]

The ghetto in Clark's view is not simply a poor place, not simply one in which crime and disorganization and resentment prevail; it is a place in which various segments and classes of the black population are confined, walled-in, and subjugated. The residents of the ghetto, rich and poor alike, are isolated. Their subjugation makes them impotent with respect to determining their own destiny. Nevertheless, however isolated, ghetto residents are involuntarily confronted with glittering amenities from the outside world—there to view but not to possess. The ghetto is a *forced* condition, and therefore its residents, who include the whole black population except those few who live in white neighborhoods, cannot extricate themselves from their ghetto conditions by ordinary means.

The acceptance of the permanent-ghetto hypothesis is the underlying reality from which the underdeveloped-nation and neocolonial model derives its analytic force and programmatic imperatives.

The model in its general form begins with the notion that the black ghetto—a society within a society, a nation within a nation—is like an underdeveloped country caught in a poverty trap perpetuated by dependence on, and domination by, the imperialist power which drains resources from its walled-in residents. Two processes are emphasized: (1) the circularity of misery which is perpetuated by the ghetto economy, and (2) subjugation by outside forces which involves sustaining the circulation of misery and expropriation of the resources that might be mobilized on behalf of the ghetto. The economics of the model begin with the seamless web of interconnections illustrated in Figure 6.1.

Blacks have low per-capita incomes which operate negatively on the population's health and other demographic characteristics. Low

[30]K. Clark, *Dark Ghetto*. New York: Harper & Row, 1965, p. 11–12.

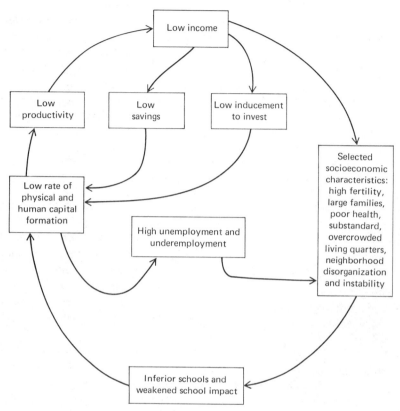

FIGURE. 6.1   Circulation of Misery

income undermines both the ability to save from current income and
the inducement to invest in large-scale domestic enterprises because
of insufficient domestic demand. To the extent that enterprises form,
they are either owned by whites or are of the high-risk, small-scale,
fast-turnover retail variety that are incapable of competing with larger-scale
operations outside the ghetto economy. The insufficiency of saving and
inducement to invest also affect the ability of the domestic ghetto economy
to absorb its labor force, whose growth is related to the high local birth
rate and immigration from rural areas. An immobile, unemployed labor
surplus in the urban context tends to produce a free-floating lumpen-

proletariat that contributes considerably to neighborhood disorganization. To the extent that the surplus labor is exported "abroad," it is exported to the low-wage "foreign" sectors, a situation not conducive to increasing "domestic" income significantly. The urban context of underdevelopment negatively affects the impact of the school system, especially in its failure to create a significant number of highly educated persons who can come to grips with the exigencies of a world dominated by sophisticated technology in need of high-grade technical skills. The various consequences of low income ultimately converge to effect an inadequate growth of the ghetto's physical and human capital—critical determinants of the population's low productivity and low per-capita income.

The Neocolonial Model

Outside forces which operate to maintain the circulation of misery propel the propensities of internal forces. The meager savings and profits which are generated in the ghetto are sucked into the white "foreign" sectors through foreign-owned financial institutions and foreign-owned income-earning assets. Moreover, the residents of the ghetto find it economically rational to import goods and services from white foreign-owned firms. This is partly due to the fact that white "foreigners" have a monopoly on the production of the more basic commodities that ghetto residents need, and partly because such imported goods and services are cheaper than those made available by indigenously-owned ghetto firms. In addition, the "demonstration effect" operates to encourage ghetto residents to ape the consumption proclivities of the white foreign culture at the expense of internal spending or saving. Thus, the general exchange between the black underdeveloped ghetto society and its white foreign controller is between the ghetto's export of low-paid labor surpluses for higher-priced imported goods and technical services. The consequences of this particular pattern of trade tend to be periodic balance-of-payments crises in the form of a ghetto deficit. The deficits are met in two ways: (1) by foreign aid in the form of welfare payments by the "imperial" controllers, used to keep the "natives" compliant, and (2) by the relative cheapening of the ghetto's main exportable commodity—surplus labor, a large portion of which is frozen within the boundaries of the ghetto. The cheapening of labor reduces the deficit by decreasing the import capacity of the ghetto residents. The reduction of the import capacity of the ghetto realized by decreasing the relative price of labor has culminated in what has been identified as the "crisis ghetto."[31] In the context of the crisis ghetto, more "primitive" and "irrational" ways operate to meet the deficit (that is, the imbalance between ghetto receipts and ghetto expenditures). In the framework of the neocolonial model, riots, rebellions, theft, and other crimes against the foreigners operating in and adjacent to ghetto territory are viewed as forceable transfers of wealth.

The power of the neocolonial model in relation to the black ghetto lies in its synthetic quality. It is a model which incorporates the realistic assumption that the black ghetto appears to be a permanent cluster for the foreseeable future. It is a model from which pragmatic proposals can be derived, while it embraces, at the same time, an attack on the structural dimensions of inequality in all areas of black life. The model appears consistent with the needs of black aspirations, given the black population's historic legacy and ongoing subordinate position. The model, finally, has the additional quality of leading to development propositions that can be pursued by means of reformist steps or revolutionary strides. No other analytic paradigm has that virtue.[32]

While we believe that the neocolonial model is the most comprehensive of the general models frequently discussed, it cannot pass without some critical qualifications. Our purpose in making these qualifications is not to dismiss its validity, but to encourage its development in more realistic and useful ways.

---

[31]A special census report conducted in Cleveland in 1965 showed:

unexpected social and economic changes in the five years since 1960. What was most significant was a sharp economic polarization among the city's Negroes. A substantial number had moved up to a more affluent life; but the group in the worst part of the ghetto was at a level of poverty that was actually *below* the one recorded in 1960. . . . These five years saw rapidly rising real income and falling unemployment for the city as a whole—but not for the very poor. The gap between haves and have-nots widened strikingly; and the most rapid widening was among Negroes—between those outside the slums who were rising, beginning finally to cash in on the American dream, and those still in the hard-core ghetto, on limited rations of income and hope.

W. Williams, "Cleveland's Crisis Ghetto," *Transaction,* September 1967, p. 33. Emphasis original.

[32]For the developmental implications of the neocolonial model, see Chapter 11.

Evaluation of the Neocolonial Model

The neocolonial model is derived from a classical colonial situation. The nature of classical colonialism was aptly summarized by Robert Blauner in his provocative article relating internal colonialism to ghetto riots:

> *Colonialism traditionally refers to the establishment of domination over a geographically external political unit, most often inhabited by people of a different race and culture, where this domination is political and economic, and the colony exists subordinated to and dependent upon the mother country. Typically the colonizers exploit the land, the raw materials, the labor, and other resources of the colonized nation; in addition, a formal recognition is given to the difference in power, autonomy, and political status, and various agencies are set up to maintain this subordination.* [33]

The critical point is that the standard colonial mode of domination involves a minority with superior technological power dominating a majority. This takes place in a context in which the majority exists as a separate geopolitical unit which, however subjugated, has the potential of becoming a completely self-governing society in all realms of activity. Comparison of the classical colonial situation with the *de facto* black one in the United States has produced various objections that can be grouped into the following five interrelated criticisms:

1. Blacks, as a dominated group, are geographically dispersed among their exploiters and, therefore, there is less potential for the development of a concerted, cohesive political movement capable of achieving the consciousness and autonomy needed to control their own resources and destiny.
2. Because the black population is not sufficiently isolated physically, spontaneous economic drains from the black to the white community (for example, income, savings, physical and human capital) are much greater than in the colonial situation. In the standard colonial situation, the potential development of a protective tariff system or the development of strict controls on the importation of superfluous goods is

[33]R. Blauner, "Internal Colonialism and Ghetto Revolts," *Social Problems*, Spring 1969, **16**, p. 395.

allowed for. In general, the underdeveloped country, in contrast to the less segregated ghetto, has a significantly greater potential capacity for insulating itself from the competitive and distorting influence of the developed countries. The balance-of-payment problem between developed and underdeveloped sectors is difficult to correct under the most favorable circumstances. With circumstances infinitely less favorable, correcting the deficit seems fairly close to impossible.

3. The black population is not culturally isolated. This means that the "demonstration effect" cannot be avoided; that is, the black population cannot avoid internalizing white consumption styles, which are derived from a society with significantly higher income levels. Aping white consumption habits makes it extremely difficult for the black population to develop an internal ethic conducive to saving and austerity, a prerequisite and accompaniment to the developmental thrust.

4. There is little possibility that the black population can acquire the degree of fiscal and monetary autonomy, for example, taxation powers, control of their own money supply, credit-creation capacities, that are needed to fulfill the political, social, and economic goals derived from a revolutionary development program implicitly suggested in the neocolonial model.

5. Blacks are a minority dominated by the majority, a fact that affects the potential power they can mobilize against their white oppressors, even under the most favorable circumstances.

The impact of the sum of these criticisms represents a rather decisive blow against a literal application of the neocolonial model to the black-white situation in the American social order. When the model is applied too literally, a gross separation tends to develop between rhetoric and reality which, in the end, debases the essential relevance of the model.

While we do not wish to end this discussion about the black ghetto and its meaning and prospects on such a pessimistic note, it is unavoidable as long as the black plight is viewed within standard approaches—whether revolutionary or reformist. The reason for being pessimistic is that none of the models often elaborated adequately considers the broad forces that affect the American social system. These forces simultaneously transcend the problems of the black community and determine the ebb and flow of the movements and conditions within it. These forces need analysis if the black community is to be understood and to develop an optimum response to the barriers it faces.

CHAPTER 7

Selected Impressions of the Post-World War II Period: A Digression

Salvation schemes developed for blacks by whites or for blacks by blacks cannot be viable if they are divorced from a close analysis of the broader cultural and institutional network which shapes the social order. This follows from our belief that black problems are too pervasive and entrenched to be solved without basic changes in American society that will affect the way whites relate to each other as well as to blacks. No particular "solution" to the relative status of blacks is possible without a more general "solution" to what ails the American society.[1] This

[1]Our discussion of the economic gains made by blacks in the short period during World War II (see Chapter 4) illustrates the kind of argument we believe must be pursued by those who are concerned with black progress. The war created emergencies that required planning, full mobilization of resources, and social "togetherness." Black demands were more specifically related to black needs, but could be made consistent with the war mobilization drive if it included meeting aspects of these needs. If war mobilization requirements had been contrary to black economic demands, they would have been met in a very different way by the powers-that-be. This means that the defensive and offensive positions taken by blacks must be closely linked to their estimate and analysis of the tendencies at work in the other parts of the system.

suggests that the acquisition of power by blacks and the pursuit of change will have to be consonant with, or complementary to, changes sought by other groups and classes who are confronting the social order for the purposes of solving *their* problems. This broader context of ferment, change, and social conflict provides possibilities for the black community in its own efforts to build a viable movement capable of achieving its objectives.

What follows is a sketch and critique of selected aspects of American society and institutions as they have evolved since World War II. Our purpose is to shed light on the ways structural forces have thus far culminated to affect the general conditions which blacks must understand in order to clarify their own orientation toward the American social order.

Post-World War II Depression Fears: 1946–1950

In the short period after World War II from 1946 to 1950, considerable skepticism prevailed about the economy's capacity to continue its war-level performance. At the highest levels of government, this skepticism was expressed by the legislature in the form of the Full Employment Act of 1946: the government, in principle, as if to allay popular fears, assumed the responsibility for maintaining full employment. Since the bill included no specific machinery to accomplish its purpose, it merely reduced itself to a moral commitment.

On the individual level, there was the case, albeit extreme, of Sewell Avery who, as director of Montgomery Ward, absurdly piled up the liquid reserves of the company in order to meet the exigencies of the assumed imminent depression. His hope was that Montgomery Ward would be in an advantageous position to buy up his defaulting competitors as they went down with the crash and depression which only Sewell Avery would have had the foresight to withstand. A more common-type crisis admonition was expressed by Dean Acheson:

> We cannot go through another ten years like the ten years at
> the end of the twenties and the beginning of the thirties. . . .
> We have got to see that what the country produces is used
> and sold under financial arrangements which make its production

> *possible. . . . We cannot have full employment and prosperity in the United States without . . . foreign markets.*[2]

A number of factors combined abruptly to dissipate the doubts inherited from the Great Depression: the monetization of the debt and the backlog of unfilled needs derived from the war, the high rate of capital investment (especially in the Far West), the dramatic increase in military outlays associated with the Korean War, and last but not least, the development of Marshall Plan aid that assured extensive market opportunities for U.S. capital. All these factors converged to generate and sustain a high level of aggregate demand relative to the system's supply capabilities. By the early fifties, the shadow of the Great Depression finally faded into oblivion. The complacent decade was launched.

Euphoric Fifties

What emerged was a new American profile. It had begun with the New Deal in the form of partial innovations and was completed and assimilated by the mid-1950s.

For the typical professional economist, with his cautious, eclectic, and pragmatic outlook, the profile was defined in terms of basic structural changes: (1) the emergence of a more liquid economy associated with the centralization of the banking system; (2) the elimination of reckless speculation on the stock market and the development of the Securities and Exchange Commission; (3) the rise of a host of built-in stabilizers which acted to modify the business cycle; and (4) the establishment of a high level of government spending and of a set of fiscal policies that were conceived as independent of fluctuations of national income generated by the private sector. These institutional changes, along with the assimilated wisdom derived from the Keynesian revolution in economic knowledge, combined to permit the average, technically oriented economist to rest his faith in the short-run tinkering process, that is, in manipulating the interest rate by controlling the money supply and by moderate adjustments in government spending and taxes. Put somewhat differently,

---

[2]D. Acheson. Cited by W. Appleman, *The Tragedy of American Diplomacy*. Cleveland: World Publishing Co., 1959, p. 148.

it enabled the state authorities to proceed as if they could readily control the level of employment and output by the manipulation of a few aggregate variables, and thereby indirectly control or contain any social unrest that might occur.

More popular versions of the new optimistic profile centered on the culmination of one hundred years of industrial growth in a private enterprise context.[3] According to this historic-panoramic view, this growth had produced more goods and leisure, sources of communication, cars and means of transportation, and educational opportunities than in any other country in the world. Although evils associated with industrial capitalism were admitted, it was argued that they had been arrested by such corrective developments as social legislation, public services, trade union activity, changes in the attitudes of businessmen, and the logic of mass production itself. This configuration had tended to produce a more nearly classless society, that is, one in which income and status differences between the rich and the poor were assumed to have narrowed to the point where the majority were now deemed members of the great middle class. Specific versions of the profile concentrated on such themes as the "corporate soul,"[4] "countervailing power,"[5] "new competition,"[6] and "people's capitalism."[7] In one way or another, the popular pundits drew optimistic conclusions by projecting their pet postwar "discovery" into the indefinite future.

What the new profile symbolized, of course, was the development of a new liberalism that was essentially a rationalization of things that actually occurred. The brokers of this new creed summarized it in such phrases as the "welfare state" or the "mixed-enterprise system" or the "pluralistic society." (For extended discussion of this in relation to blacks, see Chapters 9, 12, 13.) They generally argued that the good society, at least in the mundane sense had arrived, and that therefore no valid argument could be made for fundamental change. To ex-political radicals, it spelled the "end . . . of domestic politics for those intellectuals who

---

[3]See F. L. Allen, *The Big Change*. New York: Harper & Row, 1952.

[4]A. A. Berle, Jr. *The 20th Century Capitalist Revolution*. New York: Harcourt Brace Jovanovich, 1954.

[5]J. K. Galbraith, *American Capitalism: The Concept of Countervailing Power*. Boston: Houghton Mifflin Company, 1952.

[6]D. E. Lilienthal, *Big Business: A New Era*. New York: Harper & Row, 1952.

[7]V. Perlo, "People's Capitalism and Stock-Ownership," *American Economic Review*, 1958, **48** (3), pp. 333–347.

must have ideologies or utopias to motivate them to political action."[8] The selection of evidence that "proved" this new mood of relative domestic tranquility was nourished by the economic logic of J. M. Keynes and an optimistic "climate of opinion."

The general acceptance of the welfare state and the emergence of the giant corporation as a clean-cut, reasonable edifice manned by men with M.B.A. degrees from the ivy league graduate schools of business converged inside a postwar social atmosphere in which vast middle layers of American society energetically fought to climb career ladders. For adults who managed to miss being drafted in World War II, the period between 1941 and 1945 was an economic blessing, especially when contrasted with the memories of the 1930s. These adults found lucrative occupations and businesses that escalated their economic status and eliminated their *de facto* economic insecurities—however psychologically doubtful they may have been about their economic fate upon the war's end. As for the returning young war heroes between the ages of 20 and 40, they displayed a compelling drive to make up for the time lost during the war. Given these predispositions, the traditional lure of success and material gain went to work with a vengeance to produce a very narrow and limited social ethos for the vast majority of the American people representing all walks of life.

In the context of relative affluence, some observers saw in this process the arrival of the bland society. Team work and "groupishness" operated, it was alleged, to undermine initiative and the willful madness of individual genius. The price demanded for success was a calculated drive to belong and to work cooperatively with others, especially when "others" meant those representing authority. The ordinary citizen sought security. The "rugged" businessman was caught inside an organizational complex. Suburbanites competed with other suburbanites in the game of imitation. And last, but not least, the younger generation was lamentably observed as silent. In general, a good portion of the decade was either periodically celebrated, or simply described in terms of caution, careerism, and conformity. To some moderate critics whose values were more attached to the past than the future, it meant the death of America's innovative spirit. Whether the mood of the fifties was interpreted positively or in a moderately critical way by the popular writers of the day, it was rarely expected that the mood would change precipitously for the worse.

[8]S. M. Lipset, *Political Man*. Garden City, N.Y.: Doubleday, 1960, p. 443.

While the above picture, admittedly, is a caricature and as such could be readily punctured by the inclusion of such events and phenomena as the Korean War, McCarthyism, the Berlin Blockade, the Hungarian Revolution, the media cynicism concerning Eisenhower's grammatical syntax and golf course escapades, the U-2 incident, the impact of Sputnik, and finally, the general fear of nuclear war, the fifties received these events and phenomena for the most part as exogenous to the American system. Except for Sputnik, these events rarely stimulated a serious examination of the internal working of any major institution. Thus, in spite of many particular reasons for gloom or social action, the central domestic tendency of the fifties was one of complacency, though not without some underlying uneasiness, which, as a matter of fact, began to manifest itself in more self-conscious ways as the decade came to a close. Some serious doubts concerning American complacency began to surface among various segments of the public. Alvin Hansen, a liberal Keynesian, for example, stated the matter simply: "We are living in an age . . . of disillusionment. We are trying to escape from reality. We do not like to face cold facts. . . ."[9] Similar outcries, some of which no doubt were more elegant, elaborate and involuted, emanated from persons representing very different persuasions.

Some professional economists, for example, doubted the apparent economic well-being and began to review the pattern of unemployment that had defined the labor market from at least 1955. The peaks of the prosperity periods, as observed from approximately the mid-fifties to the end of the decade, were accompanied by an abnormally high rate of unemployment which suggested a stagnation tendency associated with a long, downward swing in the economy. The matter was suggested by Moses Abramovitz, a highly respected economist on business cycles, at the 1959 hearings of the Congressional Joint Economic Committee:

> *The rate of growth of output . . . has not been great enough to absorb the growth in the labor supply and in the stock of capital. We are passing through a period of low rate of growth, after allowing for business cycles, and it is in that sort of period that we begin to accumulate idle resources, both of labor and capital. . . . The culminating event of each period of retarded growth has been a business depression of unusual severity and*

[9]A. Hansen, *Economic Issues of the 1960s.* New York: McGraw-Hill, 1960, p. 82.

> almost always of unusually long duration. . . . Indeed, each long
> swing of which we have a definite record has ended in a depres-
> sion of unusual duration.[10]

In essence, the fear was that the economy was suffering from an endemic disease which prevented full recovery, even though all the parts of the system appeared to be operating "normally." It was a sign of "creeping stagnation" that was not sufficiently dramatic to generate bold policies but sufficiently troublesome to produce general anxieties.

Other professional economists, less concerned with the business cycle per se, focused on the issue of structural unemployment—that is, unemployment that could not be absorbed simply by the standard procedure of increasing aggregate demand. On the popular level, the structural question was elaborated in terms of the possibility that automation was making less skilled portions of the labor force completely superfluous. On numerical tables, the human statistics showed that prosperous, "full" employment peaks did not significantly absorb the black portion of the total labor force. Chronic and long-duration unemployment was observed as a permanent condition for a significant part of the black population. Also, many discovered that blacks were dropping out of the labor force and, therefore, were left statistically unaccounted for in the measurement of black joblessness. This resulted in a serious understatement of the precarious position of the black community's future. At times, welfare rolls appeared to increase unabated in both prosperous and depressed periods.

To some social scientists, writing as general critics of the social scene, the eroding influence of affluence, which they associated with an overdeveloped private sector and an underdeveloped public one, became a critical issue. The culmination of this view was presented in John Kenneth Galbraith's Affluent Society.[11] In one sense, this book represented an extension of the complacent mood established in the early fifties; in another, it was a projection of some doubts and trepidations that culminated in the mid- and late sixties. On one level, Galbraith was saying that the American system had arrived; it had solved all our major domestic

---

[10]M. Abramovitz, Employment, Growth, and Price Levels. April 7–10, 1959, pp. 460, 412, 414.

[11]J. K. Galbraith, The Affluent Society. Boston: Houghton Mifflin Company, 1958.

problems in general, although there remained specific pockets of misery. But these pockets of misery were so unique that they did not lend themselves to general solutions; therefore, they did not require a political and social movement to eradicate them, but rather needed delicate instruments used by specialists, for example, social workers and mental health professionals. Thus, Galbraith was in tune with the "end-of-ideology" school which tended to view the approaching domestic crisis in narrow technical terms.

On another level, Galbraith was arguing the view of a "creeping socialist" and succeeded in raising some very serious questions. The public sector needed embellishment, according to Galbraith, not because capitalism had failed but because it had succeeded. The private sector had produced such great abundance that, on the margin, additional goods generated in this sector did not really provide satisfaction. In the jargon of the economist, he suggested that the marginal utility of goods produced in the private sector was approaching zero. While most economists in the profession sneered at this assertion, Galbraith demonstrated his proposition by pointing to the fact that producers must create wants through advertising, which, if they were not artificially manufactured, would not naturally or spontaneously occur or be sustained. The need to nurture wants or maintain a conditioning process to sustain them was a function of the "fact" that capitalism had fulfilled its historic mission, that is, the elimination of scarcity of those basic and urgent requirements related to economic survival. From this reasoning Galbraith derived his attack on conventional wisdom which is identified with a preoccupation with production to overcome scarcity. Unfortunately, and herein lies Galbraith's particular insight, the affluence created in the private sector was at the expense of the public sector, which had now become critical to the survival of an overcrowded urban civilization. The public sector had a vital role and mission. Further increases in the productive capacity of the system had to be absorbed for use by the state. This meant that the public sector had to grow both absolutely and relatively, and thereby increase its relative control over the resources of the nation.

When Galbraith suggested how this was to be accomplished, he became completely indecisive. He did not even recommend the need to curb, let alone eliminate, the influence and power of the private corporation, the main source of the superficial want-creating malaise that he identified. Nevertheless, by relating the deficiency of the public sector to the corporation that dominates the private one, Galbraith touched upon a critical nerve center of the system.

Finally, social scientists began dealing with urban issues in more fundamental terms, for example, school segregation, housing, poverty, and the aged. The anxiety level escalated, at least among more sensitive writers such as Michael Harrington. Some of the better-known social scientists of the early fifties who described why and how our country had "made it," though ritualistically critical of the complacent mood, became, in the full swing of the sixties, preoccupied with foreign crises, nonconformity, violence, black poverty, and militarism. Moreover, the treatment of these issues, more often than not, was related to the "system" or to structural rigidities in the society. In other words, especially in contrast to the fifties, the particular problems were not seen as isolated blemishes on an otherwise reasonably clean surface, but were seen increasingly as manifestations of broad social undercurrents and intransigent power structures that could not be controlled or readily extricated by habitual political routines.

One further aspect of the fifties which deeply affected the following decade warrants identification, and represents a strange paradox which writers who celebrated the fifties have not, and perhaps cannot, explain. In the midst of this complacent and prosperous decade, in which most Americans were insularly preoccupied with the pursuit of success, which saw the Communist Party, radical action groups, and radical thought decline to oblivion, there occurred an obsession with an alleged subversive menace. This general obsession was so inversely related to the general reality that it became necessary to reflect on the matter in terms of some gigantic and inexplicable myth that "somehow" gripped the American political mind. Carey McWilliams' observations on this point are very apt:

> The alleged communist issue has been investigated at every level, state, federal, and local, and in every walk of life, law, science, the ministry, education, the military, labor, industry, the arts, entertainment, the mass media—not once but again and again. . . . It has been "exposed" ad nauseam. . . . The phoniness of the issue has been ridiculed and satirized so often, and so widely, that our obsession with it has become an international

stock joke. All the while . . . the sleuths of HUAC . . . [*have*]
enormous difficulty in flushing out a few relics now and then
to exhibit at [*their*] *hearings.*

The American consensus on communism [*has been*] *so*
massive that the issue [*was*] *not debatable; there* [*was*] *no*
"opposition" to debate it. The fact is that we debate [*d*] *only*
the degree of hatred that all proper Americans are expected
to exhibit when the subject [*was*] *mentioned. "Liberals" and*
"conservatives" alike campaigned on the "anti-communism"
issue, which . . . [*was*] *a cover for the lack of platform or prog-*
ram. . . . Yet in volume and weight it remain [*ed*] *the most massive*
one in American politics—undebated, unchallenged, and mean-
ingless. No better proof is available of the fatuousness of Ameri-
can politics than our underlying obsession with this non-issue.[12]

While the detailed reasons for this deranged political preoccupation
with a non-issue are beyond the scope of this discussion, the matter cannot
be entirely neglected. As we have indicated, the preoccupation of American politics with communists was in the direction of a collective pathology;
it was inversely related to the *de facto* power of any domestic communist
or even radical activity. In fact, it was the absence of a significant radical
movement following World War II that enabled the political and social
life of the American people to become obsessed with a fiction. Nevertheless, this involvement served a very important consensus function. It
partially satisfied conservatives and nascent fascists who were against
the welfare state and so-called Rooseveltian socialism. It partially satisfied
anticommunist socialists, radicals, and New Dealers, all of whom became
completely disillusioned with the Soviet Union, Stalinism, and the Communist Party of the 1930s. Anticommunism partially satisfied the postwar
welfare-liberals who conformed to the anticommunist impulses on the
foreign front by supporting right-wing tyrants in the Third World in
exchange for a few domestic welfare programs of limited scope. Last
but not least, it partially satisfied the needs of the military and business
establishments.

This motley crew, many of whom became ex-socialists, ex-radicals,

---

[12]C. McWilliams, "Time for a New Politics." *The Nation*, May 26, 1962, p. 461.

ex-New Dealers, ex-believers in utopias and the perfectability of man, eventually became ideologues of the Democratic Party. As a result, the party lost its original identity and meaning and whatever political imagination and energy it had possessed. As the Democrats ran out of ideas and programs, their differences with modern Republicans became primarily quantitative, and therefore, uninspirational even to their own politically conscious constituencies. Because this process occurred in a political context which was devoid of a left-wing movement and in a social context characterized by negativism and cynicism, American society drifted to the right. The fifties closed on a note of political bankruptcy. In this political climate, John F. Kennedy, given his youth and manufactured political style, became a beacon to rank-and-file Democrats. Even then, he barely out-contested a totally detestable and empty political personality, Richard M. Nixon, whose narrow defeat was probably due less to Kennedy's political strengths than to Nixon's bad make-up and poor showing in the first Kennedy-Nixon TV debate.

Turbulent Sixties

The welfare-liberal ways of worrying as the sixties got underway were manifested in John F. Kennedy's campaign speeches which emphasized the need to get the country moving again. On the domestic front, the "new frontier" slogans advertised the need for growth. Kennedy's eventual commitment to the policy of cutting taxes to stimulate aggregate demand without a corresponding cut in government spending was a triumph of Keynesian economics consciously articulated for the first time by a president in order to cope with the sluggishness of domestic demand. The Manpower Development and Training Act and Area Development Programs were Kennedy's remedy to the academic concern with structural unemployment.

On the foreign front, the Cuban Revolution helped Kennedy take notice of the nationalistic and insurgent mood of the Third World. The now defunct Alliance for Progress was his answer to the implications of the Cuban Revolution. The Alliance was an effort to give vitality to the middle position in a polarized context in which the middle was not viable. This middle position was articulated by Walter Lippman in the following terms:

> *We cannot compete with Communism in Asia, Africa, or Latin America if we go on doing what we have done so often and so widely, which is to place the weak countries in a dilemma where they will stand still with us and our client rulers or start moving with the Communists. This dilemma cannot be resolved unless it is our central and persistent and unswerving policy to offer these unhappy countries a third option, which is economic development and social improvement without the totalitarian discipline of Communism. For the only real alternative to Communism is a liberal and progressive society.*[13]

As if not to take any chances, the rhetoric about the middle way was at the same time supplemented by Kennedy's interest in and growing endorsement of counterinsurgency warfare. Kennedy gradually came to see Vietnam as a place to test our capacity to crush the revolutionary path to reform and nation building. In so doing he set in motion the bureaucratic momentum that would make direct, large-scale military intervention inevitable, a position that he was purportedly against.[14]

   The possibility that the public architect of the most inhumane and most imperialistic involvement of our history should be publically endorsed by young welfare-liberals stationed in the Democratic Party was foreseen by a welfare-liberal himself as early as 1947. John Fairbank Jr., Harvard's Chinese expert and occasional consultant to the State Department, predicted the implications of our anticommunist pathology in the following way:

> *Our fear of Communism, partly as an expression of our general fear of the future, will continue to inspire us to aggressive anti-Communist policies in Asia and elsewhere, and the American people will be led to think and may honestly believe that the support of anti-Communist governments in Asia will somehow defend the American way of life. This line of American policy will lead to American aid to establish regimes which attempt*

[13]W. Lippman. Cited by N. Podhoretz, "America and the World Revolution," *Commentary*, October, 1963, p. 278.

[14]R. J. Barnet, *Intervention and Revolution*. New York: The World Publishing Co., 1968, p. 212.

to suppress the popular movements in Indonesia, Indochina, the Philippines, and China. . . . Thus, after setting out to fight Communism in Asia, the American people will be obliged in the end to fight the peoples of Asia.

This American aggression abroad will be associated with an increasing trend toward anti-Communist authoritarianism within the United States, which its victims will call fascism. This American fascism will come . . . because American liberals have joined the American public in a fear of Communism from abroad rather than fascism at home as the chief totalitarian menace.[15]

Needless to say, the New Frontier's domestic and foreign policies were woefully insufficient to cope with the deep social malaise that was growing in the domestic and international arena. Thus, it was possible for James Reston, who was not unsympathetic to Kennedy, to write in the midst of the short-lived Kennedy years in the White House that a gap had developed:

. . . between reality and public pronouncements. The result is that they talk moderately and optimistically in public and radically and pessimistically in private. This poisons the atmosphere in Washington and debases the whole political process.[16]

From the point of view of getting Congress to act, Kennedy's assassination accomplished what he himself had been unable to accomplish before his tragic death. Lyndon Baines Johnson managed to push through Congress, in a relatively short period, all of Kennedy's proposals—plus a few of his own—as a result, partly, of his sweeping victory over Goldwater, and partly as a result of a political debt which Congress felt was owed to the Kennedy legacy.

Yet, in spite of the "innovations" which were heralded as unparalleled in the history of the nation, the credibility gap noted by Reston about Kennedy was reiterated by Reston to describe the Johnson years.

[15]J. Fairbanks, Jr. Cited by N. Chomsky, "Cambodia," *The New York Review of Books,* June 4, 1970, p. 39.

[16]J. Reston, "The Credibility Gap." *New York Times,* Oct. 23, 1963, p. 40.

The sta.idard welfare-liberal rhetoric and corresponding programs appeared incredible because the unfolding events were beyond the analytic capacities of those who legislated from the confines of the existing institutional framework. The anxieties and great doubts that have mushroomed into the public arena in the sixties do not reflect a personal disillusionment with individual leaders, though.that is the standard way in which the die is cast. They are actually related to real fears that our existing routines, defined by the institutions to which the leaders are confined, will not be able to manage, let alone resolve, the imminent crises of our time.

Hinterland and Inner City

American society and the economic system that drives it have been simultaneously hit by two crises. One is the threat of the revolutionary movements in the Third World. This exists, of course, in the hinterland of our empire. The other is the explosive nature of our inner or central cities, and reflects the dimensions of race-class segregation, black poverty, black powerlessness, and black cultural degradation.

A Marxist might argue that both crises emanate from a common denominator: the system's inability to create productive, meaningful, and useful work for large numbers of people.[17] Whether the crises have a common cause or not, they have converged to undermine the relevance of our existing institutions, the leadership that mans them, and the ideology that justifies them. They have shaken the confidence of the American ruling classes.

For different reasons, the crises of the hinterland and that of our central city have led to an examination of the American corporation: on the one hand, its international role in determining our foreign policy and in affecting the character of the Third World societies; and on the other, its domestic role in determining the character of government and ghetto in the mixed-enterprise system or the welfare state (see Chapters 10 and 11).

The hinterland crisis is related to the fusion of a permanent layer of national-security managers with large parts of the American industrial

[17]P. Baron and P. Sweezy, *Monopoly Capital*. New York: Monthly Review Press, 1966.

system. The racial crisis is connected to the welfare state, as initiated by the Democratic Party.

Our political instrumentalities, reflecting the exigencies of our economic system after World War II, have lavished status upon, and given power to, a military apparatus. This apparatus has now acquired a momentum which cannot easily be stopped by the political rhythms characteristic of the Democratic and Republican Parties or by the marginal efforts of those outside these parties. The military has combined with industry to form deep vertical enclaves involving thousands of prime contractors and subcontractors, whole states and state legislatures, universities, middle-range technicians of all kinds, national politicians, and labor unions representing millions of ordinary workers. One of the main outcomes of this process is that we habitually see all upheavals in the Third World as contrary to our economic, political, and military interests. Those who have economic power are the prime benefactors of these developments. They are in a position to get the state to bequeath to them the additional property rights, contract rights, privileges, and protection that are necessary to carry on the business of international management. Since that business is the whole world, the world has become the playground for its penetration.

While not all business enterprises have the scope and depth of interests of Standard Oil of New Jersey, it is worth describing the extent of this corporation's tentacles:

> *Standard Oil of New Jersey has a budget exceeding $15 billion, or double the GNP of Cuba. More powerful than many sovereign states, it has 150,000 agents, organizers and hired hands operating 250 suborganizations in more than 50 countries. It is part of an international syndicate which controls the economic lifeblood of half a dozen strategic countries in the underdeveloped world. In itself it is a major political force in the key electoral states of New York, Pennsylvania, New Jersey, and Texas, and it has close links with other syndicate members that are major political forces in California, Ohio, Louisiana, Indiana and elsewhere. Its agents and their associates occupied the cabinet post of Secretary of State in the Administrations of Eisenhower, Kennedy, and Johnson, and at the same time had influence in the CIA and other foreign-policy-making organizations of govern-*

ment at the highest levels. It has its own intelligence and paramilitary networks, and a fleet of ships larger than the Greek Navy. It is not a secret organization but it is run by a self-perpetuating oligarchy whose decisions and operations are secret. And these affect directly, and significantly, the level of activity of the whole U.S. economy.[18]

The market penetration of Third World economies by giant corporations has led to a deep social disequilibrium in the underdeveloped world. It has produced a revolutionary backlash that we sought to contain by building an imperial political edifice in order to complement and protect the private corporate interests that preceded it. As a result, we have become entangled in a global network that is now beginning to follow the path of the Roman Empire in its declining years. Joseph Schumpeter, writing in 1918, describes Rome's internal mood in its decades of demise:

> *Here is the classic example of that kind of insincerity in both foreign and domestic affairs which permeates not only avowed motives but also probably the conscious motives of the actors themselves—of that policy which pretends to aspire to peace but unerringly generates war, the policy of continual preparation for war, the policy of meddlesome interventionism. There was no corner of the known world where some interest was not alleged to be in danger or under actual attack. If the interests were not Roman, they were those of Rome's allies; and if Rome had no allies, then allies would be invented. When it was utterly impossible to contrive such an interest—why, then it was the national honor that had been insulted. The fight was always invested with an aura of legality. Rome was always being attacked by evil-minded neighbors, always fighting for a breathing space. The whole world was pervaded by a host of enemies, and it was manifestly Rome's duty to guard against their indubitably aggressive designs. They were enemies who only waited to fall on the Roman people.*[19]

[18]D. Horowitz, "Social Science or Ideology?" *Social Policy*, September–October, 1970, p. 30.

[19]J. Schumpeter, *Imperialism*. New York: Meridian Books, 1955, p. 51.

Schumpeter went on to argue that Rome's wars of conquest made no sense from the point of view of concrete objectives. Rome continued to relate to the rest of the world in an increasingly self-destructive way because imperial institutions, gathering their own momentum, could not be stopped. In the end the empire collapsed from sheer exhaustion. The empire's limits were defined by the internal unrest of Rome's slave population and by a communication and transportation network that was unable to keep pace with the empire's outreach.

Like Rome's, our meddlesome interventionism also involves constraints of a military and ideological nature. On the military side, we are faced with the necessity of avoiding a direct conflict with the USSR. On the ideological one, we must be able to sell our interventionism to the American public. The first constraint was fixed by the outcome of World War II and enforced by the possibility of nuclear war, a result of Russia's possession of the atomic bomb. The second constraint was less formidable, less precise, and less knowable. It depended upon the system's ability to generate a consensus ideology that could either hold disparate interests together on some level or could desensitize the public and blind it to the system's exploitation of places far beyond its borders. The "cementing" ideology, as we have already suggested, was anticommunism.

The binding power of anticommunism is ceasing to function. Ideological unity on the foreign front has reached a state of accelerated dissolution. Moreover, disunity over the "proper" degree of American imperial hegemony is being matched by, perhaps, an even greater disunity over the prognosis for our central cities. This, of course, takes us into the major internal crisis of our society.

As we have already observed, the inner cities consist of concentrations of blacks who are overrepresented in the lower class, in the lumpen criminal class, in the welfare class, and in the political and culturally alienated class. The black population is too large to be integrated into the American mainstream under conditions of economic normalcy and it is too small to achieve sufficient power in its own terms. This is the predicament of the black community. It is not capable of integrating into the American society, nor is it capable of separating and acquiring autonomy—an autonomy that might not provide riches, but that would provide what Oscar Lewis observed when he returned to visit Cuba some years after the revolution:

In 1947 I undertook a study of a slum in Havana. Recently I had an opportunity to revisit the same slum and some of the same families. The physical aspect of the place had changed little, except for a beautiful new nursery school. The people were as poor as before, but I was impressed to find much less of the feelings of despair and apathy, so symptomatic . . . in the urban slums of the U.S. The slum was now highly organized, with block committees, educational committees, and party committees. The people had found a new sense of power and importance.[20]

The black tragedy is that black Americans constitute a quasi-colony. They suffer from a chronic resource drain without any serious hope of transforming their homeland, a permanent ghetto, into a self-propelling, self-developing nation or community.

Class-race conflict is affecting the viability of the public agencies that have become part of the welfare-liberal state, as well as the viability of the welfare-liberals themselves. Consciously or unconsciously, American corporate and political interests have been forced to pursue the Bismarckian welfare game, dispensing the minimum necessary benefits to maintain the social peace, while at the same time creating a vast military sector consisting of wasted resources and wasted people. That is the essence of the mixed economy at this stage in our history.

Since the costs (political, social, and economic) of maintaining our present foreign posture are becoming excessive and the domestic cost for social peace is rising beyond the delivery capacities of the economy, the welfare state is "up against the wall."

The welfare state, moreover, dispenses disproportionately more welfare to the wealthy and property owners than to the poor and propertyless. Examples, among others, of such dispensations are subsidized housing, so-called regulation of industry, aid to farmers, tax laws, and licensing procedures used for granting property rights and privileges by the state. In all these, state intervention produced, in addition to stability, benefits that favored house owners over those who need houses, rich farmers over poor ones, and big businesses over small ones. These are not only our assertions, but conclusions drawn from studies conducted

[20]O. Lewis, "The Culture of Poverty." *Scientific American,* October, 1966, p. 19.

by welfare-liberals themselves and frankly admitted and understood by well-heeled property owners (see Chapter 13).

Accompanying ruling-class privileges and rigidities is the fearful contemplation by the ruling class of failure in both the international and the domestic arenas. The ensuing possibilities are leading to a systematic reliance on police instruments of control and surveillance in a social context of organized chaos and impotence. The need for such controls is becoming more pronounced because the public burden of maintaining and expanding our empire is causing unrest. The internal ideology, used to bring about adherence to the prevailing policies of the ruling establishment, is disintegrating. Its use in justifying, not only the empire, but our present composition of GNP and its inequitable distribution is likewise failing. The capitalistic ethic, while always dominant among capitalists, has been thoroughly assimilated by the professional classes, the paraprofessional classes, the skilled workers, the unskilled workers, and those who do not work. The latter group includes both the rich and the poor. The American public in toto is now demanding as much as it can get for as little effort. No economic system can afford that demand or meet such appetites. This state of affairs has caused serious doubts about the viability of the system from none other than James M. Roche, chairman of a company a little larger than Yugoslavia—the General Motors Corporation:

> *The dull cloud of pessimism which some have cast over free enterprise is impairing the ability of business to meet its basic economic responsibilities—not to mention its capacity to take on newer ones. This, as much as any other factor, makes it urgent that those of us who are in business stand up and be counted.* [21]

Rest assured that when the chairman of GM stands up to be counted, it is not going to be one man, one vote.

Conclusions and Implications

American society can no longer fight wars against national liberation and expect popular support for them. World War II was our last popular

---

[21]J. M. Roche, "Defending Big Business," *New York Times,* April 27, 1971, p. 47.

war. Wars waged against the Third World nations can no longer find a domestic ideological marketplace. The climate of domestic opinion and the quality of our social energies have been negatively affected by direct military and paramilitary policing involvement in the Third World nations.

Involvement affects the magnitude and nature of human and nonhuman resources available for internal use, but more importantly, it affects the kinds of business, social, and political leaders who acquire positions of power in our corporate, institutional, and political bureaucracies. The ideological climate determines the motivation and meaning that propel one's activities, both in civic and vocational realms. In sum, it is difficult to carry on wars against self-determination and simultaneously cultivate our best instincts at home. Ultimately, it is the struggle on the domestic front that we must undertake.

On this front, there is no other issue that pervades more aspects of American life than the one concerned with black-white relations. Put simply, no solution to the black predicament is possible until the issues of our empire are properly reduced by the defeat of American imperialism, and that cannot be accomplished only by peasants and guerrilla armies. It must be undertaken here at home in a battle for a decent and meaningful existence. But herein lies the danger: as our empire's disintegration accelerates, it will produce a stream of frustrated right-wing cadre of considerable size in all parts of the country whose energies will increasingly be devoted to politics. This demagogic cadre will have roots among middle-class whites (white- and blue-collar alike). Their fears and hatred of blacks will find political expression as blacks seek a permanent place in the political and social arena of our economically debased central cities. It is with this foreboding that we turn to examine the nature of various solutions, salvation schemes, policies, and movements aimed at overcoming the barriers shaping black-white relations and determining the black population's fate.

CHAPTER 8

Race, Black Power, and Nationalism

One major form of analysis of the black dilemma emphasizes almost exclusively the importance of race and racism. The proponents of this analysis see the existence of racism as the heart of the problems of blacks. To them, white racism is of such continuing and overwhelming importance that other considerations, such as ethnicity and class, play at best a minor role in determining the position of the black man in the United States. According to the proponents of this form of analysis, even the basic structure of the social system is only a secondary consideration; a change of economic and political forms would mean little to the black man. As long as the system is a predominantly white one, the argument goes, it will be hostile to black needs and interests. Racism is carried by whites in all realms and situations, and therefore the bases of all programs, analyses, and solutions must rest on the matter of race difference.[1]

[1] We shall call the adherents of this view race analysts or advocates.

Race Advocates

According to Robert Allen, a proponent of race analysis, the race factor is the basis of the "murder, brutality, exploitation and . . . force" upon which "the American system is based."[2] Harold Cruse is another race advocate who typifies the thinking implicit in a racial analysis while emphasizing the cultural aspects of the problem:

> *At the bottom of the whole question of the backward cultural development of America, the cultural banality, the cultural decadence, the cultural debasement of the entire American social scene, lies the reality of racism—racial exclusion, racial exploitation, racial segregation and all the manifestations of the ideology of white superiority.*[3]

The basis for the race analysis often is the perceived relationship between the treatment of blacks in the past and contemporary treatment of them, in which past treatment is viewed as the direct cause of current conditions. Color, in other words, has been the primary cause of discrimination, and the importance of racism transcends any other explanation.

The groups which view America from the perspective of a race analysis fall under two general categories: those who advocate black power and those who advocate black nationalism. These two categories are similar but not identical. While not all black-power groups are nationalists, all nationalist groups are necessarily concerned with achieving black power. Both groups, however, tend to share a common rhetoric.

Our examination will be divided into three basic parts: (1) a description of the major thematic interests common to both groups, (2) an analysis of black-power programs and their underlying assumptions, and (3) an analysis of black-nationalist programs and assumptions.

Common Themes

The speeches and writings of black-power and black-nationalist advocates share several common themes. The starting point of all race analysts

[2]R. L. Allen, *Black Awakening in Capitalist America: An Analytic History.* Garden City, N.Y.: Doubleday, 1970, p. 3.

[3]H. Cruse, *Rebellion or Revolution?* New York: William Morrow & Company, Inc., 1968, p. 116.

is the belief that any solution to the problems of blacks must be structured along purely racial lines. Since, they hold, America is a racist country and beyond redemption, the initial emphasis should be on the need to educate blacks to the importance and pervasiveness of racism. The development of racial pride and of black consciousness must come with this knowledge. This belief leads to a preoccupation with the black self-image. Unlike the NAACP or Urban League, which attempt to make the Negro more acceptable to whites, the advocacy of black consciousness involves the development of a distinct identity—historical, social, and group. The development of identity, which is seen as basic to the black man's fight for cultural freedom and economic equality, takes a variety of forms. First, the concept "black" is completely reevaluated and redefined in terms of beauty and strength rather than submission and inferiority. For example, in discussing the Lowndes County Freedom Organization, Stokely Carmichael states:

> *When [it] chose the black panther as its symbol, it was christened by the press "The Black Panther Party"—but the Alabama Democratic Party, whose symbol is a rooster, has never been called the White Cock Party. . . . A black panther is a bold, beautiful animal, representing the strength and dignity of black demands today. A man needs a black panther on his side when he and his family must endure—as hundreds of Alabamians have endured—loss of job, eviction, starvation, and sometimes death, for political activity.* [4]

Second, the black man is made aware of his connections with the nations of Africa. Race advocates stress both the rich heritage of Africa's past and its recent successes in achieving independence through its own efforts. Malcolm X reminded us that the Mau Mau was also a minority, a microscopic minority, "but it was the Mau Mau who . . . brought independence to Kenya." [5]

Finally, and most important, the black man is imbued with an ethos of power and self-respect that grows from self-discipline, commitment to a great cause, and being part of and identified with a black movement that is engaged in a history-shaking journey.

[4] S. Carmichael, "What We Want," *The New York Review of Books*, September 22, 1966, pp. 5–6.
[5] J. Illo, "The Rhetoric of Malcolm X." *Columbia University Forum*, Spring 1966, 9, pp. 10–11.

This emphasis on the development of a new black identity and sense of power leads to the second major theme of racial analysis: the need for self-determination of blacks, for a concentrated attempt to place black people in positions of leadership on all levels in order to facilitate black control of all institutions which affect black people's lives. An often-repeated cry is the insistence that "we must determine our own destiny."[6]

The demand for self-determination is often linked to an analogy with colonialism, a third major theme (see Chapter 6). The black community is thus seen as "struggling for its [political] self-determination as a colony against an imperial power."[7] It is seen as a colony largely because of the lack of control blacks have over their environment:

> *In these cities, we do not control our resources, we do not control the land, the houses or the stores. These are owned by whites who live outside the community. These are very real colonies, as their capital and cheap labor are exploited by those who live outside the cities. White power makes the laws and enforces those laws with guns and nightsticks in the hands of white racist policemen and black mercenaries.*[8]

These three themes—the need for a black identity, for black self-determination, and the colonial analogy—all lead race advocates to argue for independent political and economic action. In economic terms, this leads to an emphasis on economic cooperatives and on the development of a racially-based economy in which black consumers buy from black producers in segregated markets. Politically, race advocates all argue

[6]SNCC position paper on black power. "Who Is the Real Villain—Uncle Tom or Simon Legree?" in T. Wagstaff (ed.), *Black Power: The Radical Response to White America.* Beverly Hills: Glencoe Press, 1969, p. 115. According to this position paper, "If we are to proceed toward true liberation, we must cut ourselves off from white people."

[7]J. Turner, "Blacks in the Cities: Land and Self-Determination." *The Black Scholar*, 1970, 1(6), p. 9. The colonial analogy also leads SNCC to its emphasis on self-determination (see SNCC position paper, in T. Wagstaff (ed.), p. 117). SNCC describes many whites as similar to the white civil servants and missionaries in colonial countries by virtue of the paternalistic attitude toward blacks which both those groups adopt. Evidence of the primacy of racism in the United States is gathered from the fact that American whites often support anticolonialism in other countries, but view black Americans as racists when they have similar goals.

[8]S. Carmichael, Speech at a meeting of Latin American revolutionaries in Cuba, 1967. Cited by R. L. Allen, p. 7.

for some kind of independent political action, movement or bloc-voting strategy.

Finally, the race advocates see themselves in opposition to several other major approaches to black problems. They are in conflict with those whom they label "integrationists," that is, those people who see a real possibility for blacks to achieve a meaningful level of equality alongside whites within American society.[9] Race advocates claim that integrationists refuse to accept the most basic fact about America—that it is essentially racist—and that because of this racism the black man has always been betrayed and will continue to be betrayed by white Americans. While such older groups as the National Association for the Advancement of Colored People (NAACP), the Urban League, and the Southern Christian Leadership Conference (SCLC), tend to emphasize working within the established legal and social order, the advocates of a race analysis, viewing such attempts as hopeless, often postulate the need to work outside the system. This sometimes involves either a covert or an unconcealed threat of violence. Such rhetoric, while not necessarily a logical outgrowth of the racial focus, seems almost inevitably to flow from it.

The race emphasis is also opposed to the ethnic model (see Chapter 9), within which blacks are regarded as parallel to other immigrant groups. While many white immigrant groups have become incorporated into the system, race advocates do not believe blacks can repeat this success because of the racist character of American society. A race emphasis also implies a rejection of Marxist class analysis (see Chapter 10) on the ground that it ignores some very crucial facts about the nature of American capitalism and about the American labor movement. In their critique of Marxian class analysis, the race advocates maintain that black and white workers have been partially or wholly coopted by the consumerism of American capitalism. Since American labor, and especially American labor unions, is among the most discriminatory and racist groups in the United States, the race advocates reject the Marxist view of the labor movement as an instrument of revolution leading to a transformation of the black condition. According to them, the failure to understand this has often cause blacks to be used as pawns by the Marxian socialists.[10]

---

[9]An important distinction here is that between 'integration" and "assimilation." The former implies equality in all areas, the latter, the loss of cultural identity. All groups, including the integrationists, reject the latter; it is the former, the belief in integration, that is the issue.

[10]For a discussion of the relationship between Negroes and the Communist Party, see H. Cruse, *The Crisis of the Negro Intellectual.* New York: William Morrow & Company, Inc.,

Black Power

Turning to an analysis of the black-power movement, two things become clear. First, while all black-power advocates accept at least some of the themes mentioned above, most of them emphasize one or several at the expense of others. For some, black power is related to organizing blacks to vote; for others, it implies the search for economic power; for still others, it implies the use of violence. For many it is a call to black people to reorient their values and regain the pride and power which black people had in Africa before it was dominated by the Europeans. For most, black power is a combination of several of these themes.

The adherence of black-power advocates to a race analysis leads to a deep tension between their radical rhetoric and their relatively conservative programmatic activities and proposals. In terms of *economic* programs, for example, the Congress of Racial Equality (CORE) has developed a number of cooperatives around the country such as the one in Opelousa, Louisiana, where it has organized over 300 black farmers into the Grand Marie cooperative.[11] Yet the credit unions and cooperatives established by black-power groups are not very different in principle from programs such as Operation Breadbasket developed by SCLC, an organization to which black-power advocates are theoretically opposed. The *political* programs emanating from a race analysis show no greater consistency between rhetoric and practice. In some cases black power has resulted in an emphasis on "the organization of voters into self-interested units."[12] The Student Nonviolent Coordinating Committee (SNCC) was formerly most active in breaking down various legal barriers which had hindered blacks. Even Robert Williams, at one point regarded as an ultra-militant, speaks of the need for blacks to work within the system: "It is a grave error," he writes, "for militant and just-minded youth to reject struggle-serving opportunities to join the man's government services, police forces, peace corps, and vital organs of the power structure." Williams justifies this by his belief that "Militant change can be more

1967. For a fictionalized rendering of this relationship, see R. Ellison, *Invisible Man*. New York: New American Library, 1952.

[11]C. V. Hamilton, "An Advocate of Black Power Defines It," in T. Wagstaff (ed.), p. 128. CORE's adoption of black capitalism at its 1968 convention is a further example of this tendency.

[12]J. Bond, *Rights and Reviews*, Winter 1966–1967. Cited by H. Cruse, *The Crisis of the Negro Intellectual*, p. 555.

thoroughly effectuated by militant pressure from within as well as without."[13] Stripped of the rhetoric, such proposals differ little from some proposals of the early civil rights movement. It is interesting to note that Stokely Carmichael, one of the first to use the term "Black Power," now regards the early civil rights movement as irrelevant in terms of objective solutions; its only usefulness, he claims, was in heightening the contradictions in America and raising black consciousness.[14] Ironically, the only part of the black-power political program that might not be acceptable to some of the traditional leaders is the call for an independent political party. In general, despite the rhetoric, the race analysis has not in fact led black-power groups to any radically new programs. Black-power programs in general stand in complete contradiction to the rhetoric of black-power groups. Carmichael and Hamilton present a further example of this tension in their rhetoric of power and of "taking care of business," and their concrete programs, which could be advocated by any traditional pluralist.[15]

A further inconsistency in the race emphasis has to do with the role it assigns to the federal government. On the one hand, race rhetoric emphasizes that American society, especially the American government, is totally corrupt, racist, irredeemable. At the same time, there is a continued emphasis on the need for help from the government. Harold Cruse points out that:

> In the New York Post of August, 1967, a news item stated that Floyd McKissick, Wilfred Ussery, and Roy Innis demanded that the U.S. Department of Labor "develop a crash program for jobless Negroes and a living allowance until jobs are found." They also demanded that anti-poverty funds be increased by a billion dollars. These are all Black Power advocates, but they are also showing a whole lot of reliance on the capitalist government to secure Black Power reform.[16]

[13]R. F. Williams, "An Interview with Robert F. Williams," The Black Scholar, 1970, 1(7), p. 13. Recently, Williams has indicated that what concerns him most about the present situation is "the lack of dialog between the races, a gulf widened by new feelings of separatism among Blacks." See J. Dreyfuss, "Former Militant Sees Cause for Hope," New York Post, Aug. 3, 1971, p. 6.

[14]S. Carmichael, "We Are All Africans," The Black Scholar, 1970, 1(7), 16.

[15]S. Carmichael and C. V. Hamilton, Black Power: The Politics of Liberation in America. New York: Vintage Books, 1967.

[16]H. Cruse, Rebellion or Revolution? p. 235.

If one is to take the rhetoric of the race advocates literally, then any attempt to get support from the federal government is a contradiction in terms, since the government is assumed to be overwhelmingly racist. One is also inclined to wonder in what way the demand for federal involvement differs from programs such as the domestic Marshall Plan put forth by the National Urban League in 1963, or from A. Philip Randolph's Freedom Budget. The value or lack of value of such programs is not the question here. Rather, it is the fact that the rhetoric of race advocates is inconsistent with their actual programs. Even Charles Hamilton, one of the early theoreticians of black power, points out that "It is clear that Black people will need the help of whites at many places along the line."[17] If the racial analysis is correct, such help will never be forthcoming from a basically racist white America. While Hamilton points to the efforts of a group called NEGRO (National Economic Growth and Reconstruction Organization) as a good example of black power in action, it should be noted that its activities include a hospital in Queens, a chemical corporation, a textile company, and a construction company. These projects are all far from "revolutionary"; in fact, they are all projects that even the most establishment-oriented, middle-class reformer might applaud. In a telling detail, Hamilton describes NEGRO as "following the Puritan ethic of work and achievement." Although in a later sentence we learn that NEGRO "believes that Black people will never develop in this country as long as they must depend on handouts from the White man,"[18] it is hard to see how the racial model has led to anything new or revolutionary. Cruse makes it very clear that while such programs may be valuable, they are completely within the reformist tradition:

> *This is not to say that the achievements of the direct actionists are not valuable bases upon which other things can be structured, but they are still* reformist *and gradualistic ideas with which not a single NAACP-er nor King passive resister could argue.*[19]

Cruse's summary of black power as "the economic and political philosophy

[17]C. V. Hamilton, p. 132.

[18]C. V. Hamilton, p. 129.

[19]H. Cruse, *The Crisis of the Negro Intellectual,* p. 546. Emphasis original. Robert Allen makes a similar point in his book *Black Awakening in Capitalist America.*

of Booker T. Washington given a 1960s militant shot in the arm and brought up to date" is probably accurate.[20]

There is a more basic contradiction in race analysis as it is used by black-power groups. On the one hand, the explanation of the black man's situation is couched in racial terms. On the other hand, black-power programs are precisely those that would be feasible within an open, pluralist society, which the race analysis denies as existing in America. Pluralist theory implies an open society in which various groups compete on a relatively free and equal basis. If the United States is in fact a pluralist society, then the logical thing for each group to do is to pursue tactics that would increase its ability to compete with and exert pressure on other groups. A consistent race analysis, however, denies such a possibility. If the all-encompassing racism that pervades America makes it impossible for black groups to have the power or the opportunity to compete, then any programs based on a belief in pluralism are doomed to failure.

Nevertheless, many black-power advocates who believe all doors are closed to blacks simultaneously indicate their acceptance of a view of America as a pluralist society. Carmichael and Hamilton, in one of the initial definitions of black power, write:

> Before a group can enter the open society, *it must first close ranks. By this we mean that group solidarity is necessary before a group can operate effectively from a bargaining position of strength in a* pluralistic society.[21]

In the same book they also claim that "Politically, black power means what it has always meant to SNCC: the coming together of black people to elect representatives and to force those representatives to speak to their needs."[22] But this is, of course, precisely the strategy inherent in pluralist politics.

This underlying acceptance of pluralism leads to the kinds of black-power programs already mentioned. The most severe criticism of such programs is not that they are reformist, but that they are based on assump-

---

[20]H. Cruse, *Rebellion or Revolution?* p. 201.

[21]S. Carmichael and C. V. Hamilton, p. 44. First emphasis original, second emphasis added.

[22]S. Carmichael and C. V. Hamilton.

tions about the nature of American politics that contradict the view such groups claim to hold. If racism in the United States is in fact so overwhelming, then clearly blacks will never be able to operate in the same manner as other organized interest groups, no matter what tactics they adopt; they cannot proceed as if the United States were, in fact, a pluralist society.

If the race advocates are correct, there is virtually no room for blacks to maneuver within the system. The only possible resolution to this dilemma is complete separation, which, in our view, is unattainable and therefore utopian. The race advocates are caught between Scylla and Charybdis. They speak with the rhetoric of race but are forced to act on the assumptions of pluralism. Thus, black-power advocates who seek programmatic solutions in the form of community control turn to the federal government, since community projects tend not to be viable without federal financing. It is no surprise that, in the end, Robert Williams was "convinced that the Federal Government offers the only real hope that the Negro has of winning any large measure of his civil rights,"[23] or that Carmichael and Hamilton believe that the black struggle will see meaningful gains only when those gains are strengthened by black-white alliances.[24] This process of consolidating group strength and then bargaining to form alliances with other groups is precisely what pluralism means. The most ironic statement of the situation can be found in a book by Nathan Wright, chairman of the 1967 Newark Black-Power Conference. In the name of black power, Wright urged blacks to work together:

> *to seek executive positions in corporations, bishoprics, deanships of cathedrals, superintendencies of schools, and high-management positions in banks, stores, investment houses, legal firms, civic and government agencies and factories.*[25]

Wright has been rightly criticized by the black left on the ground that his program is primarily for the black middle class.[26] More important,

---

[23]J. Mayfield, "Challenge to Negro Leadership—the Case of Robert Williams," *Commentary*, April 1962, p. 300.

[24]S. Carmichael and C. V. Hamilton, p. 6.

[25]N. Wright, Jr., *Black Power and Urban Unrest*. New York: Hawthorn, 1967, p. 43.

[26]See R. L. Allen, p. 50

Wright's policy is simply an extreme example of the reformist *practice* inherent in most black-power proposals, which, as noted, is in contradiction to the rhetoric of race advocates.

Theodore Draper has accurately pointed out how unfeasible many black-power programs are:

> *All these plans have one curious characteristic. They serve notice in advance that they want and need the good offices of the present federal government in order to make the black population independent of that government. . . . These terms imply that the federal government is expected to aid and abet the disruption and dissolution of the existing American nation. Such a strategy may seem clever to its proponents, but the likelihood of its being clever enough to work would seem to be very slight.*[27]

Unfortunately Draper is right, though his tone is sour and even snide. Such programs are not suggested because they are considered "clever," but because the black-power advocate finds so little room within which to maneuver that he is ultimately forced to grab at straws and act inconsistently.

Black Nationalism

In addition to black-power groups, there are nationalists who are likewise preoccupied with the race analysis. In some sense, black nationalism, a term which has generated enormous confusion, is the most basic expression of the racial emphasis.

Historically, the concept of nationalism has been directly tied to ownership of, and control over, a specific land area. Black nationalism in the United States has taken two forms: The first is concerned with external emigration, that is, complete physical separation from whites by emigration outside the boundaries of the United States. Such a position was held by, among others, Martin Delany in the nineteenth century and Marcus Garvey in the early twentieth century. The second form, which is a variation of this theme, is one which calls for "internal emigra-

[27]T. Draper, *The Rediscovery of Black Nationalism*. New York: The Viking Press, 1970, p. 141.

tion," that is, physical separation within the United States. Such a position demands that a specific territory within the United States be declared as an independent black state, populated only by black people.

In the current context, however, nationalism seems to have taken on a broader meaning. The idea of external emigration has come to seem almost hopeless since, as several authors have pointed out, the majority of blacks in the United States do not exhibit a desire to return to Africa.[28] Internal emigration seems equally unfeasible. The United States does not appear even remotely interested in turning over several states to blacks. Even if it were, it is extremely unlikely that blacks could operate as an independent country within white America. For some, the rationale behind this rejection of internal emigration is derived directly from a race analysis. Carmichael, for example, points out that "there is no way we can operate as an independent island surrounded by the hostile white community with their police and military forces."[29] Whatever the reasons, the problems in such a program seem so overwhelming that it has gained little support.

As a result, most contemporary nationalist theorists do not emphasize the land question. At least one nationalist writer has defined the concept of nation largely in terms of race:

> *The national character of the Negro has little to do with what part of the country he lives in. . . . His national boundaries are the color of his skin, his racial characteristics, and the social conditions within his sub-cultural world.*[30]

The colonial analogy, which the nationalists often rely on, would seem to imply the need for a land base. Nationalist theoreticians have recourse to history to explain the absence of such a base. During slavery, black people in Africa were separated from a territory that was rightfully theirs, and this is what makes them "the archetype of a colonial society."[31] Land, in other words, is not crucial to a definition of colonial status.[32]

---

[28]See, for example, T. Draper.

[29]S. Carmichael, p. 16.

[30]H. Cruse, *Rebellion or Revolution?*, p. 78.

[31]J. Turner, p. 10.

[32]Within this framework, Draper's criticism of the nationalists for their lack of a land base seems distinctly unfair. Draper's criticism of the blacks is akin to Stalin's thinking about the

"In defining the colonial problem it is the role of the institutional mechanisms of colonial domination which are decisive."[33]

When the land question arises, it is usually in the form of a call for black cities. James Turner asserts that "without control over land, resources, and production there can be no self-determination for a people."[34] Roy Innis in 1968 argued for a number of dispersed city-states constituting "a series of islands with land separating us."[35] Another solution to the land problem has been the call for "total control of the U.S."[36] The problems involved in black control of cities will be discussed later in this book; more to the point here is the fact that, by and large, contemporary nationalism tends to deemphasize the land question and to settle for a more amorphous definition of nationalism.[37] If there is any common denominator to the various forms of nationalism in existence today, it

Jews: because the Jews did not fit Stalin's preconceived definition of a nation, he refused to recognize them as such and repressed the Zionist movement. Draper too is setting up a preconceived definition of nation and criticizing blacks for failing to meet his criteria. The Jews thought of themselves as a nation even though (until 1947) they had no more specific territory than American blacks have today. Yet that belief undoubtedly helped to unite the Jews, and this unity was certainly instrumental in their final acquisition of their own territory. See T. Draper, *The Rediscovery of Black Nationalism.*

[33]J. H. O'Dell, *Freedomways*, 7(1). Cited by R. L. Allen, p. 8. Another attempt to avoid the problem of a lack of territory is presented by Roy Innis: "Oppression can occur in one's homeland or in the homeland of the oppressor and the latter has been suffered only by two great peoples—the Jews and the American Blacks" (cited by J. Turner, "Blacks in the Cities: Land and Self-Determination," p. 10).

[34]J. Turner, p. 13. The difficulties of such a program have also been pointed out. Examining the approximately 25 all-black towns in existence in America today, Arthur Tolson believes that "they were doomed to failure primarily because black separatism or black nationalism as such provided no permanent solution of the black question within the framework of American capitalism" (A. L. Tolson, "Black Towns of Oklahoma," *The Black Scholar*, 1970, 1(6), p. 22).

[35]R. Innis. Cited by R. L. Allen, p. 187.

[36]The 1969 National Black Economic Development Conference in their Black Manifesto. Cited by T. Draper, p. 176.

[37]Another variant of nationalism, which will be developed elsewhere, was advanced, rather surprisingly, by the communists in the United States in the 1920s. The concept of a "black belt" was based on the fact that at that time the blacks in 184 southern counties constituted 44.8 percent of the total population. In this "black belt," and in this area only, the communists felt that it was correct to stress as its primary theme the right of blacks to self-determination. In this the communists were clearly departing from their traditional class analysis and accepting some of the tenets of race analysis. Such a concept was an anomaly within the Communist Party's class analysis, but it was a direct forerunner of some contemporary varieties of nationalism.

is not so much a demand for black territory as it is the more general emphasis on self-determination for black people.

The nationalism of today has three main strands and a subsidiary one. The main strands are economic, political, and cultural. The subsidiary strand is religious. Each particular form of nationalism tends to include all three, the distinguishing factor being one of emphasis. Thus the *economic nationalist* is likely to claim that the inferior status of blacks is due largely to their lack of control over the economic resources of the ghetto. The reason for this failure, it is claimed, lies in the inability of blacks to operate and control enterprises within white society. As a result, the only solution is to develop an economy strictly among and for blacks. Once a black economic base is established, political independence can be gained.

Cultural nationalism tends to emphasize the need for a racially oriented culture. The claim is that the cultural identity of black people as a race was destroyed by slavery. As long as this identity is left unreconstructed, it will be impossible for blacks to deal effectively with the objective economic and political realities or to relate to America as a whole in any but a subservient role. The emphasis is thus placed on establishing black cultural forms (for example, developing a black theatre), strong positive black identity, and an awareness of and identification with the African heritage.

One of the important exponents of cultural nationalism is Harold Cruse. Cruse argues that the central problem of black people in the United States is primarily cultural, and that the failure of black leaders to realize this fact has caused the current impasse within the movement. Cruse argues for a cultural revolution, which he defines as:

> an ideological and organizational approach to American social change by revolutionizing the administration, the organization, the functioning and the social purpose of the entire American apparatus of cultural communication and placing it under public ownership.[38]

Thus, Cruse's idea of cultural change involves radical change of the entire economic and administrative apparatus that is connected with any kind of cultural activity.

Political nationalism emphasizes black control of all institutions relat-

[38]H. Cruse, *Rebellion or Revolution?*, p. 112.

ing to black people. Sometimes the emphasis is on total control of cities; in less ambitious versions the stress is on control of the political institutions of the black community. Often the principle is expanded to include control of institutions not normally included in a strict definition of "political." This would include community control of schools, police, health facilities, and so on. The call for community control seems to strike a very sensitive chord within the nation as a whole. In part this is due to the overall crisis of authority in our society, that is, to the feeling that our large bureaucratic institutions are no longer responsive to our needs.[39] The demand for political nationalism invariably leads to numerous problems. For example, if community control is to be meaningful, it will infringe on the vested interests of other groups (unions, the bureaucracy, and so on). In addition, any action will be exacerbated by the question of who should have control of the needed funds. The result is that political nationalism often becomes the cause of deep resentments and hostilities and the target of bitter attacks.

There is one other form of nationalism that does not quite fit into the above categories; it is *religious nationalism* as expressed by the Nation of Islam, popularly known as the Black Muslims. The Muslim form of religious nationalism emphasizes the redeeming nature of Islam, as opposed to the future hell reserved for whites. Elijah Muhammad describes his purpose as follows:

> My Mission—*I have been risen to raise my people here (the so-called Negroes), and to help them into the knowledge of Self, and their God Allah (who is in Person among them) and the devils (their open enemy).*
>
> My objective—*I am doing all I can to make the so-called Negroes see that the* white race *and their religion (Christianity) are* their open enemies, *and to prove to them that they will never be anything but the devil's slaves and finally* go to hell with *them for believing and following them and their kind.*[40]

[39]For a full discussion of the concept of community control, see A. A. Altshuler, *Community Control: The Black Demand for Participation in Large American Cities*. New York: Western Publishing Company, 1970; and M. Fantini, M. Gittell, and R. Magat, *Community Control and the Urban School*. New York: Praeger, 1970.

[40]Elijah Muhammad. "The Supreme Wisdom." Cited by E. U. Essien-Udom, *Black Nationalism: A Search for an Identity in America*. New York: Dell Publishing Co., 1969, p. 147. Emphasis original.

The Muslims' separatism, their emphasis on race, their distrust of whites, all show the clear influence of preoccupation with race. They explain American society, both past and present, in terms of race, and within this framework consistently espouse separatism, black power, and the development of black consciousness. The Muslims, in other words, tend to accept *de facto* segregation and try to achieve a degree of independence and dignity within the confines of a segregated society. They may be the true heirs of Booker T. Washington, though with a religious twist. In some ways the Muslims are best understood not in terms of nationalism, but in terms of their religious emphasis. Cruse has pointed out the Muslims' substitution of religion for politics.[41] Indeed, the Nation of Islam can best be compared to the Millenarians, one of the many revivalist religious sects that arose in the United States in the eighteenth century. Like the Millenarians, the Muslims have withdrawn from what they see as a corrupt society, await the coming of God's vengeance, and exhibit the same hard-working, Puritanical streak. Like the Millenarians too, the Muslims depend on one central figure—Elijah Muhammad—and it is not at all clear what will happen to them when that leader dies. The Millenarians, after the death of their leader, for the most part split up and went out of existence. This is also a critical possibility for the Nation of Islam.

In general, the majority of nationalist groups which accept the racial analysis are hindered by the same contradictions that plague the black-power groups—the inconsistency between their racial rhetoric and their traditional reformist programs. An example of the black-nationalist political program is nationalist and separatist. Yet if we look at his program what Jones has done is to turn his energies in the past few years to rather traditional forms of political involvement in the Newark area, for example, voter registration, support for black candidates, and campaigning (successfully) for the election of Newark's first Black mayor. James Turner's suggestions run along similar lines. He calls for the formation of political cadres to organize black people in urban areas and to develop independent black political organizations with the hope of gaining control over all institutions within black areas. Turner, like Jones, emphasizes the need to use political elections to place black people, especially black nationalists, in positions of power. In addition, he would like to see estab-

---

[41]H. Cruse, *The Crisis of the Negro Intellectual*, p. 548.

lished what he calls "autonomous city states" in black areas.[42] Again, with the exception of the idea of city states, there is nothing in Turner's view that does not mesh with the general nature of the *given* system.[43]

If we look at a sophisticated cultural nationalist perspective, such as that enunciated by Cruse, whose efforts at realism are more pronounced than those of some other nationalists, we can again detect some basic contradictions. First, Cruse's formulation of "basic organizational objectives" to be pursued in Harlem, for example, include the following: business cooperatives, citizens' committees to fight crime and drug peddling, a new political party, the need to create a new black middle class. With the possible exception of the call for a new political party, there is nothing here that does not fall within familiar and traditional patterns.[44] Echoing Cruse himself with respect to his comment on black power,[45] we might emphasize again that the point is not to denigrate the value of these programs but to realize their limited nature and basic inconsistency with the rhetoric of nationalism.

Cruse's position also brings up a second contradiction in nationalist theory and racial analysis. As we have seen, his explanation of the black man's plight is couched primarily in racial terms and the rhetoric of his program is nationalist and separatist. Yet if we look at his program without the accompanying rhetoric, we see a view of blacks as similar to other ethnic groups and a belief that American society is pluralist. But if blacks are *unlike* other ethnic groups, if the race factor actually makes their situation unique, how can they be compared with other ethnic groups? Such a comparison would then clearly be invalid.

Given the mutually exclusive nature of the ethnic and racial models,

[42]J. Turner, pp. 12–13.

[43]A more basic question is just how useful, given the changing nature of city government, black control of cities would be. It is not at all clear that it would help to provide any realistic solutions—which is a further problem resulting from a race analysis.

[44]There is, perhaps, a more serious problem in Cruse's rationale for cultural nationalism. The whole area of culture, he claims, is clearly the weakest link in American capitalism and therefore the proper point at which to attack the system. Yet he seems to give no evidence to prove that it *is* the weakest link, aside from the fact that it is an area where no concrete commodities are produced. Cruse's definition of "cultural" includes such areas as the mass media, but it is difficult to see the media as the "weakest link" in American capitalism, since, while they may produce no concrete commodities, they are very much involved in profit-seeking and are entrenched members of the capitalist establishment.

[45]H. Cruse, *The Crisis of the Negro Intellectual*, p. 546.

it is contradictory to find the ethnic model underlying the analysis of those who espouse the racial one. Draper interprets Cruse's position as hinging "on the ethnic, rather than the racial, character of the American Negro problem," and there is evidence to support this interpretation.[46] Cruse himself states that "America is a collection of ethnic groups."[47] At one point he denies a racial analysis completely:

> *American group reality demands a struggle for democracy among ethnic groups, rather than between two races. What is called a racial struggle over civil rights is, in reality, the contention in America among several different ethnic groups, of which Anglo-Saxon Protestants and American Negroes are only two.*[48]

Cruse makes it clear that within this ethnic model there is nothing approaching equality among groups. Nevertheless, black people form *"the pivotal American ethnic group among all others,"* and it is crucial for black leadership to realize "its group's innate potential for enforcing democratization of ethnic group status." Cruse even goes so far as to point to the experience of other ethnic groups—the Irish, the Jews, the Italians—as an example of the way in which group solidarity can help an ethnic group to gain economic power.[49]

Once the underlying ethnic analysis becomes clear, Cruse's programmatic suggestions are more understandable. The use of economic cooperatives, the creation of a middle class, the formation of citizens' committees to deal with specific problems are all measures characteristically used by ethnic groups in the past. It is not surprising that Cruse has suggested such measures, but it is surprising that he has suggested them in the context of a race analysis, which contradicts both the actual programs he calls for and the assumptions that underlie such programs.

Cruse's inconsistency is characteristic of much of nationalist theory. Solomon P. Gethers, to take only one example, stresses the need for "ethnic self-hood." He sees Malcolm X as one of the chief spokesmen of this ethnic view and believes that "the position is being further defined

---

[46]T. Draper, p. 129.
[47]H. Cruse, *The Crisis of the Negro Intellectual*, p. 317.
[48]H. Cruse, *The Crisis of the Negro Intellectual*, p. 458.
[49]H. Cruse, *The Crisis of the Negro Intellectual,* pp. 315, 318. Emphasis original.

and developed by cultural nationalists throughout the country." "Ethnic integrity" is seen as both a "key element in the Afro-American's quest for freedom" and as identical with black nationalism.[50] If the emphasis is on ethnicity, then the race and nationalist emphasis should be dropped.

Like the black-power advocates, nationalists, with their pluralistic views of American society, rely on federal money to support their programs. The national field chairman of RAM (Revolutionary Action Movement) views the struggle for community control of schools as a key tactic in the struggle for nationalism.[51] While he does not specifically mention the need for federal money, it is clear that such a victory cannot be won without it. Similarly, Floyd McKissick, in proposing a way for blacks to gain control of several states, relies almost totally on the federal government. The major need, he claims, is for the federal government to enable more black sheriffs and tax collectors to be elected in counties with a black majority. The result would be the exodus of whites, and the eventual total control by blacks.[52]

This reliance on the federal government extends even to the Nation of Islam. In some ways the Black Muslims are better able to avoid the contradictions that plague other race analysts. Muslim educational programs involve their own schools, and they are able to implement at least a large part of their self-help program without federal aid. Nevertheless, their problem, perhaps in a more subtle form, is ultimately the same as that facing all race advocates: reliance on the benevolence of an assumed racist government. First, the Muslims call for equality before the law. Second, though their position has changed on several occasions, they often have called on the federal government to provide them with land of their own. But if, as their rhetoric states, the white man is basically a devil, these demands are totally inconsistent. As a result, the Muslims have come in for some severe criticism:

Their off-and-on propounding of a "separate state" and at other times, their equally unrealistic calls for a Back-to-Africa Movement

[50]S. P. Gethers, "Black Nationalism and Human Liberation," *The Black Scholar,* 1970, *1*(7), p. 48.

[51]M. Stanford, "Black Nationalism and the Afro-American Student," *The Black Scholar*, 1971, *2*(10), p. 29.

[52]F. McKissick, *Three-fifths of a Man.* New York: Macmillan, 1969. Cited by T. Draper, p. 140.

have cost them the intellectual respect of many who never actually joined the all-Black sect but nevertheless admired the leaders' militancy, their forthright analysis of the forces behind the Negro's exploitation, and their triumphant self-emancipation from America's vast indoctrination apparatus. . . . The universal complaint today is that the Muslims are all talk and no action.[53]

It is the Muslims' racial emphasis that tends to condemn them, in one sense, to be "all talk" and no action, even though their admitted success in organizing is often neglected.[54]

Conclusions and Implications

Given the basic and important tensions within race analysis, what is the net effect of its rhetoric? Is the race analysis, adopted by both black-power and black-nationalist groups, destructive, or does it also have some positive value?

The rhetoric clearly has severe disadvantages. It is unfortunate that many race advocates adopt a rhetoric that is at variance with their programs, since more often than not it is the rhetoric which people become aware of and attack, ignoring their potential agreement with some of the programmatic efforts of such groups. The kind of rhetoric that relies on verbal violence[55] and utopian exhortations about separation, in contradiction to the modesty of the *de facto* programs, has been heavily criticized by black reformist leaders. But the weaknesses of black-power

[53]W. Worthy, "Implications of an American Insurrection," *The Realist*, September 1966, No. 62, p. 18.

[54]Cruse suggests an interesting analogy between the Muslims and Booker T. Washington. "Both," he writes, "emphasize economic self-help, separatism, etc." While Elijah Muhammad added a religious element and Washington practiced what Cruse calls "moderate accomodationist separatism" in opposition to the Muslims' "militant separatism," Cruse claims that "it is still the same separatism whose quality only changes from one era to another." H. Cruse, *Rebellion or Revolution?*, p. 211.

[55]While historically black nationalism has not called for the use of violence, this tendency seems to have changed. This is consistent with the nation-colonly analogy. If blacks are in fact an oppressed nation, then a violent anticolonial struggle seems likely. Julius Lester, for example, after describing blacks as a colonial people within the United States, goes on to claim that "The concept of the black man as a nation, . . . will become reality when

and black-nationalist rhetoric go beyond the matter of overkill.[56] It not only leads to unprincipled conflict with reformists, but often turns the racial advocates against themselves by driving them to meaningless verbal escalation which is comprehensible only to those who follow the infighting of sectarians. The net result is ideological chaos.

Lest our criticism of the race advocates' general orientation be interpreted to mean that we see no rationale in black-power or nationalist expressions, it is necessary to note the relevance of this rhetoric. There must be some fundamental reasons why, despite the deficiencies of black-power and nationalist theory, sophisticated critics such as Cruse still use nationalist rhetoric in their analysis of the position of American blacks. In part both black power and black nationalism can be seen as expressions of the desire to be rid of a country that has so consistently maligned blacks. It also represents an attempt to redefine American blacks in their own terms, rather than in the terms imposed upon them by the larger society (see Chapter 14). It helps in some respects to goad blacks to act as other ethnic groups have in the past. Finally, the race analysis provides a useful counterpoint to other perspectives which deemphasize the purely race aspects of the black position in American society.[57] In

violence comes" (see Lester, J. *Look Out, Whitey! Black Power's Gon' Get Your Mama!* New York: Grove Press, 1968, p. 140). This belief in violence is often based on the theories of Frantz Fanon in regard to Algeria's fight for independence. Yet there are some obvious inconsistencies here. Fanon was discussing peasants in an agricultural country who, he felt, had nothing to lose and who were in the majority. Blacks in the United States are not a majority, are mostly located in urban ghettos, and many not only feel they have a great deal to lose but are also very interested in participating equally in the American capitalist, consumer-oriented society. Cruse believes that blacks must take into account both the colonial element and the nature of Western social conditions. The dual element of the problem, Cruse claims, can be seen in the nature of urban riots, which always end by requests for more aid from the federal government. This, of course, is a basic dilemma resulting from a race analysis.

[56]At least one NAACP official sees black power as "designed to create chaos." (H. L. Moon. Cited by H. Cruse, *Rebellion or Revolution?*, p. 200.) Bayard Rustin, speaking from a class perspective, attacks black power as utopian and reactionary because it would "give priority to the issue of race precisely at a time when the fundamental questions facing the Negro and American society alike are economic and social."—B. Rustin, "Black Power and Coalition Politics," *Commentary*, September 1966, pp. 35–36. Cited by T. Wagstaff (ed.), *Black Power: The Radical Response to White America*, pp. 104–105.

[57]As we show in the two subsequent chapters, both the ethnic and class approaches deemphasize contemporary racism to the point where the analysis of the black question is distorted so as to *avoid* the race variable.

the end, in stressing nationhood, neocolonialism, black pride, and even violence, both the black nationalists and black-power groups, whatever their many conceptual inadequacies and inconsistencies, are making the larger white society face up to the discrepancy between what it professes as a democracy in general, and what it in fact does to the black population specifically.

CHAPTER 9

Race, Ethnicity, and Making It in the American Mainstream

Our main concern in this chapter is with the ethnic model, which is often used to explain the position of blacks in the United States. This model is based on the belief that power at the local level is fragmented and dispersed among contending interest groups. Given this situation, various ethnic groups have been successful, not by giving up their identity and assimilating, but by acting as an interest group or power bloc and exerting various forms of pressure, both economic and political. Those who espouse this position believe that the ethnic model provides the best way of understanding the conditions of blacks in northern urban areas.

The ethnic model is of crucial importance today. Many of its proponents are influential in both academic and government circles and play a significant role in determining government policy toward blacks. Unfortunately, the ethnic model they use is an inadequate analytic tool. It has the potential of impeding black progress by shifting the focus of government efforts away from the removal of crippling barriers facing blacks and toward an emphasis on black progress as totally dependent on "self-improvement" within the black community. All too often the ethnic model provides a rationale for inaction, a way for American society to avoid taking responsibility for its continuing racism.[1]

One of the most influential formulations of the ethnic model was put forward by Daniel Patrick Moynihan and Nathan Glazer in 1963.[2] Moynihan and Glazer argued against the commonly held view of America, and particularly of American cities, as a "melting pot," that is, a place in which immigrant groups achieved success as they lost their particular ethnic identity and merged into the larger American culture. Equally influential in this area are Edward Banfield and James Wilson,[3] who are among the primary theorists of pluralism.[4]

The Ethnic Model

In the ethnic model, the experience of blacks is viewed in terms of the experience of other immigrant groups in the United States. Members of such groups are seen as sharing certain national characteristics, traits and preferences, a common life-style and culture.[5] Traditionally, such

[1]The great popularity of the ethnic model stems from two factors: the general popularity of pluralism as an explanation of city government, and the fact that, in ethnic formulation, the problems of blacks do not seem insurmountable but will be solved in time and with little more effort than was necessary in the case of earlier immigrant groups. Racism and discrimination thus take a back seat in this model. While prejudice does exist, it too will pass—just as prejudice toward the earlier immigrants inevitably disappeared.

[2]N. Glazer and D. P. Moynihan, *Beyond the Melting Pot: the Negroes, Puerto Ricans, Jews, Italians, and Irish of New York City*. Cambridge, Mass.: The M.I.T. Press, 1963.

[3]E. C. Banfield and J. Q. Wilson, *City Politics*. New York: Vintage Books, 1966. This is one of the most influential studies of urban politics available. For the purposes of this chapter we will confine ourselves largely to a discussion of their views as they relate to the ethnic model, despite the much greater range of their interests.

[4]While the theories of these four men are not identical, we will present, in this chapter, certain broad themes that characterize the work of all four, even though there may be differences among the authors in their individual presentation of these themes.

[5]One problem, however, makes itself felt from the outset: Glazer and Moynihan's basis for characterizing Negroes as an ethnic group is never made clear. In the first edition of

groups have entered the political system by using bloc voting and political machines, and by capturing a particular industry in which nepotism could be used to employ and promote the immigrant to higher ranked jobs. Blacks, by virtue of their migration from the rural South to the urban North, are seen as functioning just like any other ethnic group; many of the factors that now hinder blacks are the same that stood in the way of earlier immigrants. Wilson, for example, speaks of:

> the operation of those same factors which have delayed the entry of other, earlier, ethnic groups. . . . Resistance to Negroes is not, in part, different from the general resistance put up by the Irish political leadership of the big city to the demands for political recognition expressed by Poles, Italians, or Germans.[6]

The major difference seen between blacks and other immigrant groups is that black immigration took place well after the early waves of immigration; this is sometimes seen as the root of the problem.[7] Nevertheless,

Beyond the Melting Pot, Glazer argues that blacks could not view themselves as members of an ethnic group because they had no values and culture of their own; they were completely a product of America. If this is true, it is hard to see how blacks can be viewed as an ethnic group. In the second edition of the book, Glazer says that he did not mean that there were no Negro values and culture, but that since those values were American in origin, the Negro had no strong incentive to create institutions to preserve a basically foreign culture. (This still provides no basis for labeling them as an ethnic group.) Glazer then says that even this statement is incorrect. While the Negroes' view of themselves as Americans might, to some degree, have inhibited the development of strong ethnic organization, it is still possible to be an ethnic group without having a foreign origin, as are, for example, the Mormons. Presumably, then, the basis for black ethnicity is their distinctive experience in America. It can easily be argued that this is the same as saying that they are an "ethnic group" because of "race"; but how does that differ from defining the problem as a racial one? This whole issue is deeply confused, and Glazer never really makes clear how black ethnicity differs from race. (See N. Glazer and D. P. Moynihan, "Introduction to the Second Edition: New York City in 1970," Beyond the Melting Pot, (2nd ed.), pp. xix–xx.

[6]J. Q. Wilson, Negro Politics: The Search for Leadership. New York: The Free Press, 1960, p. 24.

[7]In a similar vein, Irving Kristol differentiates blacks from other immigrant groups on the ground that blacks "are technically very old Americans indeed." Nevertheless, "The real tragedy of the American Negro today is not that he is . . . black, but that he is a late-comer." I. Kristol, "The Negro Today Is Like the Immigrant Yesterday," in N. Glazer (ed.), Cities in Trouble. Chicago: Quadrangle Books, 1970, pp. 143, 152.

the final prediction of the ethnic model is optimistic: Just as other immigrant groups met and overcame prejudice in the past, so will blacks be able to do so.

Unfortunately, as Glazer and Moynihan admit, the predictions which they made in 1963, on the basis of the ethnic model, have not been borne out by the events of the sixties.[8] They have therefore been forced to identify the reasons for the apparent failure of the ethnic model. One possible reason they offer, which we would accept, is that the ethnic model has not worked for blacks because of the persistence of racism in the United States. Institutionalized racism makes it virtually impossible for blacks to be effective in the traditional ways of other immigrant groups. But the very nature of the ethnic model precludes such an explanation. In their attempt to identify blacks with other immigrant groups, the ethnic analysts are invariably forced to deemphasize the importance of race as a determining factor in the position of blacks,[9] to wit: "There is, of course, a 'race problem,' but it is not an all-encompassing phenomenon that adequately comprehends the major internal strains of our society."[10]

One result of this position is an intense opposition to a race analysis:

Only a fear of being thought illiberal may prevent us from considering that the probability of a riot is increased by demands for "Black Power," by a constant reiteration that white bigotry and racism are at the root of all the problems besetting the Negro, by the reaffirmation of the (untrue) assumption that most Negroes live wretched lives, and that matters are going from bad to worse, by constantly predicting apocalyptic violence if "something isn't done," and by "discovering" the nontruth that all Negroes are alike in their hatred of "whitey" and their tacit or open approval of extreme solutions for their plight.[11]

[8]N. Glazer and D. P. Moynihan, "Introduction to the Second Edition."

[9]Curiously, Glazer is willing to allow for the role of race insofar as it is the chief reason why poverty has become a "major issue"—but that is different from a view of race as the major *cause* of the actual situation of blacks. (N. Glazer, "Paradoxes of American Poverty," *The Public Interest,* Fall 1965, No. 1, p. 77.)

[10]J. Q. Wilson "The Moynihan Memo Revisited—Notes from an Academic Friend," *New York,* April 27, 1970, p. 44.

[11]J. Q. Wilson, "Why We Are Having a Wave of Violence," in N. Glazer (ed.), *Cities in Trouble,* p. 61.

A second result is a crucial distinction within the ethnic model between past and present causes of the black man's position. The ethnic analysts accept racism as a historical cause; they casually use such phrases as "three centuries of injustice."[12] But when Glazer and Moynihan analyze the present, the weight of history to which they give lip service miraculously dissolves; they argue that there is "no major obstacle . . . in the form of a massive, institutionalized racism. There was prejudice, of course, but other groups had met that."[13]

The refusal to accept the importance of contemporary racism is at the heart of the problems inherent in the ethnic model. Faced with the apparent failure of the model, but unwilling to accept the massive evidence of continuing racism, the ethnic analysts are forced into a strange bind; they often end up by relying on convoluted and far-fetched arguments to defend the sanctity of their model. This can be illustrated by the examination of certain key themes.

Racism Deemphasized

The first of these themes, as previously discussed, is the continual tendency to deemphasize the importance of contemporary racism. Throughout the writings of the ethnic analysts there are disclaimers to indicate that the authors are not unaware of the existence of racism. But such disclaimers are then followed by a discussion which completely ignores racism. "In addition to political resistance stiffened by personal hostility and prejudice," Wilson writes, "there are the difficulties of political organi-

[12]D. P. Moynihan, *The Negro Family: The Case for National Action.* Washington, D.C.: United States Department of Labor, 1965, p. 47.

[13]N. Glazer and D. P. Moynihan, "Introduction to the Second Edition," pp. x–xi. Moynihan rather cleverly manages both to appear to link past and present and at the same time to shift the weight of the current problem to factors other than racism. Thus he identifies the chief product of historical racism as "deep seated structural distortions in the life of the Negro American" and concludes that "at this point, the present tangle of pathology [among blacks] is capable of perpetuating itself without assistance from the white world." (D. P. Moynihan, *The Negro Family,* p. 47.) So, while racism is the original cause in the distant past, the emphasis today is on other problems, with scant attention given to the relationship of current racism to the problem.

zation among Negroes."[14] This juxtaposition is almost symbolic; racism is not only mentioned in the weaker term of prejudice, but it is sandwiched between two other considerations which receive infinitely more attention throughout Wilson's book.[15] In line with this tendency, racism is often defined in only the narrowest of terms. Moynihan's now-famous report on the Negro family begins with the assumption that "we have gone beyond equal opportunity."[16] One is reminded here of John Lewis' comment that the report "takes too much for granted in its assumption that discrimination and racism are no longer a real problem."[17] Yet that is indeed the assumption implied by Moynihan's statement.

Subjectivity of Black Problems

A second major theme in the ethnic model is the oft-repeated assertion that the problems of blacks are subjective rather than objective. The ethnic analysts often start with the assertion that the objective reality is in fact much improved for blacks. (In both Wilson's and Moynihan's terms, blacks have made "extraordinary progress."[18]) Since objective conditions are clearly getting better, a good part of the problem must lie in the way people perceive reality. And that is in fact what the ethnic

[14]J. Q. Wilson, *Negro Politics*, p. 25.

[15]A similar example of this use of the disclaimer is Irving Kristol's comment: "The fact that their 'ethnicity' is racial rather than cultural and the corollary fact that racial prejudice seems more deeply rooted than cultural prejudice, are certainly not to be minimized." Yet the rest of Kristol's analysis deemphasizes the importance of contemporary racism. I. Kristol, p. 150.

[16]D. P. Moynihan, "Introduction," *The Negro Family*.

[17]J. Lewis. Cited by L. Rainwater and W. L. Yancey, *The Moynihan Report and the Politics of Controversy*. Cambridge, Mass.: The M.I.T. Press, 1967, p. 200.

[18]See D. P. Moynihan, "Pre-inaugural Memo to Nixon, January 3, 1969," *New York Times*, March 11, 1970; and "Memo to Nixon on the Status of Negroes, January 16, 1970," *New York Times*, March 1, 1970. See also J. Q. Wilson, "The Moynihan Memo Revisited," p. 42. One basic argument here is that each year thousands of blacks are moving out of poverty and even into the middle class and the population of the central city ghettos is constantly decreasing. In sum, "During the second half of the 1960's Negroes made probably the most rapid economic and occupational gains in their history." (N. Glazer and D. P. Moynihan, "Introduction to the Second Edition: New York City in 1970," p. xii.) Moynihan is reported as wondering, in 1964, "why in a time of decreasing unemployment, the *plight of the urban*

analysts claim has happened. In terms of blacks' perception of reality, Glazer and Moynihan claim that even though the blacks' economic position "has not deteriorated either in real or in relative terms," that in fact, "just the opposite took place," still "the *perception* of well-being seems not to have accompanied the reality."[19] Banfield and Wilson blame this misperception on a rising level of expectation which in turn leads to an increase in the militancy of civic action.[20] The problem, in both cases, is purely a perceptual one.

Those whites who perceive the black condition as worsening are also deluded; their delusion is based on the fact that things are getting objectively better. The ethnic analysts reason as follows: The increased income of blacks has made it possible for them to expand their living

---

Negro was getting worse." (D. P. Moynihan, *The Negro Family.* Cited by R. Evans and R. Novak, "The Moynihan Report." Cited by L. Rainwater and W. L. Yancey, *The Moynihan Report and the Politics of Controversy,* p. 141. Emphasis added.) However, in 1970, in the famous "benign neglect" memo, Moynihan claims that "In quantitative terms, which are reliable, the American Negro is making extraordinary progress. In political terms, somewhat less reliable, this would also appear to be true." In a similar vein, Irving Kristol asserts that "In comparison with previous waves of immigrants to the great cities, they are 'making out' not badly at all." (I. Kristol, p. 157.)

But these assertions are less than reassuring in light of the information that since 1960 there has been very little decline in poverty in New York City, and even less of a decline in other American cities. (See D. M. Gordon, "Income and Welfare in New York City," *The Public Interest,* Summer 1969, No. 16, p. 79.) In a footnote to the "Introduction to the Second Edition" of *Beyond the Melting Pot,* Glazer and Moynihan mention Gordon's article. But the matter, they say, "is still not beyond dispute" (p. xcii). That may well be, but it is a very shaky basis for an assertion of "extraordinary progress." One also wonders how Banfield's and Wilson's assertion that "the cities have fewer slum dwellers now than ever before" (*City Politics,* p. 11) can be aligned with Bayard Rustin's claim, in 1967, that "The black slum proletariat has been growing in numbers and density. As agricultural mechanization and other factors continue pushing Negroes out of the South, the urban ghettoes expand each year by half a million; only 40,000 Negroes annually find their way into the suburbs. This trend has not been affected at all by any antipoverty or Great Society programs." (B. Rustin, "A Way Out of the Exploding Ghetto," in N. Glazer (ed.), *Cities in Trouble,* p. 203.)

[19]N. Glazer and D. P. Moynihan, "Introduction to the Second Edition," p. xii. Emphasis original.

[20]E. C. Banfield and J. Q. Wilson, *City Politics,* pp. 302–303. See also Wilson's assertion that "Viewed in historical perspective, and taking American cities as a whole, the conditions of urban life have, by most measures, been getting steadily better, not worse." (J. Q. Wilson, "The War on Cities," *The Public Interest,* Spring 1966, No. 3, pp. 31–32.)

space; this expansion has made the problem more visible to whites and has thus led to the incorrect conclusion that there is a growing "slum problem." Again, the problem is purely perceptual: Things appear worse because blacks are now more visible (though in 1965 Glazer argued that it was the "invisibility of poverty" that made it possible to persuade people "that there is much more [poverty] than there is."[21]) It would seem that almost anything can be used to prove that the problem is basically one of subjectivity on the basis of incorrect perceptions. Again, only scant attention is given to the role that racism plays. To give it more than a perfunctory mention would be to destroy the rhetoric of the entire ethnic model.

Rationalizing the Model's Failure

The emphasis on subjective factors extends into a third theme. In their search for possible reasons for the failure of their model, the ethnic analysts greatly exaggerate the influence of elements that are at best only marginally important. They thus place the blame on an assortment of groups: (1) the mass media, which are said to encourage riots because they "offer an opportunity for immediate expressive gratification,"[22] (2) the intellectuals who become intrigued by the sensational, and therefore abandon an objective analysis of the situation,[23] and (3) the rhetoric of black militants.[24] Again, however, the ethnic analysts fail to raise the possibility that the cause of such rhetoric may be the kind of massive ongoing racism that they ignore.[25] The ethnic analysts would do well

[21]N. Glazer, "Paradoxes of American Poverty," p. 71.

[22]J. Q. Wilson, "Why We Are Having a Wave of Violence," pp. 59–60. This critique is echoed by Irving Kristol and Paul Weaver, who charge the mass media with deciding beforehand that the basic pattern of the urban crisis will be a series of confrontations between blacks and the establishment. (I. Kristol and P. Weaver, "Who Knows New York?—and Other Notes on a Mixed-Up City," *The Public Interest,* Summer 1969, No. 16, p. 44.)

[23]N. Glazer and D. P. Moynihan, "Introduction to the Second Edition," p. xvi.

[24]Glazer and Moynihan speak of "a pervasive sense of deprivation and impending doom among the more vocal and militant elements of the New York City population. This, too, was a reality, and had the effect of reality." ("Introduction to the Second Edition," p. xii.)

[25]N. Glazer and D. P. Moynihan, "Introduction to the Second Edition," pp. xxi, xxii. Glazer and Moynihan's primary evidence for placing the blame on black militants is the contrast between 1962, when "It was becoming *routine* for Negroes to have 'a place on the slate' " (as, for example, in the democratic nomination of Edward Dudley for Attorney General),

to heed the warning of such scholars as Peter Rossi and Zahava Blum, who argue that it is important not to underrate "the effects of the punishment of discrimination at the hands of the major institutions . . . as a source of feelings of . . . anger and rebellion.[26] The ethnic analysts' attack on the intellectuals, the media, and black militants is therefore contrived.

"Endemic" Differences

The search for a place to lay the blame for blacks' insufficient progress extends even further and creates a fourth major theme within ethnic analysis. If one continues to regard the ethnic model as a valid explanatory device, then one possible reason for the failure of blacks to live up to that model is some deficiency within blacks themselves. This is a common theme running throughout ethnic analysis. According to Glazer and Moynihan, one important reason why blacks have not duplicated the experience of the early immigrant groups is because of their failure "to develop and seize the political opportunities that were open to them as, for example, in their tendency to abstain from voting."[27] Wilson offers a possible interpretation of this phenomenon (although in a slightly different context) when he notes that many blacks "doubt that politics offers them any real opportunities."[28] Despite the obvious difficulties blacks face in regard to political action, many of which Wilson himself points out elsewhere in his book, the ethnic analysts seem to present black skepticism regarding political action as a misperception, almost an internal flaw. Wilson's position is typical: "Some of the important obstacles to civic action are products of the Negro's own community and way of life."[29]

---

and 1970, when it was considered a "chancey thing" to nominate a Negro for Lieutenant Governor. They claim this supposed difference in attitudes was caused by the rhetoric of black militants: "Only after a decade of intense preoccupation with injustice done to black people, with 'white racism,' 'genocide,' and the rhetoric of social revolution did it become a chancey thing to nominate a black for the least significant of statewide posts." "Introduction to the Second Edition," p. xxii.

[26]P. H. Rossi and Z. D. Blum, "Class, Status and Poverty," in D. P. Moynihan (ed.), On Understanding Poverty. New York: Basic Books, 1969, p. 59.

[27]N. Glazer and D. P. Moynihan, "Introduction to the Second Edition," p. xviii.

[28]J. Q. Wilson, Negro Politics, p. 25.

[29]J. Q. Wilson, Negro Politics, p. 6. In some way the key to the ethnic model—or, at least, to Moynihan and his use of such a model—may well lie not in his theoretical constructs, but in an underlying theme which pervades all his writing: the need for stability, for peace,

Conspicuously missing is a detailed exploration of the possibility that this skepticism is an understandable response to objective conditions, that is, that the prevalence of white racism has made traditional black political action relatively ineffective. Instead, the effects of racism are downplayed: "The Negro may live in a prison, as a Negro author wrote, but 'the prison is vast, there is plenty of space.' "[30] Thus the emphasis shifts: White racism is alluded to in Wilson's introduction, but the rest of the book is devoted to an examination of what he calls the "Negro problem," completely apart from considerations of the effects of racism. In the ethnic analysis white racism all too often appears as being partly the fault of blacks. Moynihan's contention is that "apart from white racial attitudes" (again the familiar disclaimer) antisocial behavior among young black males is "the biggest problem black Americans face." Moynihan then goes on to state that such behavior helps to "shape white racial attitudes."[31] The implication would seem to be that racism is a problem, but in large part it is a result of the behavior of blacks themselves.

for order. The two adjectives he uses most commonly to describe different groups are "stable" and "unstable"; the consequences, if we do not attend to the problems he discusses, will be "no social peace in the United States for generations." In 1967 he delivered a speech entitled "The Politics of Stability," in which he urged liberals to see that their main interest lay in "the stability of the social order." "Given the present threats to that stability," he said, "it is necessary to seek out and make much more effective alliances with political conservatives who share that concern." (Speech to National Board, Americans for Democratic Action, September 23, 1967, p. 5.) Hence Moynihan's deep hatred for both black and white militants, since they bring with them connotations of conflicts at the least, and violence at worst. Hence, too, his preoccupation with the seeming chaos of the ghetto and his concern for what he constantly interprets as fragility—of the family, of the universities, of the social order. It is indicative that, faced with the turmoil of the sixties, Moynihan suggests an alliance with conservatives. Charles Valentine's critique of Moynihan is pertinent here. "Thus," writes Valentine, "does the 'politics of stability' resolve itself into a strategy for strengthening existing centers of power and privilege, offered to the affluent so that they may preserve their advantages against a threat from the poor." (C. A. Valentine, *Culture and Poverty: Critique and Counterproposals*. Chicago: The University of Chicago Press, 1968, p. 42). Moynihan's suggested alliance with conservatives is a chilling reminder of Gans' warning about the pitfalls of the concept of lower-class culture: "the judgment that behavior is cultural lends itself to an argument against change. But if data are not available for that judgment, the researcher indulges in conceptual conservatism." (H. J. Gans, "Culture and Class in the Study of Poverty," in D. P. Moynihan (ed.), *On Understanding Poverty*, p. 214.)

[30]J. Q. Wilson, *Negro Politics,* p. 6. The phrase Wilson quotes is from C. McKay, *A Long Way from Home*. New York: L. Furman, 1937, p. 145.

[31]D. P. Moynihan, "Memo to Nixon on the Status of Negroes."

The tendency to place the blame on blacks can also be seen in the emphasis on ghetto pathology and the culture of poverty as the key impediments to black progress.[32] The roots of this theory can be seen as early as the original edition of *Beyond the Melting Pot*. While slavery and past discrimination are mentioned in passing, the major emphasis is on such problems as black incapacity in business and lack of educational achievement, and (the major cause for black educational under-achievement) "the home . . . family and community."[33] Moynihan's later report on the Negro family, perhaps the most influential statement of this theory, identifies the problem of family instability as one of the primary, if not *the* primary cause of the ills of the urban ghetto. At points he seems to be saying that family instability is the *cause* of familiar ghetto problems such as unemployment, poverty, crime, and juvenile delin-quency. Charles Valentine points out that within the Moynihan report itself there are sufficient statistics to prove that the economic problems are the cause of family instability rather than *vice versa*. Yet Moynihan claims that the weakness of the family structure "will be found to be the *principal* source of most of the . . . behavior that did not establish but now serves to perpetuate the cycle of poverty."[34] The Moynihan report has been discussed at length elsewhere, and we do not wish to enter the quarrel about the validity of Moynihan's description of black families.[35]

[32]The basis of the "culture of poverty" theory is the belief that there is something inherent in the culture that arises in the ghetto that makes it impossible for poor people to take advantage of the opportunities available to them. In Moynihan's formulation, for example, the heart of the problem lies in the Negro family, which he characterizes as unstable. The cause of this instability is the fact that lower-class black men have no stable place in the economic system. As a result, they cannot be strong husbands and fathers, and black families come increasingly to center around women. The children, lacking a stable home to grow up in, do badly in jobs and in schools, and perpetuate the so-called cycle of poverty.

[33]N. Glazer and D. P. Moynihan, *Beyond the Melting Pot* (2nd edition), p. 49.

[34]D. P. Moynihan, *The Negro Family*, p. 30. Emphasis added. Once again the disjunction in the ethnic model between past and present causes is clear. Racism is the original or past cause, but the current cause is within blacks themselves. This inconsistency between past and present causes is well summed up by Valentine: "So we come back to the same essential contention: Whatever forces may have been at work in the past, today the main plight of the poor and the despised is the internal deficiencies in their own way of life." (C. A. Valentine, *Culture and Poverty*, p. 33.)

[35]For a full discussion of the Moynihan report, see L. Rainwater and W. L. Yancey, *The Moynihan Report and the Politics of Controversy*. The Moynihan report has been criticized again and again as having racist implications, and we do not wish to perpetuate that criticism.

The important point is not whether Moynihan's description is accurate. Rather, as Valentine points out, this analysis directs attention away from what society is now doing to the poor and focuses instead on what blacks are doing to themselves through their own defective culture.[36] Banfield and Wilson repeat this emphasis, that black family structure is the heart of the black problem, and they are therefore subject to the same criticism.[37]

Perhaps the most crucial indication of the tendency to blame blacks for their problems is the ethnic analysts' choice of words in discussing the problems of the ghetto. "What are we to do," Glazer and Moynihan ask,

with the large number of people emerging in modern society who are irresponsible and depraved? The worthy poor create

It seems clear that Moynihan's purpose was not to cast a racial slur, but to goad the government toward greater efforts to reduce unemployment. But the difficulties inherent in an interpretation of the report can be seen clearly from Nathan Glazer's comments on it; even he seems to question both Moynihan's basic premise and the thrust of the report. He asks, "Do we know enough about family life and the significance of any kind of intervention within it to sanction a large effort to restructure or reform the lower class or Negro family? I doubt it." In the sentences that follow he seems to assume that Moynihan's argument is for direct intervention in the Negro family itself, rather than Moynihan's claim that it is toward intervention in the economy. "There are parts of the society," Glazer writes, "that are more legitimately subject to governmental intervention than the family." (N. Glazer, Foreword to E. F. Frazier, *The Negro Family in the United States* (revised and abridged ed.). Chicago: University of Chicago Press, 1966. Cited by L. Rainwater and W. L. Yancey, *The Moynihan Report and the Politics of Controversy,* p. 313.)

[36]See C. A. Valentine, *Culture and Poverty,* p. 32. Moynihan also falls into the trap pointed out by Herbert Gans. Gans' claim is that any research on the culture of the poor must include data on both their behavior and their aspirations. If the people involved in a lower-class culture adapt out of necessity but in fact want something else, "then ascribing their adaptation to a lower-class culture is inaccurate." (H. J. Gans, "Culture and Class in the Study of Poverty," p. 214.) We might also point out here another criticism by Gans of the Moynihan report: that it is not at all clear that the phenomena Moynihan points to are in fact pathological, that "it may well be that instability, illegitimacy, and matriarchy are the most positive adaptations possible to the conditions which Negroes must endure . . . one could argue that at present, the broken and matriarchal family is a viable solution for the Negro lower-class population." (H. J. Gans, "The Breakdown of the Negro Family: The "Moynihan Report" and Its Implications for Federal Civil Rights Policy." In L. Rainwater and W. L. Yancey, *The Moynihan Report and the Politics of Controversy,* pp. 450–451.)

[37]E. C. Banfield and J. Q. Wilson, *City Politics,* p. 295.

no serious problems—nothing that money cannot solve. But the
unworthy poor? No one has come up with the answers.[38]

If the "worthy poor" present only a problem of money, then the "unworthy poor" must be the group that is caught in ghetto pathology, in the culture of poverty. To characterize people as "irresponsible" is to imply freedom of choice—despite Glazer and Moynihan's assertions elsewhere that the poor are literally trapped in the culture of poverty. Glazer and Moynihan thus seem at bottom to be saying that the "unworthy poor" have chosen to live in poverty and are therefore beyond help. In a similar vein, Wilson claims that despite overall black economic progress, there is still a group of blacks who "*will not* or cannot escape" from poverty.[39] In adding the possibility that blacks "will not" escape, Wilson is at least suggesting that they have a choice. The implication is almost that they have a moral flaw which prevents them from making the "right" choice and escaping from poverty. In that case not only is current racism irrelevant, but even the effect of past racism seems relatively unimportant. The ethnic analysts would do well to follow Herbert Gans' warning. Gans himself is willing to accept the term "culture of poverty," though he makes it clear that such a concept must be very carefully defined. He warns that if the culture of poverty is to be viewed as "those cultural patterns that keep people poor" (and this certainly seems to be the way the ethnic analysts view it), then it is also necessary to include in the definition:

> *the persisting cultural patterns among the affluent that, deliberately or not, keep their fellow citizens poor. When the concept of a culture of poverty is applied only to the poor, the onus for change falls too much on them, when in reality the prime obstacles to the elimination of poverty lie in an economic, political, and social structure that operates to protect and increase the wealth of the already affluent.*[40]

All too often the effect of the ethnic model is to absolve whites of any

---

[38]N. Glazer and D. P. Moynihan, *Beyond the Melting Pot* (2nd ed.), p. 64.
[39]J. Q. Wilson, "The Moynihan Memo Revisited," p. 43. Emphasis added.
[40]H. J. Gans, "Culture and Class in the Study of Poverty," p. 216.

continuing and current responsibility for the problems faced by American blacks.[41]

Ethnicity-Class Confusion and the Culture of Poverty

The emphasis of the ethnic analysts on the culture of poverty leads to still another problem. In many cases the discussion of the culture of poverty relies not on the concept of ethnicity but on the concept of class. This is the fifth theme which is characteristic of ethnic analysis: the tendency to ignore the ethnic model completely when it is convenient to do so, and to switch the analysis to one based primarily on class problems. Sometimes the ethnic analysts use the rhetoric of ethnicity but the substance of class analysis. At other times they ignore the ethnic model entirely and rely solely on class. The former produces a clear contradiction. The latter might be acceptable if it represented a change in their views, but none of these men has ever rejected the ethnic model, and as late as 1970 Glazer and Moynihan still indicated an acceptance of that model.[42]

Moynihan's report on the Negro family is the primary example of this. Despite Moynihan's belief in the ethnic model, his analysis of the problem is in terms of class. The heart of the problem for Moynihan is not the Negro family structure in general, but the family structure of the Negro lower class, which he characterizes as "highly unstable and, in many urban centers . . . approaching complete breakdown."[43] Throughout Moynihan's writings on the pathology of the ghetto he is always careful to indicate that pathology is an affliction of the *lower class,* not

[41]A contrast to such a one-sided view might be the position of someone like Kenneth Clark, who agrees with the importance of ghetto pathology but combines this with a careful discussion of the role of current racism and with suggestions for change in major American institutions. (K. Clark, *Dark Ghetto: Dilemmas of Social Power.* New York: Harper & Row, 1965.) In opposition to the whole "culture of poverty" concept is the argument of Rossi and Blum, that "the empirical evidence from our review of the literature does not support the idea of a culture of poverty in which the poor are distinctively different from other layers of society. Nor does the evidence from intergenerational mobility studies support the idea of culture of poverty in the sense of the poor being composed largely of persons themselves coming from families living in poverty." (P. H. Rossi and Z. D. Blum, "Class, Status and Poverty," p. 43.)

[42]N. Glazer and D. P. Moynihan, "Introduction to the Second Edition."

[43]D. P. Moynihan, *The Negro Family,* p. 5.

of the middle class, and presumably not of the working class which he later characterizes as the silent black majority.[44] But if black pathology really plays the central role that Moynihan claims; if, as he says elsewhere, the black lower class represents approximately one half of the total black population; and if, as he seems to say, the black middle class poses relatively few problems, then his analysis is relying on class and not on ethnicity. This tendency becomes even sharper when he describes "lower class violence" as "purely a matter of social class" which has "nothing to do with race."[45] Not once in this work does he mention ethnicity.

In a similar vein, Wilson has recently argued that "we are seeing the emergence of such a deep and fundamental *class* cleavage among black Americans that race alone is no longer an accurate or particularly useful description of the problem."[46] Wilson might more accurately have said that ethnicity too is no longer an accurate or particularly useful description of the problem. While his article speaks extensively about class, it never mentions ethnicity. The depth of this tension becomes clear from the fact that in Banfield's latest book, *The Unheavenly City,* he poses the problem entirely in terms of *his* definition of class and avoids ethnicity altogether.[47] The implication appears to be that in practice adherents of the ethnic model find that model less than satisfactory as a way of explaining the problems of the black ghetto.

The Black-Uniqueness Thesis

Wilson's emphasis on a class cleavage among blacks is indicative of a sixth theme within the ethnic model. At the same time that the ethnic analysts describe blacks as basically just another ethnic group, their analysis depicts blacks as unique; at times this unique quality is so pervasive that it negates the original depiction of blacks as similar to other ethnic groups.

This emphasis can be seen most clearly in the ethnic analysts' discussion of the relationship between the black middle and lower classes.

[44]D. P. Moynihan, "Pre-inaugural Memo to Nixon." There is often great confusion in the ethnic analysts' characterization of class, particularly with respect to the lower and working classes.

[45]D. P. Moynihan, "Pre-inaugural Memo to Nixon."

[46]J. Q. Wilson, "The Moynihan Memo Revisited, p. 44. Emphasis original.

[47]E. C. Banfield, *The Unheavenly City: The Nature and Future of Our Urban Crisis.* Boston: Little, Brown & Company, 1970.

Banfield and Wilson, discussing problems of organizing among blacks, see the split between middle- and lower-class blacks as a major problem. This split is supposedly so great that it leads not merely to different goals, but to a clear conflict of interest between the two groups.[48] Wilson describes these conflicts of interest in great detail.[49] Similarly, both Glazer and Moynihan assert that the black middle class is unable to provide the necessary leadership for blacks in general. This belief runs throughout their work, but it is especially important in regard to their view of ghetto pathology as the core of the problem. They are thus very careful to distinguish between the stable black middle class and the unstable black lower class.[50] But this view of a serious disjunction between classes is totally different from both the basic premises of the ethnic model and the reality of the earlier immigrant experience. One of the basic premises of the ethnic model is the belief that ethnicity cuts across class lines for immigrant groups; this is said to be a major source of their strength. Such was the case, in fact, for other early immigrants. But the disjunction between classes for black people is a new element. If it is true that the two classes are so far apart, then blacks by definition cannot fit into the ethnic model since they lack one of the most important attributes of an ethnic group.

A similar comment can be made about the general emphasis on ghetto pathology and the culture of poverty. In *Beyond the Melting Pot* Glazer and Moynihan emphasized the problem of family instability far more for blacks than for any other ethnic group; Banfield and Wilson reiterate this view in *City Politics*. The whole view of a culture of poverty has arisen as an attempt to explain the black ghetto situation. But if the culture of poverty presents a more serious—even insurmountable—obstacle to blacks than to other immigrant groups, then blacks must be basically different from other ethnic groups.

The same problem arises in the ethnic analysts' description of blacks' failure to engage in extensive political activity. Involvement in politics is one of the main prerequisites of the ethnic model. If blacks in fact do not follow this pattern (for whatever reason) then it seems useless to try to build an extended comparison with the previous immigrant groups. The cumulative effect of these factors is to take blacks completely

[48]E. C. Banfield and J. Q. Wilson, *City Politics,* p. 298.

[49]J. Q. Wilson, *Negro Politics.*

[50]N. Glazer and D. P. Moynihan, "Introduction to the Second Edition."

out of the original ethnic framework. All the things the ethnic analysts emphasize indicate that blacks are substantially different. To make predictions about the future on the basis of the ethnic model is thus fallacious. It is ironic that all the evidence for this conclusion has been presented by the ethnic analysts themselves. Yet they fail to see the implications of their own work.

The Changing Cities

There is a seventh and final criticism that must be made of ethnic analysis. Banfield and Wilson have devoted a great deal of attention to an analysis of the changing nature of American cities. Glazer and Moynihan have at points agreed with many of the specifics of this analysis and with the general principle that the nature of city government has changed drastically.[51] All four seem to agree that American cities are no longer what they were when earlier immigrants came to live in them.

If this is true, it is difficult to see how the ethnic model can still be considered applicable to blacks since the model is based on the experiences of immigrants in the old-style cities. If those cities in effect no longer exist, there is no basis for a parallel between the current black situation and that of earlier immigrants. The ethnic analysts are perfectly willing to point out the changing conditions, but they do not go the one step further to recognize that those conditions may nullify their model. Instead, they continue to believe that comparing the experience of blacks to that of other immigrant groups is "enough . . . to justify an ethnic rather than a racial or 'internally colonized' self-image,"[52] and they continue to believe that, as more and more blacks come to the cities, they will gain increasing amounts of power and their position will improve accordingly.[53]

To summarize, all the themes of ethnic analysis are the product of the basic dilemma of the ethnic model. In order to compare blacks

[51]Among the basic elements of this change are the erosion of the urban tax base, the decline of machine politics, the changing nature of the American conception of politics, the changed position of the mayor, the growth of the metropolitan area concept, and the loss of power of city government. (See Chapter 12 for further discussion.)

[52]N. Glazer and D. P. Moynihan, "Introduction to the Second Edition," p. xiv.

[53]J. Q. Wilson, *Negro Politics,* p. 22.

to other immigrant groups and thus fit them into the ethnic model, ethnic analysts are forced to deemphasize the importance of race. Faced with the shortcomings of the ethnic model, but unable to use race as an explanation for that shortcoming without destroying the validity of the model, the ethnic analysts try to salvage the model by claiming that things have in fact improved (as they had predicted), and that the problem is that people simply do not perceive the improvement. But since black progress has fallen short of the prediction, the ethnic analysts are forced to place the blame on the intellectuals, the mass media, black militants, and finally, on blacks themselves. Their own analysis of black problems —which causes the failure of the ethnic model—leads them outside the boundaries of that model. The result is that they are often left with the rhetoric of ethnicity and an analysis based on class. In the end, they manage to define blacks out of the ethnic model completely, and at the same time continue to use a model based on urban conditions that no longer exist.

Ironically, many of the major themes within ethnic analysis point to the importance of racism in the United States. If the pathology of the ghetto is related to unemployment, and if, as Moynihan claims, one half of the black population is lower class, this at least might be an indication of the continued existence of racial barriers to employment and uncontrolled market forces. If blacks remain aloof from politics, it might be because racism has, in the past, prevented them from obtaining any meaningful gains through traditional political efforts. If black militants impede the progress of blacks by their shrill and angry rhetoric, that rhetoric might in part be a response to the continued experience of discrimination. The negative reactions of whites to rhetoric might be an indication of a basically racist tendency on their part to ignore the concrete realities of injustice and to reject the legitimate claims of blacks merely because of what they perceive as an unpleasant tone. Even the alleged predilection of intellectuals for the sensational and the preoccupation of the mass media with black riots can be seen as a reflection of racism. Both things fit into the all too familiar racist pattern of fascination with the so-called savage nature of blacks.

The ethnic analysts, trapped by a model that is too limited to offer an adequate explanation of the situation of blacks, are unable to include in that model a real analysis of the effects of contemporary racism. Charles Wilson's claim is that "commonly accepted views of New York City politics as a medium and arena for the adjustment of ethnic groups stand in sharp contrast to the real political history of the black community."[54] The major difference between the black experience and the experience of other ethnic groups, he suggests, is the "dependency relationship" which has characterized black-white relations. Wilson is implicitly pointing out the enormous effects of racism, but the ethnic analysts continue to use a model that simply does not describe the situation. As a result, however accurate some of their descriptions may be, the overall effect is invariably one-sided and incomplete. Wilson's claim that some blacks "will not" escape from poverty seems, in this light, to be almost an expression of petulance and frustration. Despite the lengths to which the ethnic analysts have gone to preserve the ethnic model, blacks simply will not fit within its boundaries.

Programmatic Implications

If we turn to an analysis of the programmatic solutions proposed by the ethnic analysts, we are faced with further problems. One program involves an emphasis on black self-help, which can be seen as early as the original edition of Beyond the Melting Pot. It is curious that, writing in 1963, Glazer and Moynihan could conclude that the need for protest had passed. Protest, they felt, could lead only to diminishing returns; they saw few additional gains to be made in the city through such action. Instead, what was needed was "a period of self-examination and self-help, in which the increasing income and resources of leadership of the group are turned inwards."[55] They particularly emphasized the role of the black middle class in providing leadership for this kind of movement.[56] Wilson also emphasizes the need for stronger leadership: "In some sense," he writes, "Negro critics of their own leaders may be right: There may well be a scarcity of able and creative leadership."[57] In a later work, Glazer indicates that the major source in overcoming poverty will have to come from the black community (although the money will come from the federal government). He then goes on:

[54]C. E. Wilson, "Negro Leadership at the Crossroads," in L. C. Fitch and A. H. Walsh (eds.), Agenda for a City. Beverly Hills, Calif.: Sage Publications, 1970, p. 552.

[55]N. Glazer and D. P. Moynihan, Beyond the Melting Pot (2nd ed.), p. 84.

[56]For a critique of the emphasis on developing black middle-class leadership see C. E. Wilson, "Negro Leadership at the Crossroads," pp. 547–556.

[57]J. Q. Wilson, Negro Politics, p. 7.

> *It is axiomatic to me that Negro organizations . . . can potentially do far, far more with Negro clients than can government organizations. It is in the stimulation of individual and group effort . . . that I see the most productive course we can follow to overcome poverty.*[58]

The call for self-help is consistent with the ethnic model. But, as Charles Valentine points out, it involves Glazer and Moynihan in a complete contradiction, especially in its emphasis on the role of the black middle class. Elsewhere, Glazer and Moynihan indicate that self-help is impossible, precisely because of the pathology of the ghetto:

> *The magnitude of the problems in the lower class and disorganized sectors of the population is so great that the middle-class element is inadequate to deal with them, as other middle-class elements of other ethnic groups dealt in the past (and deal today) with their problems. It is not likely we will see a massive self-help effort.*[59]

We agree with Valentine's point, but would add an even more basic one. If Glazer and Moynihan are convinced, as they seem to be, that blacks cannot help themselves to a sufficient degree, then, as we have pointed out, this places blacks outside the ethnic model.

The emphasis on black self-help leads to a further flaw that is characteristic of the ethnic model: the tendency to place the blame, and therefore the responsibility for change, on blacks. Black responsibility

[58]N. Glazer, "Paradoxes of American Poverty," p. 81. There is a very real irony here. Glazer and Moynihan are strongly opposed to a race analysis. While they support increasing black self-assertion insofar as it fosters a feeling of pride, they vigorously oppose its tendency toward separatism, and they see the rhetoric of black militants as one of the reasons why blacks have not duplicated the record of earlier immigrants. Yet, as we pointed out earlier, one of the primary functions that the rhetoric of race analysis has served is to goad the black community into acting as a strong ethnic group, and the programs that emanate from such an analysis—however much they may contradict the rhetoric—are precisely those that would logically emanate from the ethnic model. The irony becomes complete when Glazer proposes exactly the kind of self-help program that the race analysts propose. It is a measure of the one-sidedness of the ethnic analysts that they cannot see this.

[59]N. Glazer and D. P. Moynihan, *Beyond the Melting Pot (2nd ed.), pp. 52–53.* For Valentine's critique of this position see C. A. Valentine, *Culture and Poverty*, p. 28.

is emphasized at the expense of a detailed discussion of the objective obstacles standing in their way. Charles Wilson accurately characterizes the proposal to strengthen black middle-class leadership as bringing "a genuinely tragic dimension to the present crisis." His summary of such proposals is dramatic, but nevertheless accurate and important: "It is now seriously proposed," he writes, "that, instead of dealing with the real issues and basic relationships of our city, municipal officials employ city resources to affect the kinds, styles, and goals of Negro-black civic leadership."[60]

A second programmatic contradiction arises in regard to the role of the federal government. Many of the programs of the ethnic analysts rely on federal initiative. Moynihan has claimed that the chief purpose of his report on the Negro family was to push the government to act in regard to unemployment. Wilson's programmatic suggestions also rely largely on federal involvement. The federal government, he says, should place a floor under the ability of Americans to acquire such basics as housing, food, clothing, and medical care. Central cities should receive block grants from the state or federal government to provide services for the poor, for example, education and police protection. The federal government can, through special incentives, encourage experiments with various user charges to see that nonresidents pay their share of the services they use in the cities.[61]

Combined with this emphasis on federal involvement is an increasing note of pessimism about such involvement, and more and more of a belief that government should play at best a limited role. Despite Moynihan's interest in increasing federal involvement in 1965, by 1969 he began to be disillusioned with this involvement. One of the first signs of this can be seen when he wrote: "Rightly or otherwise—and one is no longer sure of this—it is our tradition in such circumstances to look to government."[62] In the same article he emphasized the need to strengthen local government. This tendency was stronger in Moynihan's pre-inauguration memo to Nixon, where he talked about the importance of deescalating the rhetoric "about those problems . . . which Government has relatively little power to influence in the present state of knowledge

[60]C. E. Wilson, "Negro Leadership at the Crossroads," p. 548.

[61]See J. Q. Wilson, "The War on Cities."

[62]D. P. Moynihan, "Toward a National Urban Policy," *The Public Interest*, Fall 1969, No. 17, p. 5.

and available resources."[63] To be sure, he makes it clear that he is not calling for diminution of governmental efforts. Yet the areas he suggests in which government is relatively powerless are curious: crime, *de facto* segregation, and low educational achievement. The curious fact is that crime and low educational achievement are the very problems Moynihan identified earlier as caused by the Negro family structure, and he had suggested that they could be alleviated by government intervention to reduce unemployment. Since Moynihan had not renounced that earlier view, his later pessimism on the role of government seems to create a real problem within his analysis. It is especially hard to square such pessimism with Glazer and Moynihan's introduction to the second edition of *Beyond the Melting Pot*. They start out with a characteristic disclaimer: "It would be a foolish man who would say that more could not have, should not have, been done." But they then go on: "And yet what impresses us is the creativity, relatively speaking, of the American political response all through the decade."[64] The Moynihan writing here seems to be a completely different man from the Moynihan who felt that the government's lack of knowledge in setting up the War on Poverty "brought about social losses that need not have occurred."[65]

The same pessimism can be seen in Banfield and Wilson according to whom the government's hands are tied for several reasons. As the middle class moves out of "gray areas," the lower-class will move in and will change these areas into low-density slums; the central city will deteriorate still further. Banfield and Wilson see no way for government to stop this. Several of the forces at work such as "changes in technology, in location of industry and population, and in consumer tastes and incomes . . . are all largely beyond the control of government in a free society." While these are all the "most fundamental problems" of the cities, the ones that make up "a life and death crisis," Banfield and Wilson feel that such problems cannot be solved or even relieved by government action at any level (local, state, or national).[66] If, as Glazer and Moynihan assert, blacks cannot develop a strong self-help movement, and if federal intervention seems of limited value, then one obvious conclusion is that

---

[63]D. P. Moynihan, "Pre-inaugural Memo to Nixon."

[64]N. Glazer and D. P. Moynihan, "Introduction to the Second Edition," p. xiv.

[65]D. P. Moynihan, *Maximum Feasible Misunderstanding: Community Action in the War on Poverty.* New York: The Free Press, 1970, p. xiv.

[66]E. C. Banfield and J. Q. Wilson, *City Politics,* p. 344.

things are very bleak indeed—a conclusion that is in opposition to the inherent optimism characteristic of the ethnic model.

The final problem with which we are concerned involves the ethnic model's assumptions regarding the nature of American politics. The ethnic analysts avoid the inconsistency of race advocates who reject pluralism on the rhetorical level but often accept it at the programmatic one. The ethnic analysts are explicit in their emphasis on pluralism. But as they implicitly admit, pluralist theory does not adequately explain the position of blacks in urban ghettos. In point of fact the black experience has been different from that of other immigrant groups, and thus the standard pluralist processes have not functioned in their favor. In light of this, the validity of the ethnic analysts' reliance on pluralism is questionable. Even if pluralism is an accurate description of the functioning of local communities, it does not seem to be a useful way to understand the position of blacks.

The basic reasons for doubting that blacks will follow the past immigrant groups within the context of the pluralistic system can be put in more schematic terms developed in an official government document, *The Report on the National Advisory Commission on Civil Disorders*.[67] The Report notes the following reasons:

1. The American industrial system has gone through its youth and middle-aged expansionary phases. These phases, and their attendant occupational upgrading and opportunities, coincided with the arrival of large numbers of foreign-born immigrants. However, "since World War II, . . . America's urban-industrial society has matured, and therefore, the Negro migrant, unlike the immigrant, found little opportunity in the city; he arrived too late, and the unskilled labor he had to offer was no longer needed" (p. 278).
2. While discrimination against past ethnic groups was considerable, it was not "so pervasive as the prejudice against color . . . which has formed a bar to advancement, unlike any other" (p. 279). Race represents an ineradicable mark of identification that cannot be readily removed by those who have power to provide opportunities. As Langston Hughes suggested many years ago in *Simple Speaks His Mind*, you can always change your name, but you can't paint your face.
3. Political opportunities; if not closed, have narrowed. Not only are

---

[67]*Report of the National Advisory Commission on Civil Disorders.* New York: Bantam Books, 1968, pp. 278–282.

the present local political organizations stagnant but they have increasingly less power over job opportunities. This, of course, results in a scarcity of patronage jobs and less willingness on the part of the political machinery to share those patronage jobs which do exist —especially with the new, black, city "immigrants."

4. Whereas foreign-born immigrants who did not speak English found their handicap a blessing in disguise, blacks, native-born "immigrants" who spoke English, found their blessing a handicap in disguise. The reason for this ironical paradox was stated in the following way: "Since the immigrants spoke little English and had their own ethnic culture, they needed stores to supply them with ethnic foods, and other services. . . . Since [blacks] spoke English, they had no need for their own stores; besides, the areas they occupied were already filled with stores (p. 280).

The importance of this last point cannot be underestimated. A store, a shop, a restaurant, an enterprise, however small, is a producing unit, demanding chores from all members of the family. Thus, the store not only served to hold the family "together" by demanding that each member pitch in, but also enabled one or two members of the family to get second jobs while income from the store provided the minimum needs. Moreover, there was always the possibility of the small "store" becoming "big business" through hard work and much luck. In these ways the foreign-born immigrant had opportunities unlike those facing the black population.

An important addition to this list of barriers is the professionalization of job requirements associated with the reforms of the 1920s, 1930s, and 1940s which were undertaken to eliminate nepotism. Licensing procedures and civil service examinations, whatever their virtues, have not always been beneficial to blacks compared to the nepotistic opportunities afforded foreign-born immigrants. Finally, the minority immigrant groups were part of the majority with respect to the pervasive nature of poverty during the 1920s, 1930s, and 1940s. Specific minorities and the majority suffered and endured a common problem. Today the relatively impoverished black minority stands alone and contrasts its fate with the relatively more affluent majority. Viewed as a whole, the barriers facing the black community are qualitatively more difficult to overcome than those faced by the earlier immigrant groups.

In the end, we are left with an ethnic model that describes neither the specific group in question nor the objective conditions that blacks must deal with. In their emphasis on the culture of poverty, on the lack of black leadership, on the problems of the lower class, on the role of the media, the intellectuals, and black militants, the ethnic analysts present a tacit admission that the ethnic model has failed in relation to blacks. Their attempts to salvage the model have led them in increasingly peculiar directions that often bear little relation to and even ignore the dynamics of the ethnic model. The convoluted and inconsistent nature of many of their arguments implicitly points to the importance of *both* the historical legacy *and* ongoing racism. Yet they continue to reject, or at best pay lip service to, the race factor. In so doing, they make it all too possible for government to conclude that the primary responsibility for change must rest with blacks, that white America has no responsibility for the effects of contemporary racism. They provide, in short, the perfect "cop-out" for a society that would prefer not to have to think about the problems of the black ghetto, and that does not want to face up to its own complicity in perpetuating those problems.

CHAPTER 10

Race, Class, and Social Change

There are probably few concepts that have taken on such a broad range of meanings as that of class. For some theorists, the concept involves purely objective factors, while for others it involves primarily subjective psychological attitudes. This flexibility of interpretation can be seen most clearly in the viewpoints of the different groups that have adopted a class concept to explain the position of blacks. One version of class analysis, a subjective one, has become influential among conservative government and establishment circles. It is used to justify total government inaction at worst, and gradual, slow, incremental change at best. A second version, an objective one, is the theoretical backbone of the various Marxist and socialist groups that are opposed to American capitalism and its government. These groups use a class analysis to justify radical social change.

The original Marxian definition of class relied primarily on economic factors. "We are concerned here,"

Marx says in the preface to *Capital,* "with persons only in so far as they are the personifications of economic categories, carriers of certain class relations and interests."[1] The most extreme divergence from the Marxian formulation can be found in a group of subjective theories which include within the concept of class the role of the individual psyche and of individual values.[2]

Within this wide range of definitions, two patterns of analysis tend to emerge as explanations of the inferior position of American blacks. Almost every analyst dealing with the black condition uses the class concept in some way. As the emphasis on race increases, however, the emphasis on class frequently decreases, and vice versa. Where the emphasis on race predominates, as among the race analysts, the emphasis on class as a primary determinant of the problems of blacks diminishes. When race advocates use the concept of class (usually defined in terms of income level), it is seen primarily as a result of racism. As we move away from racial analysis toward ethnic analysis, the importance of race recedes and class becomes more important. The ethnic analysts often assert that black problems stem in large part from the fact that so many blacks are lower class, and at times this emphasis becomes so dominant that ethnicity is virtually disregarded.[3] As we move toward the other end of the spectrum, class predominates at the expense of both race and ethnicity. Some versions of Marxist theory, for example, emphasize only the concept of class.

[1]K. Marx, *Das Kapital* (new ed.) Berlin, 1953, p. 8. Cited by R. Dahrendorf, *Class and Class Conflict in Industrial Society.* Stanford, Calif.: Stanford University Press, 1965, p. 145. The proponents of social-stratification theory altered this formulation in order to define class by such criteria as wealth and the conditions of the individual's existence. The proponents of structural analysis modified the original definition to include the concept of social role.

[2]One example of the various "subjective" theories of class might be called the "social-psychological" class concept, by which an individual is seen as belonging to the group which he feels he belongs to. But as Dahrendorf points out, most scholars who hold to a "subjective" class theory regard these psychological phenomena as socially structured; the determinant of class is in reality not the individual but the social relations in which he and others are involved. See R. Dahrendorf, *Class and Class Conflict in Industrial Society,* pp. 145–148.

[3]While ethnic analysis is essentially different from class analysis, the importance of class takes on additional significance among ethnic analysts and at times seems to contradict the ethnic model.

The Subjectivist View: Banfield's Class Analysis

One of the most influential proponents of a "subjective" class analysis is Edward Banfield. Banfield's class theory has helped to form, and often serves to justify, the major outlines of both the conservative position vis-à-vis blacks and the Nixon administration's view of the problem. The Nixon administration has emphasized increasingly the relative inability of government to alleviate the problems of the black ghetto. Its major focus has been on strengthening the middle class through such programs as black capitalism (see Chapter 11). Both these themes are the outgrowth of the view put forth in Banfield's book *The Unheavenly City,* a book that has served as the theoretical justification for the increasingly conservative trend of the early 1970s.[4] Banfield's influence, in our view, is pernicious and should therefore be studied with great care. His view is also important as an illustration of the link between the ethnic and subjective class approaches to the black question. As we indicated earlier, the ethnic analysis shows an increasing, albeit uncomfortable, interplay between the concepts of ethnicity and class. Banfield's earlier writings were within the ethnic framework and very much along the lines of the work of Moynihan, Glazer, and Wilson (see Chapter 9).

Banfield's definition of class is unique. A person's class is determined by what Banfield calls his "orientation toward the future" (p. 47). This orientation is a product of two things: the individual's ability to imagine a future, and his ability to discipline himself enough to sacrifice his immediate pleasure in the interest of long-range goals and satisfactions. The upper-class individual is future-oriented; he has the ability to imagine a distant future and to deprive himself of immediate gains in the interest of that future. The lower-class individual is present-oriented; he has little ability to conceive of the future or to make sacrifices for the sake of it.[5] Banfield thus rejects the usual objective criteria of wealth, income,

---

[4]E. C. Banfield, *The Unheavenly City: The Nature and Future of Our Urban Crisis.* Boston: Little, Brown & Company, 1970. All further references to Banfield in this chapter are to this book unless otherwise noted.

[5]Between these two extremes are the working and middle classes who are less present-oriented than the lower class but more than the upper class. Insofar as an individual has

and so on to define a person's class position, using instead the subjective criterion of orientation toward the future.[6]

Banfield's main thesis is that because of the nature of the lower-class person there is little that can be done to improve slum conditions. According to Banfield, poverty is often the result of the present-orientation of the lower-class person. Poor people who are present-oriented will never be able to rise above the poverty level because they lack the ability to discipline themselves and to postpone immediate gratification in favor of future rewards. Because many poor people are also lower class, there is little that can be done to help them. Giving them money is wasteful, since they will spend it all immediately. Improving housing conditions is useless, since their present-orientation makes it impossible for them to take care of such housing and prevent it from turning into a slum.

In short, Banfield is saying that because the slums have a high percentage of lower-class, or present-oriented, people, we will not be able to change slum conditions. In order to reach this conclusion it is crucial that he define the lower-class person as *psychologically unable* to conceive of the future. It is not enough to say that a person's behavior indicates that he is present-oriented, because his behavior might change if the situation changes. An obvious example of this would be the person who fails to plan for the future because in reality he has no chance for a decent future. If his environment were to change, if circumstances

a greater and greater capacity to imagine a future and plan for that future, he is more and more upper class. Banfield does see a rough correspondence between the usual views of upper and lower class based on income and his own definition. His rationale is that because the upper-class person (in his definition) tends to plan for the future, he will obtain the necessary education, and so on. The lower-class person, incapable of looking ahead, is likely to be poor and unskilled. Despite this rough correspondence, the two views need not be identical: "A person who is poor, unschooled, and of low status may be upper class; indeed he *is* upper class if he is psychologically capable of providing for a distant future. By the same token, one who is rich and a member of 'the 400' may be lower class; he *is* lower class if he is incapable of conceptualizing the future or of controlling his impulses and is therefore obliged to live from moment to moment" (p. 48). (Emphasis original.)

[6]Banfield reinforces this emphasis on subjective qualities, as opposed to behavioral manifestations, in his list of the secondary characteristics of each class culture. These include attitudes toward authority, self-improvement, risk, and violence, all of which are purely subjective states of mind. Interestingly, the one objective criterion used in this list of secondary characteristics is that of distinctive forms of social organization, especially family structure—the favorite whipping boy of the ethnic analysts. The subjective nature of Banfield's criteria is reinforced, too, by his assertion that a poor person can be upper class and vice versa.

were such that he could realistically envision a good future, then his attitude might change. If this were the case, Banfield's conclusion that little can be done to help lower-class people would be inaccurate since it would be necessary only to change the objective conditions of poverty in order to change the present orientation to a future orientation.

Banfield is well aware of this problem and he tries to avoid it by setting up a distinction between *ability,* on the one hand, and *actual performance,* on the other. He thus stresses that a person can be considered lower class only if he is *psychologically incapable* of conceiving of the future (p. 47). He cannot be considered lower class just because he *behaves* as if he were unconcerned about the future.

This principle, that a person's class position can be judged only on the basis of his ability to conceive of the future and not on the basis of his performance, is crucial to Banfield's theory. Had he simply adhered to this definition of the lower-class person as psychologically unable to conceive of the future, he would at least be logically justified in his conclusion that we can do little to alleviate slum conditions. But he does not, and therefore the conclusion and the major thrust of the book are invalid.

Subjective-Objective Inconsistencies

The fatal internal contradiction in Banfield's work arises from his inclusion of three types of present-orientation within the lower class: cognitive, situational, and volitional. He defines these as follows:

Cognitive: a person who is *"psychologically incapable* either of taking account of the future or of controlling impulses."

Situational: a person who is *"psychologically capable* both of taking the future into account and of controlling his impulses. He lives from moment to moment because he believes his situation to be such that investment in the future is either impossible or unprofitable."

Volitional: a person who, "despite being *psychologically capable* of providing for the future, and despite being in a situation which (as he perceives it) may afford excellent opportunity for investing, nevertheless lives from moment to moment simply because he prefers that style of life" (p. 217. Emphasis added).

It is clear that only one category, cognitive present-orientedness, involves a psychological inability to conceive of the future. Each of the other two categories, volitional and situational, describes people who are *psychologically capable* of conceiving of the future, but fail to do so for other reasons. The contradiction is obvious: While Banfield had originally warned that a person could be defined as lower class only on the basis of psychological inability to conceive of the future (cognitive present-orientedness), he is including in the lower class two other types, volitional and situational, who are capable of conceiving of the future but fail to do so. When Banfield includes these two types in the lower class he is doing so on the basis of what a person does, that is, his performance, and thereby ignoring his own stipulation that "The criterion . . . is ability, not performance" (p. 47).[7] He has quietly switched from subjective to objective criteria in contradiction to his own definition. This contradiction shows up clearly in his summary of the three types. He says that they are all "unable *or unwilling* either to control impulses or to put forth any effort at self-improvement" (p. 217. Emphasis added.) But even if a person is unwilling to plan for the future, he may still have the ability to do so; to include the "unwilling" with the "unable" in the lower class is to destroy his own definition and analysis.

This contradiction leads to other inconsistencies throughout the book. At one point, for example, Banfield writes that both the "tastes" and the "situation" of the lower-class person will tend to make him present-oriented (p. 218). But to include "tastes" and "situation" as causes of present-orientation is again to ignore the original principle that psychological inability to conceive of the future is the sole criterion of the lower-class position. This principle would make considerations of "tastes" and "situation" irrelevant.

Pointing out these inconsistencies is more than an academic exercise because it is these inconsistencies that enable Banfield to come to what, in our view, are some very destructive conclusions regarding the problems of black ghettos. This begins to be apparent when Banfield states that "most lower-class people in the large cities are black" (p. 237), (meaning people who, for reasons that remain obscure, lack the *ability* to conceive of the future and to control their impulses). Since he cites no evidence for this statement, one can only conclude that he is either using lower-class in the conventional (but by his theory contradictory) sense of income level, or that he comes to his conclusion on the

[7]Banfield makes his actual reliance on performance explicit when he says, in regard to the three types, "An individual of one type acts very much like one of another. . . . The types differ according to the *cause* of the individual's present-orientation" (p. 217. Emphasis original.)

basis of performance (rather than ability); that is, since so many blacks are poor and live in ghettos, a large number are present-oriented. In either case, his position is inconsistent.

Banfield goes on to compound this felony by concluding: "The main trouble with the 'ghetto' (when it is without walls) is that so many of its residents are lower or lower working class" (p. 82).[8] Banfield has gone from a dubious theory of class to a broad generalization about the ghetto without offering any evidence that ghetto residents are lower class by his definition of the term. Without this evidence it is hard to escape the conclusion that, contrary to his own theory, Banfield is working backward. Starting with the concrete objective situation of the ghetto, he is assuming that these conditions are the result of present-orientedness and then concluding that there must be a large number of "lower-class" people in the central cities.

Banfield barely considers the possibility that the conditions of the ghetto are the product of some external force. He ignores the possibility that the supposed present-orientedness of the ghetto dweller (assuming that such is the case) is purely the result of the objective reality that he faces, that the ghetto Negro in fact has no real control over, or hopes for, the future. Elsewhere Banfield states that "a rational person does not exchange present for future satisfaction if the world appears so full of uncertainty as to make a return on the investment most unlikely" (p. 220). One could wish that he had carried his own statement to its logical conclusion instead of being so quick to characterize lower-class culture as "pathological." Instead, he uses his already flawed theory to come to the rather remarkable conclusion that poverty is the effect rather than the cause of lower-class culture (p. 125).

This theory has had enormous implications for urban policy-making. Given its importance, one would expect Banfield to have developed, tested, refined, and retested a comprehensive method for determining a person's orientation toward the future. We have a right to expect, at the least, that Banfield indicate clearly how to distinguish between ability and performance.

Banfield's major methodological discussion, however, consists of a list of three possible ways to determine whether a person's present-

---

[8]If Banfield's comment is combined with a whole series of similar comments—for example, "For the lower-middle-class person a car pool will do—the upper-middle-class person, however, finds that distasteful." (p. 60)—one begins to get a sense of the kind of condescending attitude that underlies Banfield's book.

orientedness is cognitive, situational, or volitional. The most convincing test, he claims, is to give the person powerful incentives to provide for the future and then observe his behavior. When he discusses these "powerful incentives," he indicates that good jobs would provide such an incentive, but he rejects that as impractical and instead moves on to a second method, which involves an implausible psychological test. In this test the subject would be asked to tell a story in which "the span of time covered by the action of the story is taken as a measure of time-orientation" (p. 305). An obvious and immediate problem is that it is not clear if failure to tell a story with a long time span ("long" being undefined) is to be equated with the inability to plan for the future. More important, Banfield admits that such tests yield uncertain results, yet he is perfectly willing to elaborate a whole theory of the pathological nature of lower-class culture on the admittedly flimsy evidence of story-telling.[9] The test Banfield relies on for his primary evidence has not been administered to very many blacks in ghetto areas, or anywhere else as a matter of fact. Nevertheless, he still insists that "most lower class people in the large cities are black" (p. 82). His approach could be the subject of comic ridicule if it didn't have such dangerous implications.

Poverty: Effect Not Cause

Banfield claims that a good part of his concept of class culture depends heavily on the work of Herbert Gans, and especially on Gans' book *The Urban Villagers*.[10] Even here the inconsistencies abound. Discussing his theories in a later essay, Gans does stress the present-orientedness of the lower class, but he does not make the psychological orientation the primary determinant of class.[11] Yet it is this psychological incapacity that is at the heart of Banfield's theory. Gans points out that there is

---

[9]Banfield's third method is equally flimsy. If an examination by a cultural anthropologist "of 'the entire way of life of a people' reveals that way to be present-oriented, it is safe to conclude that the present-orientedness of persons socialized into that way of life will be cognitive, whatever else it may be" (p. 223). No evidence is offered for this statement.

[10]H. J. Gans, *The Urban Villagers: Group and Class in the Life of Italian-Americans*. New York: The Free Press, 1962.

[11]H. J. Gans, "Culture and Class in the Study of Poverty: An Approach to Anti-poverty Research," in D. P. Moynihan (ed.), *On Understanding Poverty: Perspectives from the Social Sciences*. New York: Basic Books, 1969.

a direct relationship between a person's aspirations and the material conditions of his existence; these aspirations can be tested only if economic conditions are favorable to their realization. Banfield in part admits this when he says the best way to determine the particular type of present-orientation is to provide powerful incentives to provide for the future. Nevertheless he rejects that test and, despite Gans' warning, is still willing to settle for what, by his own admission, is the uncertain evidence of psychological tests. Gans' warning about the dangers of class culture theory is remarkably applicable to Banfield:

> *Analyses that define class positions on the basis of situational responses, but ascribe it to culture, make ad-hoc behavior seem permanent and may assign people to long-term class positions on the basis of data which in fact describe their short-term response to a situation. For example, if poor people's inability to plan is a situational response rather than a behavioral norm, it cannot be used as a criterion of lower-class culture, although it might be considered a pattern associated with lower-class position.*[12]

In short, Banfield appears to have fallen into the very trap that Gans describes. At one point, Banfield appears to doubt the whole theoretical edifice: In the interest of objectivity and balance he warns that "It may turn out that the lower class . . . does not exist . . . or that it exists among so few persons as to be inconsequential" (p. 223).[13] However, ignoring his own qualification, the major themes of his book are the direct product of his theory of the lower class. The "fact" that many ghetto residents are lower class leads Banfield to the conclusion that the existence of poverty and the conditions of the ghetto are the fault of the

---

[12]H. J. Gans, "Culture and Class in the Study of Poverty," pp. 216–217.

[13]The full quotation reads as follows: "It may turn out that the lower class that has figured so largely in this book does not exist (that whatever present-orientation exists is neither cultural in origin nor cognitive in nature) or that it exists among so few people as to be inconsequential." Banfield seems to be saying here, as in the original definition, that lower-class present-orientation must be cognitive in nature, that is, that it must involve psychological inability to plan for the future.

poor. He implicitly admits this when, speaking about lower-class culture, he asserts that "poverty is its effect rather than its cause" (p. 125).[14] The number of lower-class residents, Banfield claims, is the reason why ghettos are full of rats, garbage, bad schools, noise, and disorder. It is not at all clear why an inability to plan for the future is the cause of these phenomena, but Banfield goes even further. In an amazing and inexplicable leap of logic he manages to blame both inadequate police protection and the charging of higher prices for low quality goods on the supposed present-orientation of lower-class culture. A theme that had been lying just beneath the surface in the writings of the ethnic analysts becomes explicit in Banfield: Many ghetto dwellers are poor because of some innate psychological defect within them—in this case their present-orientedness.[15] (It should be noted, in passing, that this is a functional equivalent of the presently less fashionable genetic explanation of the black man's lower socioeconomic status.) It is present-orientedness that causes lower-class workers to leave jobs without notice and to steal, as well as engendering the supposed lower-class tendency to squander money and engage in violence. If the lower class were to disappear, so too would the most pressing urban problems disappear.

Having "proved" the existence of this lower class, Banfield goes on to assert that most attempts to improve the ghetto are doomed to failure:

> So long as the city contains a sizable lower class, nothing basic can be done about its most serious problems. Good jobs may be offered to all, but some will remain chronically unemployed. Slums may be demolished, but if the housing that replaces them is occupied by the lower class it will shortly be turned into new slums. Welfare payments may be doubled or tripled and a negative income tax instituted, but some persons will continue to live in squalor and misery. New schools may be built, new curricula

[14]For an opposing view see Rossi and Blum, who argue that if there is a culture of poverty its cause lies in "the exigencies of being relatively without resources and of being negatively evaluated by the larger society." P. H. Rossi and Z. D. Blum, "Class, Status, and Poverty," in D. P. Moynihan (ed.), p. 56. See also C. A. Valentine, *Culture and Poverty: Critique and Counter-proposals*. Chicago: University of Chicago Press, 1968.

[15]Banfield admits that some "middle-class" people are also trapped in poverty, but his major emphasis is on the lower class.

> *devised, and the teacher-pupil ratio cut in half, but if the children who attend these schools come from lower-class homes, they will be turned into blackboard jungles . . . (pp. 210–211).*

It is only one step to his final, inevitable judgment that government not only cannot solve the problems of the cities, but "is likely to make them worse by trying" (p. 257). This belief is a natural concomitant of any theory that holds that an inner defect in the poor, rather than a structural defect in society is the cause of poverty. It is a theme that first began to appear, however tentatively and disguised, in the writings of the ethnic analysts. Thus Banfield can state unequivocally: "The government cannot eliminate slums, educate the slum child, train the unskilled worker, end chronic poverty, stop crime and delinquency and prevent riots. In the main these problems are not susceptible to solution."[16] While he denies that the purpose of his theory is to provide a rationale for inaction, he certainly seems to present such a rationale. His conclusions, moreover, are especially invalid in the light of the fact that his theory, by his own admission, is based on a relatively small number of people.[17] Given the relatively small number of people involved in this lower-class culture, it is difficult to understand why Banfield is presenting the theory at all.

Banfield's concrete programmatic suggestions reflect both his pessimism and his continued reliance on the lower-class concept. The majority of his suggestions are designed to decrease crime. Two others emphasize the need to deescalate any rhetoric that tends to "raise expectations to unreasonable and unrealizable levels," that emphasizes racism, and that "exaggerates" the seriousness of the social problems. At the same time, poverty must be redefined to mean "hardship" instead of "relative deprivation." A third group of suggestions involves ways in which the number of lower-class people can be reduced, either by providing more

---

[16]E. C. Banfield, "Why Government Cannot Solve the Urban Problem," *Daedalus,* Fall 1968, p. 1232. (Part of this article appears in revised form in *The Unheavenly City.)*

[17]Banfield admits that the number of present-oriented people is small both in absolute numbers and as a percentage of the whole population. Further, his claim is that "most Negroes are not improvident, do not live in squalor and violence, and therefore are plainly not lower class," and he says that these same people are often the inhabitants of ghettos. This leaves only a minority, yet from that minority Banfield draws the conclusion that little can be done to improve the ghettos (p. 211).

birth control information or by paying "problem families" to send their children to day-care centers.[18] In short, the vast majority of Banfield's proposals have nothing to do with changing the concrete conditions within which the (black) poor are forced to live. In a long list, there are basically only two suggestions to improve the objective conditions of the ghetto.[19]

Class versus Ethnic Interpretations

Banfield's emphasis on lower-class culture ties in with, and is strengthened by, tendencies that were evident in Banfield's earlier use of the ethnic analysis. One of the most striking features of *The Unheavenly City* is its tendency to use the lower-class concept to magnify and emphasize themes that were present in the ethnic analysis, though in a more muted form.

Banfield's close ties with the ethnic analysts can be readily identified. He claims that the ghetto is characterized by the fact that "many of its residents are lower or lower working class" (p. 82). He adopts the argument that the main disadvantage of the black ghetto dweller is the fact that "he is the most recent unskilled, and hence relatively low-income, immigrant to reach the city from a backward rural area" (p. 68). In his earlier book, *City Politics,* written within the ethnic framework, Banfield was able to point to various factors, such as the political machine and

[18]For the full list of Banfield's proposals, see *The Unheavenly City,* pp. 245–246.

[19]One of these—the proposal to bring all income above the poverty level—is seriously weakened by Banfield's belief that current poverty is mainly a matter of "relative deprivation." Raising incomes above his newly defined "hardship" level might in practice turn out to be only a minor improvement. In addition, the value of the proposal is offset by the solution Banfield appends to it, that we distinguish between the competent and the incompetent poor and, where necessary, either encourage or require some of the latter to live in an institution or semi-institution. The "incompetent poor," according to Banfield, includes "the insane, the severely retarded, the senile, the lower class (inveterate problem families) and unprotected children." This grouping of the lower class with the retarded and insane is consistent with Banfield's view of lower-class culture as pathological, albeit the morality is somewhat dubious. Banfield's other major attempt to change objective conditions is the proposal that if it is feasible, the unemployment level should be kept below 3 percent. If that is not possible, we can help to raise employment by repealing the minimum-wage law, ceasing to overpay for low-skilled public employment, and ceasing to harass private employers who offer low wages and unattractive (but not unsafe) working conditions to people who would not otherwise be employed.

the role of middle-class leadership, that helped to bring newly arrived immigrants into the economic and political mainstream. But given the class analysis which he adopts in *The Unheavenly City,* the fact that blacks are recent arrivals is irrelevant. The factors he earlier pointed to as helping the immigrant groups are useless if, as he claims, "most lower class people in the large cities are black" (p. 237), and "So long as the city contains a sizable lower class, nothing basic can be done about its most serious problems" (p. 210). Banfield tries to reconcile the two interpretations by stating that an individual is influenced by both his class and his ethnic culture, but he never clarifies that relationship; the use of both class and ethnic analyses is contradictory.

Banfield's close relationship with ethnic analysis also emerges in other ways. First, the ethnic analysts had claimed that race was not the crucial determinant of the black man's position in American society. Using the kind of disclaimer that ethnic analysts often rely on, Banfield also dispenses with the problem of race by stating that "The existence of ethnic and racial prejudice both past and present is a fact too painfully evident to require assertion" (p. 68).[20] Having thus protected himself, he dispenses with an analysis of racism, past or present. His real views on the subject become fairly clear from the fact that he is often unwilling even to use the term racism. Like other ethnic analysts, he usually substitutes the much milder word, prejudice, and qualifies even that by claiming that much of what appears to be race prejudice is really class prejudice. Like the ethnic analysts, Banfield emphasizes the distinction between past and present causes. His argument is that the continuing causes of black problems "are seldom purely racial and very often have little or nothing to do with race" (p. 70). His analysis therefore has the same one-sided quality that characterized the ethnic analysis.

Second, Banfield's analysis exhibits a major flaw which links him to the ethnic analysts. His refusal to acknowledge the dimensions of the urban problem leads him to ever more tortured and convoluted ways of explaining the discontent of urban blacks. Banfield's claim is that most of the problems of the so-called urban crisis are not serious, that is, they do not affect the essential welfare of the individual or the general "health of society." They are, rather, "important," that is, they have to

[20]Banfield is also similar to the ethnic analysts in his belief that the mass media are an important cause of riots (p. 198).

do with such things as comfort, convenience, and business advantage.[21] The "urban crisis," Banfield claims, again directly paralleling the ethnic analysts, is largely a subjective one. Improved conditions have led to higher standards; the problems only seem to be worse because of these new standards.[22] It is in large part this denial of the importance of racism and the belief that the poor are not so badly off that make it possible for Banfield to go on to attribute the ills of the (black) poor to their own time-orientation.

Third, Banfield parallels the ethnic analysts in his acceptance of a pluralist view of the American political system. He argues, for example, that his list of solutions is politically unfeasible because of the existence of various interest groups similar to those that supposedly forced an abrupt end to official consideration of the Moynihan report. In a typical defense of pluralism Banfield states: "That interest groups have such power does not represent a malfunctioning of the political system. When they designed the system the Founding Fathers took great pains to distribute power widely so that 'factions' would check one another, thus preventing the rise of any sort of tyranny" (p. 247).

[21]Banfield's callous disregard of the problems of the urban slum dweller becomes clear when he says that the best example of a "serious" problem he can find in the cities is air pollution. For Banfield, the vast majority of people are better off than they have ever been and there is every reason to believe that things will get better in the future. A further example of this callousness is the argument he offers to prove that riots are not as harmful as many would think. His evidence is the fact that in all the riots from 1964 to 1967 no more than 20 persons were killed by rioters. He fails to mention the fact, pointed out by Wilson, that "43 persons died in Detroit, most from police and national guard bullets." (J. Q. Wilson, "Why We Are Having a Wave of Violence," in N. Glazer (ed.), *Cities in Trouble*. Chicago, Quadrangle Books, 1970, p. 58.) Banfield's definition of danger seems not to include danger to the supposed rioters.

[22]One might well ask why Banfield is even bothering to write a book about a relatively minor, if not non-existent, urban crisis. And here Banfield's real concern becomes apparent. He is worried, in part, because "middle class-ification" seems to carry with it the tendency to view society as responsible for everything and therefore to place undue blame on it; in his view, this tendency to lose confidence in society is dangerous. There is also a very "serious" problem regarding poverty. However, Banfield is not concerned about the horrible conditions in urban ghettos, but about the dangers inherent in "huge enclaves of people of low skill, income, and status" (p. 12). Such conditions tend to produce a sense of collective self-identity which is desirable in some ways, but which is also a threat to peace and order and which could produce different, less democratic politics in the long run. One is reminded here of Glazer and Moynihan's belief that the recent increase in black self-assertion is good. But ultimately, for all these men, the underlying problem seems to be one of preserving stability and defending the established order.

Fourth, and most important, Banfield's lower-class theory is the logical culmination of the culture-of-poverty theory of the ethnic analysts. Banfield's "lower-class culture" is the extension of Glazer and Moynihan's "unworthy poor." His comment that lower-class individuals are "either unwilling or unable to plan for the future" has the familiar ring of Wilson's poor who either "will not or cannot" escape from poverty. Banfield's class analysis represents the worst side of the ethnic analysis without any of the ethnic analysts' redeeming qualities. For all their tendency to blame the poor, Glazer, Moynihan, and Wilson tried to devise ways to improve their objective conditions. But the optimism of *Beyond the Melting Pot* has been replaced by the pessimism of *The Unheavenly City,* which consistently denies the value of any attempts to alleviate slum conditions. Wilson once pointed out that it was impossible to judge the effectiveness of various plans to increase employment because they had never seriously been tried.[23] Banfield might have done well to remember that statement before deciding that slum problems were beyond help. His view of the lower class makes him all too quick to conclude that reform is impossible, a mood that is prevalent in conservative circles throughout the country.

In sum, Banfield's theory manages to turn everything upside down. Poverty is not the cause but the effect of lower-class behavior. The poor are not unhappy because of their poverty; their "discomfort and inconvenience" are "seldom acute and persistent." Rather, "It is appearing to others and to oneself as inferior . . . that constitutes most poverty now" (p. 119). White America is guilty not because of its mistreatment and neglect of the black poor, but because it is basically too good. Banfield is worried about the future because of his belief that increasing "middle class-ification" will produce increasing numbers of people oriented to the "service" ideal of the upper class. This ideal, which Banfield claims dominates American politics, is basically altruistic; it is oriented toward the future and toward increased progress, and it emphasizes both the possibility of finding solutions to problems and the obligation to do so. As a result, middle- and upper-class culture poses just as great a problem for Banfield as does lower-class culture with respect to the question of changing the conditions of blacks. The lower class either refuses to change or is incapable of changing; the middle class, unable to accept this fact, simply makes the situation worse:

[23]J. Q. Wilson, "The War on Cities," *The Public Interest,* Spring 1966, No. 3, p. 38.

> It is the generous and public regarding impulses of voters and taxpayers that impel them to support measures—for example, the minimum wage and compulsory high school attendance—the ultimate effect of which is to make the poor poorer and more demoralized. Our devotion to the doctrine that all men are created equal discourages any explicit recognition of class-cultural differences and leads to "democratic"—often misleading —formulations of problems: for example, poverty as lack of income and material resources (something external to the individual) rather than as inability or unwillingness to take account of the future or to control impulses (something internal). Sympathy for the oppressed, indignation at the oppressor, and a wish to make amends for wrongs done by one's ancestors lead to a misrepresentation of the Negro as the near-helpless victim of "white racism" (p. 256).

It turns out that, for Banfield, the crime of white America is not its racism or its willingness to tolerate inequality. Our real crime is that, like Alexander Portnoy's mother, we are simply too nice. It is only one short step from there to a governmental decision that we have done our best, that the nature of the lower class makes it impossible to improve slum conditions. The concrete result of such a policy is exactly what we are witnessing today: decreasing government involvement in ghetto problems in favor of aid to the black middle class through black capitalism (see Chapter 11). Even the emphasis on black capitalism is more theoretical than real. While there is a good deal of talk about black capitalism, remarkably little concrete help has been given to its development.

The Objectivist View: A Marxist Class Analysis

If we leave Banfield and turn to a Marxist class analysis, the contrasts are striking. Where Banfield bases his class theory on subjective criteria, the Marxists rely primarily on objective criteria. Where Banfield represents the thinking of basically conservative "establishment" circles, Marxist theory typifies the thinking of anti-establishment critics. Banfield's pessimism led to the conclusion that the best we can hope for is gradual, incremental change. The Marxists are equally pessimistic about the future within the context of capitalism. Their pessimism leads them to believe in the necessity of revolution.

However sophisticated may be the total Marxist view of class and its implications, Marxist *practitioners* often emphasize a straight class view of the black malaise and a simple economic determinist interpretation of the historical nature of racism. Looking at American capitalism in terms of a two-class system, the strict Marxist tends to see blacks solely as part of the exploited class. Within this analysis the Marxist would not deny the historical relevance of race and racism; however, he would view it as a *manifestation* of the economic system of American capitalism. A good statement of this position is presented by Oliver Cox. Cox's position is that race prejudice serves as an "attitudinal justification" for the exploitation of another race. Racism "is the socio-attitudinal matrix supporting a calculated and determined effort of a white ruling class to keep some people or peoples of color and their resources exploitable."[24] But having given lip service to the relevance of racism as determined by economic forces of the past, Marxist practitioners proceed to devise programs which primarily emphasize class and ignore race almost entirely.

Marxist analysis rejects any explanation of the position of blacks in the United States that is based on questions of race or color; the economic position of blacks is the only relevant issue. Marxists would argue that race is used to justify the economic interests of the ruling class against the working class. Racism keeps the working class divided against itself and prevents it from understanding its real, as opposed to its nominal, interests.[25]

As a result of this theory, the proper role for a Marxist party is to show the working class, both black and white (1) that the race issue is a diversionary tactic, and (2) that the only way to liberate both blacks and oppressed whites is to overthrow the capitalist system. Marxists such as Cox argue that there is "no possibility of giving up race prejudice while still retaining the system which produced it."[26] In this they are clearly opposed to the race analysts. Any attempt to organize blacks on the basis of color would be contrary to the Marxists' straight class

[24]O. Cox, *Caste, Class and Race: A Study in Social Dynamics.* Garden City: Doubleday & Co., 1948, pp. 475–476.

[25]In order to prove their argument, the Marxists must show that racism is profitable to the dominant class. If the dominant class should discover that it is not profitable, but continues to perpetuate racist sentiments and practices, the class analysis is considerably weakened.

[26]O. Cox, p. 581.

position. To the extent that the ethnic analysts tend to accept and approve of capitalism (however modified) and to view the black problem largely in other than class terms, the Marxists would also be opposed to ethnic analysis. The difficulty of applying the orthodox Marxist class position is readily illustrated by examining some of the inconsistent positions that various Marxist parties have had in relating to black problems and needs.

The Communist Party, for example, in its early stage, looked at black problems within the standard boundaries of the Marxist class analysis. The problem of the Negro worker was thus seen as part of the overall problem of the unskilled worker.[27] Similarly, according to David Shannon, the Socialist Party "made no special effort to attract Negro members, and the party was generally disinterested if not actually hostile to the effort of Negroes to improve their position in American capitalist society."[28] The position is best summed up by Eugene Debs: "We have nothing special to offer the Negro and we cannot make separate appeals to all races. The socialist party is the party of the whole working class regardless of color, the whole working class of the whole world."[29] Such a position presents an ironic parallel to that of the ethnic analysts. For both groups, the factor of race is deemphasized or denied. Indeed, the Marxist class position goes even further in denying the uniqueness of blacks, since it views them as basically like any other members of the working class; the ethnic analysts at least give blacks the status of a distinct ethnic group.

The Communist Party and the Black Question

The Communist Party policy, even in the early period, did not remain true to a purely class position. In 1922, it discussed the American Negro in terms of the larger colonial question. Blacks were seen as having

[27]T. Draper, *The Roots of American Communism*. New York: The Viking Press, 1957, p. 192.

[28]D. A. Shannon, *The Socialist Party of America*. Chicago: Quadrangle Books, 1955, p. 52.

[29]E. V. Debs. Cited by R. Ginger, *The Bending Cross: A Biography of Eugene V. Debs*. New Jersey: Rutgers University Press, 1949, p. 260.

a pivotal place in the liberation "of the entire AFRICAN race."[30] Thus, in spite of the Communist Party's class predisposition, it was forced to give lip service to the nascent nationalist impulses arising from some segments of the black population. While the Communist Party believed that American blacks would be helped by the emergence of Africa, it also believed in international working-class solidarity, that is, it believed that "the European proletariat cannot obtain a real link with Africa except through the more advanced Negroes of America."[31] Thus, the Communist Party ultimately believed that international class interests would triumph over international race divisions.

Perhaps the most important and controversial position of the Communist Party vis-á-vis American blacks was ironically, the party's view of the black problem as a nationality question. This position was formulated and had the greatest influence during the late 1920s and early 1930s.[32] The major theoretical basis comes from Lenin's 1920 "Theses on the National and Colonial Question," in which he speaks of the need for the Communist Party "to render direct aid to the revolutionary movements in the dependent and subject nations (for example . . . the Negroes in America)."[33]

The Communist Party's policy had three basic parts: the nationality question, the black belt, and the right of the black man to self-

[30]Theses on the Negro Question. *Resolutions and Theses of the Fourth Congress,* 1922. Cited by T. Draper, *American Communism and Soviet Russia: The Formative Period.* New York: The Viking Press, 1963, p. 327. We have relied on Chapter 15 of this book, "The Negro Question," for much of the factual information presented in regard to the Communist Party.

[31]I. Jones, "Africa's Awakening," *International Press Correspondence,* June 14, 1923, p. 22. Cited by T. Draper, *American Communism and Soviet Russia,* p. 328.

[32]The earliest known statement of this possibility is a minor comment by Lenin in 1917 in which he spoke of American Negroes as "an oppressed nation," although, as Draper points out, he added the qualification that the tendency in the United States was for national differences to shrink and for groups to merge into a single nation. V. I. Lenin, "Capitalism and Agriculture in the United States of America," *Sochineniia,* 1949, Vol. 23. Cited by T. Draper, *American Communism and Soviet Russia,* p. 336.

[33]V. I. Lenin, "Preliminary Draft of Theses on the National and Colonial Question," June 5, 1920, in *V. I. Lenin: Selected Works,* Vol. X, translated from Russian as issued by the Marx-Engels-Lenin Institute, Moscow. New York: International Publishers, 1938, p. 235. Draper's claim is that this is an incorrect translation. In place of the phrase "in the dependent and subject nations," he would substitute "among the dependent nations and those without equal rights." (T. Draper, *American Communism and Soviet Russia,* p. 337, footnote.)

determination. The Communists used the basic definition of a nation which had been formulated by Stalin much earlier:

> *A nation is a historically evolved, stable community arising on the foundation of a common language, territory, economic life, and psychological make-up, manifested in a community of culture.*[34]

The territorial requirement of such a definition was fulfilled by the "Black Belt," which was defined as that area in the South which had a substantial black majority, plus an additional area where blacks made up close to one half of the total population. The requirement for a common language was fulfilled by English (that requirement, it was decided, called only for a common language, not a different one). The common economic life was that of the Negro sharecropper in the South, while a common psychological make-up and culture were seen as arising from the unique historical and social conditions of the American Negro. It was made very clear that this policy was a southern and not a northern one. The proper goal in the North was that of assimilation; the emphasis in the South was on the right to self-determination.

Such a policy clearly illustrates the difficulty of trying to reconcile a straight class approach with black realities. The official announcement of the policy by the Comintern indicated that in southern areas inhabited by the Negro masses, "it is essential to put forward the slogan of the Right of Self-Determination for Negroes."[35] But in the following sentences the emphasis seems to shift to more traditional Marxist goals:

> *A radical transformation of the agrarian structure of the Southern States is one of the basic tasks of the revolution . . . only the victorious proletarian revolution will completely and permanently*

[34]J. Stalin, *Marxism and the National Question*. New York: International Publishers, 1942, p. 12. Cited by T. Draper, *American Communism and Soviet Russia*, p. 344.

[35]Draper presents the exact statistics on which this black belt theory was based. "At that time (1930) 72.6% of all Negroes in the United States still lived in 12 Southern states, and 51.1% in the rural portions of those states. In 189 counties of the area, Negroes accounted for more than half the population. The 'Black Belt' was defined as that area in which there was a substantial Negro majority, plus a larger area of 477 counties in which Negroes constituted 44.8% of the total population." (T. Draper, *The Rediscovery of Black Nationalism*. New York: The Viking Press, 1970, pp. 63–64.)

> *solve the agrarian and national question of the Southern United States in the interests of the overwhelming majority of the Negro population of the country.* [36]

At one point, when the American Party was about to interpret the policy to allow for complete separation, it was informed by Moscow that the policy of complete separation was not permissible. [37]

The self-determination policy died out by 1935; by 1958 it was decided that American Negroes in no way constituted a nation, since they lacked either a "stable community" or a "common psychological make-up." The proper direction, it was now claimed, was toward full equality with white America. [38] Thus, the Communist Party class analysis had gone the full gamut, even to the basically nonrevolutionary demands parallel to those of the integrationists. [39]

We agree with Harold Cruse that discounting the race factor is a culpable blindness, given the nature of the American system. [40] Such a criticism is not only correct, but probably offers the most important objection to a straight Marxist class approach. Marxist analysis posits

[36]*Theses on the Revolutionary Movement in the Colonies and Semi-colonies. International Press Correspondence,* December 12, 1928, p. 1674. Cited by T. Draper, *American Communism and Soviet Russia,* p. 349.

[37]See T. Draper, *The Rediscovery of Black Nationalism,* pp. 64–65. Draper points out that the result of this confusion was that the final American version allows for the right to separate, but indicates that this does not mean that the American Negro should actually do so. Negro communists were advised that if a proletarian revolution were to take place in the United States, they should come out against separatism.

[38]*Political Affairs,* January 1959. Cited by T. Draper, *American Communism and Soviet Russia,* p. 355.

[39]The great variety of positions the Communist Party had taken can be seen from just a few examples. In 1923 Leon Trotsky told Claude McKay that Negroes should work "in a spirit of solidarity of all exploited without consideration of color." ("Trotsky on the Negro Question,"*International Press Correspondence,* March 15, 1923. Cited by T. Draper,*American Communism and Soviet Russia,* p. 340). But by 1933 he supported the right of black people "to separate a piece of land for themselves" (G. Breitman (ed.), *Leon Trotsky on Black Nationalism and Self-Determination.* New York: Merit Publishers, 1967, p. 13), while Irene Browder, writing in 1938, attacked the identification of national groups with oppressed nations (I. Browder, "For a Correct Approach to the Problems of the National Groups." Cited by H. Cruse, *The Crisis of the Negro Intellectual.* New York: William Morrow & Co., 1968, p. 149). The 1969 Trotskyist program leaves the decision up to blacks themselves (see T. Draper, *The Rediscovery of Black Nationalism,* p. 194, note 13).

[40]See, for example, H. Cruse, *Rebellion or Revolution?* New York: William Morrow & Co., 1968, pp. 76–77.

the working class as the key component of the revolution, yet it fails to take into account the very obvious existence of racism within both the labor rank and file and the labor unions. It is ironic that the Marxists of the Communist Party concur with the ethnic analysts in their common emphasis on class at the expense of race.[41]

The problem that plagued Marxist parties, that is, the tension between a class theory and the reality of particular black problems that transcend class, is a product of the basic dilemma of the black position in the United States. The black problem, whatever else it may be, is racial, and any analysis that fails to consider this is condemned to irrelevance. The dilemma of Marxist parties arises in part from their inability to synthesize the race and class analysis. The achievement of such a synthesis is difficult and beset with problems; the communists' failure is no different from other approaches that have failed.

Race and Class: The Problem of Synthesis

The difficulties involved in finding the proper race-class synthesis are also apparent in the work of Malcolm X and the Black Panthers. During some periods in his career Malcolm X clearly adhered to some form of nationalism, though the meaning he gave to the term was constantly changing. In the earlier stages of his thinking, he seemed to call for repatriation to Africa, though he also stated that an acceptable alternative would be a separate territory within the United States.[42] At other times his nationalism seemed to be purely cultural.[43] In general, the main direction of his nationalism seems to have been toward self-determination, with the concomitant call for black control of all the major areas of life in the black communities. Later, and especially after the break with the Nation of Islam, he completely abandoned the concept of a black state and moved toward a synthesis of his nationalist orientation with a revolu-

---

[41]A further criticism of Cruse's is that the communists often used blacks in the service of party objectives rather than in the interest of blacks. Again Cruse is right, but the deeper explanation of this lies not in the communists' lack of interest in blacks but in their own total confusion vis-à-vis the race-class issue. Their constant vacillation between racial and class policies resulted in their inconsistent position in regard to blacks.

[42]G. Breitman, *The Last Year of Malcolm X*. New York: Schocken Books, 1967, p. 57.

[43]G. Breitman (ed.), *Malcolm X Speaks*. New York: Grove Press, 1965, pp. 62–63.

tionary class analysis. In part, this change stemmed from his belief that black control of black communities would mean little as long as those communities were still surrounded by, and part of, the larger white society. In expanding his interests to include the larger society, Malcolm X came to the same realization that the Marxists before him had come to: that there is a causal link between capitalism and racism. "It's impossible," Malcolm said, "for a white person to believe in capitalism and not believe in racism. You can't have capitalism without racism."[44]

In this attempt to combine the race and class analysis, Malcolm was invariably forced into contradictions. On the one hand, he saw the American system as irredeemable: "It's impossible for this system, as it stands, to provide freedom right now for the black man in this country."[45] His conclusion was that revolution was necessary and, as he put it, "Revolutions are based on bloodshed."[46] On the other hand, the programmatic statement he wrote for his own group, the Organization of Afro-American Unity, leans heavily on the ethnic model in its discussion of "a larger unity transcending all organizational differences" and "ethnic intermingling."[47] His proposed tactics also included the traditional ethnic strategy of bloc voting. He thus called on the organization to:

> *organize the Afro-American community block by block to make the community aware of its power and potential; we will start immediately a voter-registration drive to make every unregistered voter in the Afro-American community an independent voter; we propose to support and/or organize political clubs, to run independent candidates for office, and to support any Afro-American already in office who answers to and is responsible to the Afro-American community.*[48]

---

[44]Malcolm X, May, 1964. Cited by R. L. Allen, *Black Awakening in Capitalist America: An Analytic History*. Garden City, N.Y.: Doubleday & Co., 1970, p. 32. Malcolm also linked to this view the belief that American blacks were the victims of domestic colonialism and should therefore see themselves as part of the international struggle against colonialism. One specific implementation that he proposed was the bringing of charges against the United States at the United Nations.

[45]G. Breitman, *The Last Year of Malcolm X*, p. 33.

[46]G. Breitman (ed.), *Malcolm X Speaks*, p. 50.

[47]Malcolm X. Cited by T. Draper, *The Rediscovery of Black Nationalism*, p. 94.

[48]G. Breitman, *The Last Year of Malcolm X*, p. 109.

Despite the call for violent revolution, Malcolm also felt that America could be the first country in history to have a "bloodless revolution." His rationale for this was a reliance on traditional political efforts:

> *The Negro in this country holds the balance of power, and if the Negro in this country were given what the Constitution says he is supposed to have, the added power of the Negro in this country would sweep all of the racists and the segregationists out of office. It would change the entire political structure of the country.*[49]

The problems Malcolm faced in combining race and class analysis foreshadowed many of the difficulties inherent in the approach of the Black Panthers, who tried to achieve a similar synthesis. The Panther program, too, had strong nationalist overtones. The first point in their program stressed the familiar call for self-determination. Echoing Malcolm's earlier desire to bring charges against the United States before the United Nations, point #10 of the Panther program sought to implement the principle of self-determination through:

> *our major political objective, a United Nations-supervised plebiscite to be held throughout the black colony in which only black colonial subjects will be allowed to participate, for the purpose of determining the will of black people as to their national destiny.*[50]

The Panthers defined black people as a nation on the grounds of (1) the subjection of all black people to similar economic oppression, (2) a common psychological make-up, and (3) common territory, that is, black ghettos.[51] They thus tied their nationalism to a concrete land base; point #10 also demanded land, though its location was left unclear.

[49]G. Breitman (ed.), *Malcolm X Speaks,* p. 57.

[50]"Black Panther Party Platform and Program: What We Want, What We Believe," October, 1966. *The Black Panther,* July 11, 1970, p. 21.

[51]Bobby Seale, at the Anti-Fascist Conference in Oakland, California, July, 1969. *The Black Panther,* February 17, 1969, p. 17.

The Panthers, like Malcolm X, found the racial analysis too limiting. They came to much the same conclusion that Malcolm X reached later—that a black state could never survive within American capitalism. The desire to synthesize both class and race analysis is evident in a statement by Eldridge Cleaver:

> *We recognize the problem presented to black people by the economic system—the capitalist economic system. We repudiate the capitalist economic system. We recognize the class nature of the capitalist economic system and we recognize the dynamics involved in the capitalist system. At the same time we recognize the national character of our struggle. We recognize the fact that we have been oppressed because we are black people even though we know this oppression was for the purpose of exploitation. We have to deal with both exploitation and racial oppression, and we don't think you can achieve a proper balance by neglecting one or the other.*[52]

Using the standard Marxist rhetoric, the Panthers thus claimed that "All members of the working class must seize the means of production."[53] They identified two basic evils which black people must fight: racism and capitalism. Within this combined race-class analysis there was also a call for revolutionary violence as a primary means of liberation.

Inevitably, the Panthers found themselves involved in a series of contradictions. Despite their revolutionary rhetoric, a large part of their program relied on federal aid. Point #3 in their program calls on the government for financial payments to the black community as restitution for past crimes against black people. Point #9 calls on the American court system to live up to the Fourteenth Amendment guarantee of trial by one's peer group. And Point #2 holds the federal government "responsible and obligated to give every man employment or a guaranteed income."[54] Their phrasing of that demand is symbolic. The traditional

[52]E. Cleaver, *Guardian,* April 13, 1968. Cited by R. L. Allen, *Black Awakening in Capitalist America,* p. 265.

[53]H. Newton, "The Black Panthers," *Ebony,* August 1969. Cited by T. Draper, *The Rediscovery of Black Nationalism,* p. 107.

[54]"Black Panther Party Platform and Program," p. 21.

demand for full employment is followed by the use of Marxist theory and the racial principle of community control to indicate the necessary alternative if full employment is not guaranteed:

> *We believe that if the white American businessmen will not give full employment, then the means of production should be taken from the businessmen and placed in the community so that the people of the community can organize and employ all of its people and give a high standard of living.*[55]

Actual Panther activities showed these same contradictions. Their emphasis on self-determination was expressed in a campaign for community control of the police force, but the method they use to achieve that goal was the traditional use of a petition campaign. Other projects—a free breakfast program and free health clinics—all fall within the framework of traditional, nonrevolutionary activities, though the Panthers attempted to justify them by revolutionary rhetoric. Bobby Seale, responding to charges of reformism, said:

> *Some people are going to call these programs reformist but we're revolutionaries and what they call a reformist program is one thing when the capitalists put it up and it's another thing when the revolutionary camp puts it up. Revolutionaries must always go forth to answer the momentary desires and needs of the people, the poor and oppressed people, while waging the revolutionary struggle. It's very important because it strengthens the people's revolutionary camp while it weakens the camp of the capitalist power structure.*[56]

The significance of the Panther program is not, as groups such as SNCC have charged, that it is "more reformist than revolutionary."[57] In substance,

---

[55]"Black Panther Party Platform and Program," p. 21.

[56]B. Seale, "The Movement, March, 1969." Cited by R. L. Allen, *Black Awakening in Capitalist America,* p. 87.

[57]SNCC. Cited by R. L. Allen, *Black Awakening in Capitalist America,* p. 267.

Malcolm X, the Panthers, and the Communist Party all shared the same dilemma. The black experience in the United States requires a creative synthesis of the race-class analysis, and a correspondingly appropriate development of programs and political strategies. This has yet to be accomplished in a viable way.

In the end, we have come full circle. While race and class analysts are in theory diametrically opposed, and while the proponents of each are in bitter disagreement, the black reality requires that they be combined.

CHAPTER 11

Race and Economic Development

While there is little disagreement among blacks about the need for economic development, there are considerable disagreements with regard to the kind of economic development that would be desirable. In this chapter we are concerned with two modes of development: black capitalism and community development planning. Although the ultimate goals of both modes overlap in some ways, there are profound differences between them.

Black Capitalism

One of the current stimuli shaping the interest in black capitalism derived from a campaign speech by Richard Nixon in 1968. Using the same argument that Abraham Lincoln had used about 110 years earlier, Nixon unwittingly developed a "Marxian" view of the relationship between human rights and property rights as they apply to blacks:

*To have human rights, people need property rights—and never
has this been more true than in the case of the Negro today.
[Blacks must have] the economic power that comes from ownership, and the security and independence that comes from
economic power. . . . [This can come about] by an expansion
of black ownership, of black capitalism. We need more black
employers, more black businesses. . . . We have to get private
enterprise into the ghetto. . . . At the same time, we have to get
the people of the ghetto into private enterprise—as workers, as
managers, as owners.*[1]

It is strange to hear a president publicly imply, however truthfully,
that human dignity and human rights in a capitalist society require the
ownership of property. Yet, Nixon's speech was heralded as one that
"could prove to be more constructive than anything yet said by the other
Presidential candidates on the crisis of the cities."[2] Nixon's speech was
also applauded by Roy Innis, leader of CORE. Thus, black capitalism
is receiving another round of endorsements by some segments of the
power structure as it has periodically in the past.

Black capitalism as an instrument of black salvation has a long
history. Like black power, it has taken on a variety of meanings. These
range from the militant blacks' grand visions of black retail chain stores,
manufacturing plants, and development banks, to the modest policies
of the Small Business Administration for what are essentially marginal
"ma and pa" stores operating within the confines of the ghetto. Black
socialists view black capitalism as the means chosen by the establishment
to assuage the demands of the black middle-class leadership at the
expense of the black masses. Which meaning one chooses largely
depends on one's conception of the purpose of black capitalism. Thus,
we might ask what is meant by "black capitalism"?

The emergence of a viable black capitalist system or sector requires
the development of a black capitalist class. As such, it must have a
strong propensity to accumulate capital in order to expand the number
and size of privately owned black enterprises. This not only means that

[1]R. Nixon. Cited by J. McClaughry, "Black Ownership and National Politics," in W. F. Haddad
and D. Pugh (eds.), *Black Economic Development*. Englewood Cliffs, N.J.: Prentice-Hall,
1969, pp. 38–39.
[2]T. Wicker, in J. McClaughry, p. 38.

profits must continuously be reinvested, but that the pursuit of profit by individual black capitalists must take place within the confines of the black economy. In other words, black capitalists must seek to maximize their firms' rate of growth. Growth is necessary if black capitalism is to absorb a growing black labor force, supply it with occupational mobility, and lead to the development of a black entrepreneurial class of sufficient size to uplift the social confidence of the black population in general. Finally, the fruits of black-owned enterprises must be kept within the black economy, that is, leakages from the black into the white economy must be kept to a minimum.

In order to understand the likelihood of developing black capitalism, it is necessary to review its past and present status. Since the existence of a black capitalist sector predates even Booker T. Washington's efforts, we might ask why black capitalism has never become sufficiently viable to alter the fundamental status of blacks. The answer lies in the characteristics of black capitalism itself, especially as it has operated within the confines of a black ghetto shaped and contained by the larger society.

The business history of the black population is one of failure. It has never gone beyond the marginal service and retail stores which operated in unstable segregated markets and were run by businessmen whose commercial and financial experience was nil. It is not surprising that the black consumer found "black proprietors inefficient, lazy, lack-[ing] education, [with] little business experience, [and] slow and discourteous."[3] Moreover, black entrepreneurial activities were often a spin-off from other lines, such as the professions, the church, or the underworld. This meant that business interests were often thought of as supplementary to other, primary interests, as, for example, a black doctor investing his surplus income in real estate.

The present outcome of this state of affairs, as one would expect, is dismal:

> *The overwhelming majority of black businesses are individual proprietorships in the retailing and services sector. Most are "Mom and Pop" stores, employing fewer than five people, and varying in value from $5,000 to $50,000. These stores consist*

[3]E. F. Frazier, *The Negro in the United States.* New York: Macmillan, 1957, p. 410. Cited by E. Ofari, *The Myth of Black Capitalism.* New York: Monthly Review Press, 1970, p. 77.

mainly of eating places, beauty parlors, apparel, liquor, and second-hand shops. Such businesses are often very shaky. They rarely accumulate significant capital for their owners and have a high failure rate. . . . [I]nvestigation in major cities such as Los Angeles, St. Louis, and Minneapolis (and 10 other cities) leads to the conclusion that in many inner-city areas the attrition rate of black merchants exceeds the birthrate. . . . [The problems are] getting access to capital, developing competent entrepreneurs, and marrying these to viable opportunities. . . .[4]

If we look at black business over a specific period of time, the picture is even gloomier. According to Dempsey J. Travis, President of the Association of Negro Mortgage Bankers, "there are fewer Negro businesses of significant size now than there were 40 years ago."[5] This absolute shrinkage in number is remarkable in view of the fact that both black population and income have risen significantly over the same period.

Because of the shortage of black equity capital, and because white banks are not prone to lend to high-risk black enterprises, black-owned banks might be expected to play a particularly important role in raising equity capital. But this is not the case. Stated simply, the reason is that there are only 20 Negro-owned banks operating in 19 cities in the country, a decline from a total of 49 operating in 38 cities in 1929. These 20 banks, moreover, are making no after-tax profits.[6] Hence, they cannot dispense much in the form of high-risk loans.

A comparison of a successful black "big" business with its white counterpart is equally depressing:

North Carolina Mutual Life Insurance Co. is the largest black insurance operation in the country today. Its assets total $97 million. By comparison, Prudential, one of White America's largest insurance companies, has assets of $25 billion. Altogether, the top five black insurance companies' combined assets, roughly

[4]J. Z. DeLorean, "The Problem," in W. F. Haddad and D. Pugh (eds.), pp. 9–10.

[5]J. M. Kirchheimer, *Christian Science Monitor.* Cited by J. Z. DeLorean, "The Problem," pp. 9–10: Mr. Kirchheimer is a Wall Street investment banker.

[6]J. Z. DeLorean, p. 16.

$268 million, equal little more than 1 percent of Prudential's assets alone.[7]

Table 11.1 summarizes the current picture of black enterprise. The number of black-owned enterprises is actually lower than it appears since these figures include a significant number of Japanese-owned and Chinese-owned establishments.

TABLE 11.1

Current Business Population

Industry	Total No. of Businesses	Nonwhite Owned	
		Number	Percent
Contract construction	500	8	1.6
Manufacturing	330	2	.7
Personal services	550	40	7.3
Other services	550	15	2.8
Retail trade	2150	65	3.0
Wholesale trade	350	5	1.5
All others	650	15	2.3

SOURCE: H. J. Samuels, "Compensatory Capitalism." In William F. Haddad and Douglas Pugh (eds.), *Black Economic Development*. Englewood Cliffs, N.J.: Prentice Hall, 1969, p. 64.

In examining the total value of black expenditure and comparing it to the volume of business done by black enterprises, it appears that blacks spend about 10 percent of their total income in black-owned stores.[8] For food expenditures, this figure decreases to approximately 3–4 percent. Since black businesses tend to charge more for less, black consumers appear to be acting as rational buyers.

If black capitalism is to emerge from the long and persistent failure of black business, its development into a vital instrument will have to come from nothing since "within the ghetto there are scarcely any models, any tradition, any experience—or, for that matter, any means for it to draw on."[9]

[7]E. Ofari, p. 77.

[8]M. Skala, "Inner-City Enterprises: Current Experience," in W. F. Haddad and D. Pugh (eds.), p. 163.

[9]J. Z. DeLorean, p. 10.

Thus, if black capitalism is to be a solution to black problems, it must be conceived in terms of a complete *break* with the past and present. Black capitalism, if it is to succeed, requires the finding and training of black entrepreneurs and managers, a radically liberalizing set of criteria for lending, bonding, and providing insurance of all kinds, and large-scale technical assistance and the identification and cultivation of profitable market opportunities. It will further require sheltered markets and subsidies reaching the heights of $20–$30 billion per year, a sustained white corporate involvement and partnership, and a reversal of the flow of capital and other resources from the central city to the suburbs. The realization of such developments implicitly requires that the thinly spread black middle class of the ghetto stay in the ghetto to lead and manage the crash program necessary to create black capitalism.

The advocates of this capitalist dream are entertaining a solution that the white power structure is most unlikely to support. If the white power structure were prepared seriously to support the development of black capitalism, it would have to undertake programs far more costly than those involving a systematic effort to eliminate barriers to job and promotional opportunities. Since the corporate structure has been unwilling to support the less costly latter programs, it is unlikely that it will underwrite the much more costly development of black capitalism. If such support *were* forthcoming, the black struggle for social freedom and equality would become a purely technical matter of fulfilling a pre-existing plan. Since this is not the case, black capitalism is a programmatic deception, a retreat from the inability of the society to respond to the black protest of the sixties. We can do no better than to quote the disillusioned words from the last article written by the late Whitney M. Young, Jr., Executive Director of the National Urban League, whose whole career was devoted to the salvation of his race along capitalistic lines. With reference to ghetto investment and business involvement, Young wrote:

> *In many quarters, "the great [business] involvement" in the [black ghetto] is beginning to look like the "great copout." In fact, our business leaders sometimes act like restless college kids, flirting first with civil-rights action, then speaking up against the war, and, now, clutching the new found environment issue to their collective bosoms. . . . Businessmen are reflecting the same qualities they find so reprehensible in others—lack of staying*

> *power and dilettantism. . . . Corporations that had never put their toes in the muddier waters of* [black] *urban problems plunged in, not nearly as deep as they should have, but at least enough to get their feet wet. Now, crying that the water is too hot, many are clambering back to shore. The result of this unseemly dash to the beach is that the motives of many corporations are called into question. . . . One company blamed its pullout on the recession. "When the red ink shows," said one executive, "anything that is not of a direct business nature is the first to go." Another corporate official showed the complacency that drives so many critics of business up the walls: "We've done our share," he said. "We've put in $100,000."*
>
> *The same businessman will pour many millions into research and development of new products. He'll only expect a 5 percent return. . . . But when he's trying to help solve social problems 400 years in the making, created by the racialist attitudes of companies and unions like his own, he suddenly expects fast returns and instant successes.* [10]

The meaning of Young's disillusionment is clear enough: American capitalism, in its rhetoric to reform itself, has proved again that far from being part of the solution, it is an intrinsic part of the problem.

Black Economic and Community Development

Given the many dimensions that constitute community development, it is not surprising that there is considerable confusion about its meaning. For example, black economic development has been interpreted to mean black capitalism. Black economic development has also been entangled with notions of self- and national-determination, the latter frequently leading to a discussion of national separatism whereby blacks see themselves as constituting a separate nation with a separate economy (see Chapter 8). Community control has been associated with black separatism or even black segregation. Moreover, community control has often been projected as being an ultimate goal or end rather than as being a means.

[10]W. Young, Jr., "The Ghetto Investment," *New York Times,* March 13, 1971, p. 29.

In other words, because some efforts to achieve community control have involved direct action, such as sit-ins or obstructing public school-board meetings, community control has been viewed as a revolutionary end, when it could also be viewed as a reformist end.

In our discussion of the neocolonial model (see Chapter 6), we suggested that it led to a more synthesized, less piecemeal program than any other interpretation of the nature of the black condition. A complete development program for the black ghetto similarly involves synthesis in the form of a multidimensional strategy which includes the participation of important segments of the black population. In such a program, tasks would be assigned to black professionals, politicians, street leaders, community organizations and action groups, church personnel, and last but not least, to blacks who have entrepreneurial ambitions and talents. The whole operation stresses the need for self-help.

A comprehensive development plan begins with a close inventory of the ghetto's sources of internally generated income (actual and potential). Income leakages associated with foreign-owned enterprises are examined, as well as those connected to imports by ghetto residents. An inventory of the demographic characteristics of the ghetto population is undertaken including the quantity and quality of the housing stock, and any other aspects of the ghetto that might provide useful information.

The information about the current state of the ghetto's economy becomes an input in the forging of criteria for selecting projects to be implemented by a local planning instrument. While plan objectives may vary with particular ghetto situations, most ghetto development plans would include the following specific objectives:

1. To create ghetto-based enterprises to absorb some portion of black unemployment and underemployment.
2. To improve the potentially competitive performance and quality of existing enterprises in the ghetto owned by black capitalists.
3. To establish a ghetto planning agency, that is, a community development corporation, to implement the plans.
4. To acquire sufficient political power and autonomy to control the flow of resources out of the ghetto, as well as to extract resource transfers from "foreign" exploiters.

These general objectives are unifying to the extent that they relate to the unemployed black masses, to some black businessmen, to black professionals and technicians who wish to employ their know-how in meaningful ways, and to black politicians and ideologues who see the need to develop black consciousness, nationalism, and/or black-power ideas in general.

The economic strategy to be employed involves selection criteria similar to those used in underdeveioped countries, that is, an integrated plan of industrial complexes involving export development and import substitution. If ghetto-based and ghetto-owned enterprises are to survive they must extend their markets. Industries must be developed that can simultaneously compete with industries outside the ghetto (export development) and replace those foreign-owned operations that presently sell to ghetto residents (import substitution). Only by reversing the terms of trade and the flow of income between the ghetto and outside market forces will the ghetto eliminate its deficit crises and dependence on unproductive "foreign" aid (welfare transfers).

The deliberations that have led to the schemes with which we are concerned culminated in the Community Self-Determination Bill, a bill created by CORE with extensive expert assistance. The bill was introduced before Congress in July 1968 but, unfortunately, faded into oblivion. Nevertheless, the ideas underlying the bill will reappear, since the conditions that brought it forth will continue to exist for the foreseeable future.

The general rationale for the bill was presented by Roy Innis, the National Director of CORE, who argued that blacks need to control the decision-making levers of their community in order to implement their own solutions to the problems of the ghetto:

> *A crucial weakness has been the lack of control by black people over the institutions that surround them: institutions that not only establish imposed values for them but also control the flow of goods and services within their communities, thereby shaping the quality of their lives. . . . Thus, schools in black neighborhoods too often do not teach, sanitation departments do not clean, employment departments do not find jobs, welfare departments do not give adequate relief, housing departments do not give decent housing.* [11]

[11]R. Innis, "Separatist Economics: A New Social Contract," in W. F. Haddad and D. Pugh (eds.), p. 51.

What is needed to correct these deficiencies, according to Innis, is a new social contract. Large, densely packed black populations in urban areas "must become political subdivisions of the state, instead of sub-colonial appendages. Blacks must manage and control the institutions that service their areas, as has always been the case for other interest groups" (p. 51).

Innis goes on to talk about separating but not segregating black economic and social interests. Segregation without control of community instruments is the prevailing condition. What Innis is suggesting is the need to control the flow of goods and services within the confines of the black community. He holds that "there must be some sort of socio-cultural renaissance if there is to be movement in any direction. There must be some sort of politico-economic development if the cultural movement is to have any base on which to acquire significance" (p. 52).

Black economic development, in Innis' view, does not commit the black community to any *a priori* style of ownership of the instruments of development:

> *It may include elements of capitalism, elements of socialism, or elements of neither; that is immaterial. What matters is that it will be created to fit our needs. . . . We say that we are willing to operate pragmatically and let the style of ownership fit the style of the area or its inhabitants (pp. 52–53).*

Put somewhat differently, what is needed is a new *degree* (not complete, not total) of black autonomy so that the many dollars that blacks earn and the tax dollars they pay will be used to provide guaranteed markets for black-controlled and black-owned enterprises to produce those goods and services needed by the community. For example, the $100 million spent servicing Harlem schools with everything from paper clips to typewriters could be contracted, in part, to black producers, or could be routed through black-owned distribution outlets if the needed items could not be produced because of the huge capital outlays involved.[12]

The Community Self-Determination Bill, mentioned previously, provided the legal framework to enable a black community to acquire control of its own community instruments. The basic concept behind the bill

---

[12]R. Innis, p. 54.

was the ownership of broadly supported community development corporations which were:

> *based in an area defined by the people themselves through a . . . referendum process. The corporation would own a family of businesses, which might range from a shoe shine stand to a major factory and which would be located both inside and outside the community area. With the profits from these enterprises, the community corporation would finance community service projects of the people's own choice, such as day-care centers, basic education, legal aid, non-profit housing, health care, and the like. To finance the acquisitions of the community corporation, the bill authorized the creation of community development banks and a national secondary financing institution, a system resembling . . . the present Farm Credit System. The community corporation would also have access to funds to enable it to hire the managerial and technical expertise, the lack of which was admittedly the most serious bottleneck to rapid progress. . . . Moreover the community corporations and their subsidiaries would pay little or no taxes. The tax-augmented profit flow would be applied only to community services and not used to line private pockets.* [13]

Another part of the bill included a tax device that would encourage white-owned corporations to set up ghetto businesses, train black workers and managers, and then sell the operation, once it became viable, to the community corporation. [14]

In sum and substance, the community development corporation is conceived as a planning instrument similar to those often created in underdeveloped countries. The planning seeks to overcome the fragmentation of the black ghetto's economy, as well as to create social and political interests in the enterprises connected to the development corporation's plans. It is possible to build these interests, not only because the community corporation itself is made up of representatives of the community, but also because its surpluses are plowed back into the creation of needed community services.

[13]J. McClaughry, p. 41.
[14]J. McClaughry, p. 42.

To illustrate the black economic-development and community-control strategy as applied to the ghetto economy, we have chosen to describe part of a remarkable study of Central Harlem which could serve as a prototype for all ghettos and relations between ghettos within regions.[15] To our knowledge, the Harlem study is the most comprehensive effort to date to apply and combine development tools and community-participation ideas in order to solve the broad socioeconomic malaise which characterizes ghetto society.

In this study, a community development corporation is conceived as one that coordinates and controls a variegated set of related, complementary activities which feed organically upon themselves. A consistent set of criteria is related to established goals for coping with ghetto problems. The need is not for job-training *per se* or for the establishment of a black enterprise *per se,* but for the development of a whole complex in which external economic, social, and political benefits are generated. The development corporation undertakes projects that must, at a minimum, be able to break even. Emphasis is placed on those projects that maximize the social benefit to the black community: projects involving the training of blacks for jobs which are not dead-end; projects that have positive effects on the morale and cohesion of the community; and finally, projects that can both be competitive with white enterprise (in and outside the ghetto) and meet important needs of the black community.

The cultivation of black political power and consciousness is central to overcoming the barriers that affect the implementation of the economic planning process. Black political power is the *sine qua non* of economic development. This is, of course, what led the authors of the Harlem study to state:

> *Since ghetto development problems are dominated by social, psychological, and political considerations, the economist's narrow focus on resource allocation is too confining and serves, in fact, to wash away the substantive issues. Whereas the economist is traditionally accustomed to formulating economic policy subject to political constraints, we have found it necessary to focus on political policy-making subject to economic constraints. . . . Economic development, wherever it takes place,*

[15]T. Vietorisz and B. Harrison, *The Economic Development of Harlem.* New York: Praeger, 1970.

> *acts as a catalyst of social and political change. . . . Conventional economic analysis treats these social effects as external—incidental to, and not very important in light of, the over-all economic infrastructure. We believe, however, that economic development of the ghetto is vital because of the social externalities that it can generate—social benefits far in excess of the mere creation of even a considerable number of sterile workplaces.* [16]

According to Vietorisz and Harrison, the elements of a ghetto development strategy involve *first,* the community ownership of "greenhouse industries," the main purpose of which are to upgrade the ghetto's labor force and economic base. These industries are "designed to create new jobs in the familiar local environment, and perform systematic skill-training functions that are coordinated with the productive operations of each establishment" (p. 67). While such training may take various forms, the most important kind is:

> *structured on-the-job training, supplemented by formal remedial classroom instruction, and followed by a period of practical job experience in surroundings conducive to the deepening of newly acquired skills.*
>
> *To qualify as a greenhouse industry, an activity must offer the proper level and mix of skills; . . . it must also fit into the developing economic base of the ghetto. The upgrading of service to the local consumer, the filling of gaps in the* [ghetto's] *economic base, and the production for local use and for outside sale are some of the requirements that greenhouse industries must beat (p. 67).*

As workers complete their training and accumulate job experience, some may be exported to make room for additional trainees. Exported workers may be recycled back into the greenhouse industry for additional training and work experience at a later time, thus enabling some to take advantage of the career-ladder structure built into the greenhouse-industry design.

---

[16]T. Vietorisz and B. Harrison, *The Economic Development of Harlem,* pp. 55, 66. All further references in this chapter to Vietorisz and Harrison are to this book.

Secondly, investment projects must meet a minimum profitability criterion. Given the broader social benefits that are related to our investment design, ghetto projects need not seek the usual success indicators of 10 to 15 percent after-tax return. Instead, a breakeven economic target is the minimum requirement. On this basis, far more projects than are generally found feasible become candidates for consideration, and the returns which accrue are, in fact, social returns which are spread over a wide range of ghetto projects. The upgrading of the ghetto's labor force and economic base will lead to the gradual increase of more sophisticated projects for development, and will also lead to the improvement of the newly formed ghetto industries. Planned industrial networks leading to extra community benefits cannot be readily measured in pecuniary terms. A little store here and a small establishment there simply do not feed into each other and, therefore, must eventually face all the risks and ill effects of operating inside a ghetto economy.

The *third* element is the financing of ghetto investment. Three financing sources are identified in this study: internally-generated funds, public funds, and funds originating from white-owned corporations. A comprehensive picture of the way in which the financing of ghetto training and industries can take place is shown in Figure 11.1. This figure also demonstrates the multidimensional nature of ghetto-development strategies. Implicit in the development scheme is a financial plan in which it is assumed that significant portions of the business and government establishment, in order to avoid chaos, will eventually find it in their enlightened self-interest to commit resources to rehabilitate the ghetto.

The heart of the financial plan in Vietorisz and Harrison's model revolves about the Harlem Commonwealth Council, a black development corporation directly linked to local black enterprises, and a consortium of outside white enterprises such as banks, insurance companies, and corporations (see Figure 11.1). The development corporation "will own, sponsor, and control ghetto investments, and will exert influence on existing ghetto businesses through technical assistance and affiliation programs" (p. 71). The development corporation's primary, long-term sources of funds are to be supplied by the federal government and the ghetto community itself. Extracting money from the government involves black political pressure; extracting money from the population of the ghetto requires black consciousness and a willingness on the part of the black population to tax itself in order to launch the corporation.

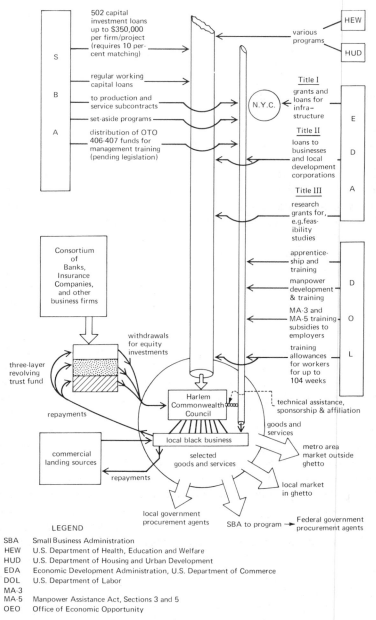

FIGURE 11.1 Prototypical Flow of Governmental and Private Financing for Ghetto Development

The development of a short-term financing mechanism takes place by means of a three-layer revolving trust fund which is the main mechanism linking the white consortium to the development corporation (see Figure 11.1). One rationale behind such a structure was to avoid the pitfalls of the Bedford Stuyvesant model in which white corporations put the black development corporation in the position of being a permanent petitioner for funds. Another, of course, was to "create black equity in new or expanded Harlem enterprises" (p. 73). These two objectives were accomplished through the establishment of a mixed-control system. That is:

> Drawings on a "black" layer would be controlled fully and exclusively by the ghetto development corporation, while drawings on a "white" layer, together with conditions of repayment, would be subject to full approval by the consortium that established the fund. There would also be an intermediate, or "gray" layer, on which drawings for specific projects could be held up by the consortium for a fixed period of time, after which the community development corporation would be free to go ahead with the project whether approved by the consortium or not. The exact apportionment of the fund among the three layers and the maximum time delay affecting the gray layer for each of several classes of projects would be determined by negotiation and incorporated in the bylaws governing the fund (p. 75).

Figure 11.1 also shows how major government programs might be employed to provide financial resources either directly to the development corporation (HCC) or to local black businesses which are assisted by, sponsored by, or affiliated with the black development corporation.

Next we face the "identification and selection of concrete development projects, involving both new and expanded ghetto enterprises" that can fulfill the broad social and political goals inherent in the development strategy, as well as meet some narrower economic criteria established by the fact that resources in the ghetto, such as land, skilled labor, and funds, are limited.

Vietorisz and Harrison hold that criteria concerning technology, training and growth, distribution and marketing, and generating employment opportunities should be seen in relation to project profitability. This means that the external benefits and costs must be seen in their totality. For example, should the development corporation pursue labor-intensive projects which maximize short-run employment opportunities but in practice tend to develop yesterday's industries involving low productivity and a low rate of savings? Or, should projects be capital-intensive, and thus generate bigger profits and a higher rate of savings, at the expense of ignoring the labor and employment needs of unemployed and underemployed ghetto workers? Development planning can address itself to these kinds of problems in ways that private-investment operations cannot.

To illustrate some of the principles that can be utilized in a planning context, we shall briefly touch upon two projects that have been explored in depth in the Harlem study: an automotive service center and a supermarket chain. The purpose here is to point out some aspects of the investment design that are ignored when serious public development planning is neglected.

Figure 11.2 identifies the departments of an automotive center. Some of the characteristics of the automotive center are as follows: (1) it can be built in segments, thus avoiding the need to raise large amounts of capital all at once; (2) it involves a need for an assortment of skills, ranging from unskilled to professionally qualified (career-ladder concept); (3) it supplies an important demand in the black community, as well as services that could be exported to the white community; (4) it supplies services needed by the city and state governments so that political pressure might induce the purchasing agents of local governments to contract the service center, thus guaranteeing a more stable demand; and (5) various segments of the center feed into each other and also provide a market for other kinds of goods and services supplied by black producers (for example, a tire recapping factory could supply the requirements of the center's tire sales department, thus also increasing its own chances of survival).

The supermarket project illustrates some of the same possibilities in the area of retail marketing and distribution. Ghetto residents pay a considerable portion of their disposable income for food and many types of related goods sold in local supermarkets.[17] Since the typical ghetto family income is low, food and related "kitchen" costs constitute a large fraction of that income. Efficient purchasing at lower costs would, therefore, significantly increase the real income of ghetto residents.

[17]See D. Caplovitz, The Poor Pay More. New York: Crowell-Collier and Macmillan, Inc., 1967.

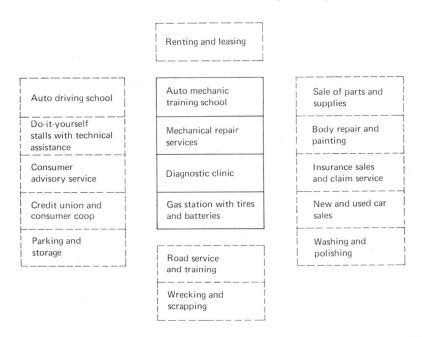

Solid lines: activities recommended for immediate implementation.
Broken lines: activities to be added.

FIGURE 11.2   Organizational Plan for Augmented Automotive Center

In a black cooperatively owned chain of supermarkets in a large urban ghetto, shelf space could be used for house brands produced or distributed by black-owned factories or wholesale distributors. The assured shelf space would reduce the advertising costs and enable some black products, for example, canned tomatoes, to compete with nationally advertised brands. As a consequence: (1) black ghetto residents would not be forced to deal with supermarket monopolies and/or inefficient high-priced grocery or durable goods outlets; (2) complementary black industries would be put in a preferential position and in a "buy black" atmosphere; (3) drains on family income would be reduced, permitting purchasing power to filter into other community cooperatives; and (4) transferable manpower skills, usable in other ghetto projects, would be developed.

The point of this discussion of ghetto development through planning and community participation is that it represents a programmatic alternative to more eclectic "solutions." Moreover, it integrates the psychological, social, and political needs of the black population with their economic needs. While this avoids complete separatism, it assumes a basic reorganization of American society. Black economic and social development, as conceived here, goes far beyond the elitism implicit in black capitalism and goes beyond the one-dimensional approach characteristic of the job-creation policies put forth by welfare liberals (see Chapter 13).

The scheme necessitates the involvement of a large number of black people in different capacities for the purpose of altering the basic profile of their own community. However, we cannot have any illusions about the problems of achieving effective black-controlled planning instruments. Sociopolitical planning on a consequential scale, however necessary in crowded urban communities, will not occur by osmosis or by a spontaneous awareness on the part of the white community. Political work must be accomplished both within and outside the black community if any planning operation is to obtain national attention, let alone national approval.

Race, Politics, and the American Political System

Most interpretations of the position of blacks in the American political system seem to share one common assumption: Any possibility for blacks fundamentally to alter their status rests on their ability to function as a strong interest group within a pluralist system of competing groups. This belief in pluralism is not always stated explicitly, and in many cases, as we have seen, the rhetoric contradicts the pluralist assumptions. Nevertheless, an acceptance of pluralism underlies many of the most common approaches to the problems of blacks. In our view, the dependence on pluralist theory is questionable, since pluralism has important weaknesses, both as a theory and as a description of American society. Traditional pluralist processes have clearly not worked for blacks up to now. Further, even if we dismiss past experience as an aberration, as something that will change as blacks develop more strength, changing conditions in the cities invalidate the pluralist approach. Finally, and this is perhaps the heart of the problem, pluralist theory in general ignores some of the most fundamental facts about the American political system.

The problems raised by pluralism are complex and intertwined, and any attempt to divide them into discrete categories or to differentiate local from national questions is artificial. In the interests of clarity and convenience, however, such a division is useful.

City Politics and Pluralism

The failure of pluralism can best be seen at the local level. If blacks are to find solutions to their problems by following the traditional path of ethnic groups within a pluralist community, as many analysts have suggested, then the traditional political avenues would be a necessary factor in their efforts. In the past, ethnic groups relied especially on the traditional party organization, the political machine. The machine fulfilled several basic functions. Given the fragmented nature of government, it served to bring together and organize "the scattered fragments of power" which are often dispersed within the political structure. The political machine was thus able to serve the needs of various subgroups within the community.[1] It provided these groups with material aid in a human, personal context, as opposed to the clinical legality of a service bureaucracy; it also served as an avenue of social mobility for the poor. The machine was traditionally strong within lower-income and immigrant groups. It was able to attract such people both through material inducements, such as money and jobs, and nonmaterial inducements, such as power, prestige, and the feeling of participation in events, though greater emphasis was placed on the first of these three. The power to provide these inducements gave the machine a large measure of political control over the people it helped; the machine was thus able to provide the politician with a locus of influence based on his control of low-income voters.

While the machine has functioned well for "foreign" immigrant groups, it has not functioned effectively for blacks. The ineffectiveness

[1]For a full discussion of this topic, see R. K. Merton, *Social Theory and Social Structure*. New York: The Free Press, 1957, pp. 71–81.

for blacks of even the well-organized traditional machine can be seen in the case of Chicago.[2] The black machine in Chicago, until recently under the leadership of William Dawson, is something of an anachronism in an era in which machine politics is dying out; nevertheless, it continues to be very strong within black wards. It functions through the traditional use of low-paying jobs, political favors, and material assistance as inducements to voters. It has been able to set up a network of obligations in the black community that includes the press, businessmen, the NAACP, ministers, and labor leaders.

In short, there is ample evidence that the Chicago machine is precisely the kind of organization that the pluralist approach would require in order to help blacks. If the pluralist model is valid for the black situation, then the position of blacks in Chicago should be significantly improved because of the existence and strength of the black machine. As matters stand presently, however, the black machine has not in fact been able to function as well for blacks as it did for other immigrant groups in the past. One reason for this is the dependence of the black machine on the existence of the overall white city machine (in James Wilson's terminology, the former is a "sub-machine"). Wilson points out that the very existence of the Dawson machine is made possible only by the existence of the city machine as the major source of authority and patronage. The prior existence of this city machine also means that the entry of blacks into politics has to take place within the rules and forms established by the white machine; thus, the "sub-machine" is left at an inevitable disadvantage.[3]

The failure of the machine to protect the interests of black people

[2]J. Q. Wilson, *Negro Politics: The Search for Leadership.* New York: The Free Press, 1960. Much of the factual information about the Dawson machine is based on Wilson's book.

[3]See J. Q. Wilson, *Negro Politics: The Search for Leadership,* pp. 85–87. Also important here is Charles Wilson's argument that while the black man's political position is in some ways like that of other ethnic groups, it is very different in that historically it has involved a dependency of blacks on whites, in which blacks take the role of "clients." Wilson's argument, which points to the failure of pluralism for blacks, is well illustrated by the history of the Dawson machine. (C. E. Wilson, "Negro Leadership at the Crossroads," in L. C. Fitch and A. H. Walsh (eds.), *Agenda for a City: Issues Confronting New York.* Beverly Hills, Calif.: Sage Publications, 1970, pp. 547–556.)

is depicted throughout Wilson's book, *Negro Politics*.[4] Wilson points out that Chicago's strong black machine has little effect on "the size of the vote delivered to Negro candidates, the percentage of the total vote polled by the winning candidate, or the number of straight-ticket votes." While a strong organization helps the leadership to control the primary vote and to turn out a large vote on ballot propositions, the more important consideration seems to be that "the strength of the organization seems unrelated to, and in some cases hinders, the ability of Negroes to secure important appointive offices, in the state and local governments" (p. 39). It seems, in short, that even a strong black machine is not able to help blacks in the areas most crucial to them. Perhaps the most telling comment on the ineffectiveness of the Dawson machine is Wilson's comparison of cities with a black machine and those with either a weak or a nonexistent machine. His claim is that the major result of strong party organization "is in the set of constraints it places on the leaders and members. . . . The primary importance of the machine lies in the way of life it creates for its members" (p. 47).[5]

The implication is that the machine is effective in setting up an organization and in controlling its members, but that the effect of that organization outside the confines of the machine is negligible. In other words, the black machine has little real influence on city politics; it may help some of its members get jobs, but it can win no major victories on the basis of its own strength. If such is the case, then the immigrant analogy offered by the pluralists is inaccurate (and it is ironic that Wilson

[4]Two primary examples of this in Chicago are the issues of judicial reform and urban renewal, in both of which the black machine was unable to protect its own vital interests. The judicial reform issue arose when Mayor Daley endorsed a plan to reform the courts, a plan which the black machine saw as dangerous to its interests. Despite this feeling, the black Democrats in the state legislature were induced to vote for Daley's proposal and against what they perceived as their real interests. Similarly, when an urban renewal plan involved the destruction of large numbers of black-occupied housing units, black politicians were unable to block it against Mayor Daley's support. In both these cases, the Mayor seemed clearly to be acting against the interests of his own party. Seemingly, then, the interests of blacks can be disregarded by the Mayor even when those interests constitute a large faction of his own party and despite the existence of a strong black machine. Only when the Mayor can be persuaded to act on certain problems is the action effective. The machine thus has no real independent strength. See J. Q. Wilson, *Negro Politics: The Search for Leadership*.

[5]The fundamental differences, he continues, "consist not so much in the final election results, but in what must be done to produce those results, what obligations members acquire for having benefited by them, and what rewards exist for those who have contributed to their attainment."

continues to hold the pluralist view despite the material presented in his own excellent book). The dependence which characterizes the black machine severely limits the potential of any plan which involves blacks acting as an independent voting bloc within the city.

Let us suppose, however, that this failure does not automatically continue. If the defects of the black machine could be overcome, the reliance on pluralism would be appropriate. Even if we accept this rather dubious assumption, we shall see that the pluralist approach has other weaknesses arising from its failure to take into account the changing conditions in the cities.

The Decline of the Political Machine

One of the deficiencies of pluralism stems from the fact that the political machine is currently on the decline and, in some places, almost nonexistent. As a result, some of the most important conditions on which the pluralist model is based are gone.

The first major cause of this decline is the fact that the inducements which the machine can offer have become less attractive. The small favors that were desperately needed by newly arrived immigrants have come to mean less and less as those immigrants have become upwardly mobile. The general prosperity of the post-war years led to an increased mobility among many segments of the population, and the kinds of jobs that the machine can offer now seem below the aspirations of this population. In addition, public welfare programs, unions, and various arms of the bureaucracy have taken over almost all the service functions that the machine used to provide. Since the machine has no influence over the services provided by these other organizations, it can do little more than provide information.

A second major cause of the decline of the machine is a changing emphasis in the predominant view of politics. Banfield and Wilson have described this in terms of the difference between two conceptions of the public interest. One of these is identified with the middle-class ethos and is called "public-regarding"[6]; it emphasizes the individual's obligation

---

[6]E. C. Banfield and J. Q. Wilson, "Public-Regardingness as a Value Premise in Voting Behavior," *American Political Science Review*, 1964, **58** (4). The original formulation of this concept can be found in R. Hofstadter, *The Age of Reform*. New York: Alfred A. Knopf, 1955, p. 9.

to the community and is concerned with the government of the entire community. In concrete political terms, this leads to the identification of "good government" with such qualities as efficiency, impartiality, and honesty. The other conception, identified with newly arrived immigrant groups and with members of the lower class in general, is essentially "private-regarding"; people who hold this view regard political relationships in terms of personal obligations, and politicians as an important source of aid for individual and family problems. This conception leads people to identify with the local ward rather than with the community at large; government, in this view, is valued not for its overall honesty, but for its ability to provide specific material benefits. This, of course, is a conception that leads directly to the strengthening of machine politics, while the former conception leads directly away from such politics.[7]

The implications of these changes are clear. Insofar as more and more people have become, and are becoming, part of the professional or quasi-professional middle class, the emphasis will be (and has been) away from machine politics and toward the various reform movements leading to a supposedly more impartial system of government. The result is the decline of machine politics in all except those areas of the city that are populated by the very poor, who are still dependent on the material incentives provided by the machine, and who still retain the older conception of politics. But that machine, as we have seen in the case of Chicago, cannot function effectively in isolation; it depends for its effectiveness on the larger political context, a context that is moving further away from machine politics. Banfield and Wilson summarize the situation when they point out that:

> *the nationally growing middle class has shown that it will use its control of state and federal governments—and particularly of law-enforcement agencies and of special districts within the metropolitan areas—to withhold the patronage, protection, and other political resources that are indispensable to the growth of political machines in the central cities. This means that the lower class will have to play politics of a kind that is tolerable to the middle class or not play at all.*[8]

---

[7]For a discussion of the relevance of this concept to voting behavior see E. C. Banfield and J. Q. Wilson, "Public-Regardingness as a Value Premise in Voting Behavior," pp. 876–887.

[8]E. C. Banfield and J. Q. Wilson, *City Politics*. New York: Vintage Books, 1966, p. 330.

A third reason for the machine's decline is a drastic decline in patronage. The use of patronage is the backbone of the machine. The withholding or awarding of patronage positions is used by the party leader to impose discipline on differing blocs and individuals in order to create a cohesive whole.[9] It is used to attract additional members, to entice members into such necessary activities as canvassing and campaigning, to increase the finances of the party,[10] and to insure the desired policy or administrative action for the party and its constituents.

The machine's reliance on patronage makes it especially vulnerable to the kinds of reforms that are consistent with the "public-regardingness" of the middle class, especially since that same middle class in large part retains political control. The merit systems that have been instituted by such reforms to replace patronage deprive the machine of the various well-paid, specialized positions which call for training and expertise. What is left to the party is a group of less desirable positions, most of which involve low pay; however, the kind of person the machine would like to attract is very often one who would not be interested in such jobs. As a result, such people are uninterested in the machine and instead go directly to the bureaucracy which controls the kinds of jobs they want.[11]

The fourth and final reason for the decline of the machine is the overall decline of the importance of local political parties. In general, the power center is shifting from the political party to the civil service, the welfare-state bureaucracy. This bureaucracy is constantly expanding and has obtained major political force through coalitions with established unions. Banfield and Wilson point out that city employees constitute one of the most important pressure groups in city politics, yet employee unions are functioning less and less as adjuncts of the party machinery.[12] They

[9]For a full discussion of this topic see F. J. Sorauf, "The Silent Revolution in Patronage," in E. C. Banfield (ed.), *Urban Government: A Reader in Administration and Politics*. New York: The Free Press, 1969, pp. 376–386. We have relied on this article for much of our discussion of patronage.

[10]Sorauf points out that when patronage was at its height, a political appointee was required to contribute close to 5 percent of his salary in return for his appointment.

[11]We do not mean to suggest that patronage is disappearing; quite the opposite is true. Rather, the *nature* of patronage appointments is changing. Not as many higher-paid positions involving specialized skills are available through patronage. This leaves the traditional machine in charge mainly of low-level and therefore poorly-paid jobs.

[12]See E. C. Banfield and J. Q. Wilson, *City Politics*, p. 213. See also W. S. Sayre and H. Kaufman, *Governing New York City: Politics in the Metropolis*. New York: W. W. Norton and Co., 1960, pp. 73–76.

are interested, instead, in making the bureaucracy as independent as possible, and they have succeeded both in reducing the amount and nature of patronage available, and in weakening the decision-making power of the political party. As the machines fade, the career bureaucrat becomes the modern-day equivalent of the party boss. As such, he may well have more power than the old boss ever had, and this increase in his power will be at the expense of the machine and the party. Costikyan sums up this process:

> [C]urrent trends are toward a nonparty system in the city. The party organization has been excluded from the governmental process. . . . The power of lateral invasion into the bureaucracy which enabled the party organization to accelerate and to stimulate government action for constituencies has been eliminated. As a result, the electorates have turned less and less to the party organization for help. As a further result, the party organizations have had less and less of a call upon the electorates for their support at the polls.[13]

With the decline of the machine, a major component of the pluralist position vis-à-vis blacks no longer exists. The consequences for blacks are numerous. In a large number of cities, a black machine will have to start from scratch, since many cities have no such machine.[14] But without the patronage necessary to build a machine, it will be much more difficult for effective machine-type political leaders to emerge from the black lower class. Those leaders who do manage to build some kind of organization and achieve a moderate degree of success will still find enormous barriers to their entrance into state and national politics. The result of all these factors will be to slow the progress of blacks in general. Pluralist theorists have underscored these problems, but they have failed to draw the obvious conclusion that the net effect is to destroy the validity of the pluralist model for blacks.[15]

[13]E. N. Costikyan, "The Mayor: Commentary," in L. C. Fitch and A. H. Walsh (eds.), p. 603.

[14]In Philadelphia, for example, there is no black political organization, nor has there ever been one. It is commonly recognized that the overall city organization determines how many and which blacks will be elected. (J. H. Strange, "The Negro and Philadelphia Politics," in E. C. Banfield (ed.), *Urban Government*, p. 409.)

[15]See, for example, E. C. Banfield and J. Q. Wilson, *City Politics*, pp. 331–333.

The Role of the Mayor

There is still another factor which acts to the disadvantage of blacks working within a pluralist framework: the changing role of the mayor. Historically, the influence of the mayor has depended on his position as "boss" of the political party. But as we mentioned, with the decline of the machine, the earlier patronage system has been replaced by a merit system of appointment, and this has in turn spawned a burgeoning bureaucracy which has become increasingly autonomous and has taken on an increasingly larger role in the governing of the city.[16] The mayor is dependent on this bureaucracy both as a source of information and as the instrument of administration. Since the bureaucracy tends to be relatively unified, it can be a powerful enemy to the mayor. To complicate the problem, the mayor has few weapons with which to deal with the bureaucracy. Career bureau chiefs have permanent tenure within the city system and are therefore little affected by the mayor. Even where the mayor has the ability to remove a key figure, he often finds that the career commissioner regards his own area of specialization as his alone and will not tolerate interference within that area.[17]

The net result is an increasingly independent bureaucracy which the mayor cannot control as he could once control the party bosses. The mayor thus finds himself caught between two conflicting needs. On the one hand, he has a political need for a strong party organization. On the other hand, he has the administrative need for a well-functioning, efficient bureaucracy. He is expected to get things done, but the power to act effectively is virtually taken out of his hands.

The mayor's power is further diminished by the lack of unity he faces within his many constituencies.[18] Three of his constituencies—the party organization, the electorate, and interest groups—are fragmented

---

[16]W. S. Sayre, "The Mayor," in L. C. Fitch and A. H. Walsh (eds.), p. 574. What Sayre calls "the bureaucratic constituency of the mayor" is made up of three groups: appointed officials in the city administration, career bureau chiefs at the head of the city's departments and agencies, and employees' unions and associations.

[17]Banfield and Wilson cite the example of Mayor Wagner to illustrate this point. After indicating a desire to send police patrols into housing projects, the mayor was informed by the police commissioner that the decision was not the mayor's to make (*City Politics*, p. 218).

[18]See W. S. Sayre, "The Mayor," for a full discussion of the role of the mayor. We have relied on his article for much of this discussion. Sayre lists six such constituencies: "The political party organizations, elected officials, and the electorates. The bureaucracies, com-

into small, competing groups over which he has little effective control. Because of the existence of so many small groups, many of which are reluctant to enter into anything more than a temporary alliance, it is almost impossible to build the effective and long-lasting coalition that is necessary for sustained action. The mayor's position is made even more difficult by the tendency of various interest groups to ally themselves with elements of the bureaucracy and effectively bypass the mayor in many transactions. This is particularly true in the areas that most directly affect blacks, for example, education, health, planning, poverty, and welfare.

The final result of this is that the mayor "is deprived of any institution capable of aggregating sufficient power to govern the city with direction and purpose."[19] It must also be remembered that the problems mentioned above are exacerbated by the need to appeal to three additional constituencies—the communications media, the state, and the national government. Because of this wide variety of constituencies, there is no force at work which can unify a large enough group to govern the city relative to its needs. The stronger party system of the past used to serve that function, but the decline of the party organization has left the mayor powerless to carve any meaningful unity out of his many competing constituencies.

This change in the mayor's position further weakens the pluralist model. While such a model does posit the existence of a wide variety of competing groups, it also presupposes that strong coalitions be developed. According to pluralist theory, the absence of a permanent and unified "power elite" dictates that effective political power can come only through the unity of several interest groups in support of a particular issue. In the past, these coalitions were able to form because of the power of the political machine and the ability of the party boss to control a large number of voters. With that power gone, the mayor is unable to focus enough support to develop a clear policy. This was not the situation facing the early immigrants. However, since it is the situation within which blacks must function today, it casts doubt on the validity

posed of high appointed officialdom, the bureau chiefs, and the public service unions. The non-governmental interest groups, organizations representing varied business, labor, geographic, ethnic, and religious blocs. The communications media, both print and electronic. The state government at Albany. The national government in Washington" (p. 564).

[19]W. S. Sayre, "The Mayor," p. 574.

of any strategy based on the pluralist model. A more realistic assessment of the situation is provided by Theodore Lowi:

> *This is, then, the new situation in which the cities find themselves. There is no Negro social dissolution in any particularly new extreme. Some would even argue that the Negro ghetto has become over-organized. Instead, there is political dissolution of the city in which the Negro finds himself. The one essential factor facing the Negro that was not facing his lower-class white predecessors is the failure of political institutions.*[20]

In sum, the possibilities for blacks within the pluralist framework have been drastically limited by changing conditions, and those conditions cast doubt on any solution that is based on an increased role for blacks as an interest group exerting pressure on city government.

Black Cities: Implications

Some analysts are more optimistic when they consider the possibility that blacks will be not merely an interest group, but a majority within American cities, a situation that seems to be clearly in the making. (This possibility is discussed in more detail in Chapter 14.) They point to the experience of such groups as the Irish in Boston, with the expectation that blacks will repeat their pattern. Such an expectation is unwarranted, not only because of the changing conditions already described, but for additional factors which we shall now consider.[21]

    The city that blacks will inherit if they achieve control is very different from that inhabited by other immigrant groups. The city that blacks may inherit is one desperately lacking financial resources; while it may

---

[20]T. J. Lowi, *The End of Liberalism: Ideology, Policy, and the Crisis of Public Authority.* New York: W. W. Norton and Co., 1969, p. 206.

[21]James Wilson, for example, writes, "The growing number of Negroes in Northern cities suggests the increased possibility that Negro political power will become a decisive factor in the quest for race goals. Political leadership based on this large electorate might presumably be a potent force for change" (*Negro Politics,* p. 22).

present them with the appearance of power, the actual power they will have to change things may be less than anticipated. One facet of this (see Chapter 5), relates to the changing surface of the metropolitan area, for example, the movement of the white middle and upper classes to new suburban communities, the flight of industry (along with job opportunities) from the central cities, and the deterioration of the central city's public facilities.[22] The city finds itself faced with a two-fold dilemma: the financial problem and the deep-seated hostility between the city and the surrounding suburbs. The split between city and country has been a consistent theme in American history. It now takes on an added importance, since the middle-class people who escape to the suburbs often feel no responsibility for the welfare of the city. They use many of the services of the city, but they are not willing to pay to support them. This conflict is heightened by a relatively new tendency which arose just a few decades ago. In earlier days the city expanded as its population moved outward and the jurisdiction of city government was simply extended to newly populated areas, providing at least some balance between the city's responsibilities and its resources. This ended when the newer areas began to incorporate as legal entities and to see their interests as totally separate from those of the city. The final result is that it is not uncommon for the city to find its major political opposition in an alliance between the suburbs and the more distant rural areas. The problem is sufficiently serious for at least one observer to predict a basic shift in geographical alignments in the United States. The older pattern involved splits between North and South, between country and town, between agriculture and industry. The new tendency may be for a cleavage "between the core city and the suburbs throughout all regions and all areas of the country."[23] In addition to the obvious effect of such a development on the city, it might also change the nature

---

[22]Banfield and Wilson identify those aspects of business which are likely to remain in the city as ones which require frequent face-to-face communications with a large and varied clientele. "A businessman, for example, may find it indispensable to be where he can talk face-to-face with bankers, public officials, and other businessmen. But the record-keeping department of his firm may very well be decentralized to the suburbs where land is cheaper and where many typists, business machine operators, and accountants live" (*City Politics,* pp. 13–14).

[23]P. F. Drucker, "Notes on the New Politics," *The Public Interest,* Summer 1966, No. 4, p. 23.

of national politics; the building of a national party would depend on bringing together enough groups from each of these basic divisions.

In simple terms, the white exodus to the suburbs produces a city with less money. At the same time, the increased demand for services leads to greater financial obligations. The result will inevitably be that if blacks are a majority in the city, they will be forced to look outside the city for financial support even more than they do now. One obvious source of this support is the state government; but the problems involved here were difficult even for immigrant groups of the past and recent deficiencies of state government have made them even more complicated. Under the best of circumstances, the relationship between city and state is a difficult one for the city. The state has both constitutional and financial supremacy over cities. Legally, the city is the creation of the state and subject to its rule. While many cities have been granted some form of "home rule," the power they receive from this is still insufficient. Many of the important decisions are made by state governors and legislatures and not by mayors and the city councils. Financially the states limit the city's economy, for example, its ability to set tax rates and borrow money. They collect revenue (a good part of it from taxpayers living in the city) and return it to the city in the form of various grants-in-aid. The overall result is that much of the power over the cities is in the hands of the state political system.[24]

The political implications of this are important. Sayre, discussing the problems of city government, characterizes the state government as "in many respects the mayor's most intransigent constituency."[25] The reasons for this are numerous. First, as the move to the suburbs and smaller cities and townships increases, the city represents a constantly decreasing portion of the state electorate, and this decreases the mayor's bargaining power and leverage with state governments. The latter are being pressed by white constituencies to employ state resources for the benefit of *their* problems. Second, state governments, like city governments, do not have adequate sources of revenue to meet the growing problems of their own white constituencies, thus making them even more unwilling to devote an increasing share to cities whose populations, far from increasing, are declining or constant. Third, there have recently

[24]See E. C. Banfield and J. Q. Wilson, *City Politics,* Chapter 5.
[25]W. S. Sayre, "The Mayor," p. 585.

occurred numerous interstate projects, sponsored by a number of states, that are administered completely independently of the cities. And finally, the decline of machine politics is just as crucial for states as for cities. Wilson points out that in many states the "informal bases" of power—favors, patronage, party discipline—are being destroyed, while the formal basis of power, that is, legal authority, is not being increased at a parallel rate.[26] Thus the state government, like the city government, is weakening.

Since the state clearly does not provide the answer to urban problems, and since these problems cannot be solved by the city alone, the final alternative is to turn to the federal government. Here we come to the heart of the issue. If any factor is crucial to an understanding of the conditions of urban blacks, it is this reliance on the national government. Whether blacks are a small or large minority within the city, whether they increase their power by increased numbers or by gaining control of the cities, the situation remains unchanged. In the final analysis the national government has the answers.

National Politics and Pluralism

The importance of the national government becomes clear if we look at a few basic facts. While localities as of 1968 collected only 7 percent of tax revenues, the national government collected 67 percent.[27] As of 1969, the national government had become the third most important source of revenue for the city, supplying 15 percent of all city revenues, and indications are that its importance as a source of revenue will increase dramatically from the 1969 level.[28] The practice of giving grants directly to the cities (and thus bypassing the state) is relatively new, in contrast to the older procedure of channeling funds through the states. These direct grants began in the 1930s, accelerated after World War II, and have increased most sharply in the 1960s.[29] This tendency seems likely to continue unchecked. Banfield and Wilson accurately predicted that "if

[26]J. Q. Wilson, "Corruption: The Shame of the States," *The Public Interest,* Winter 1966, No. 2, p. 38.

[27]F. F. Piven and R. A. Cloward, "What Chance for Black Power?" *The New Republic,* March 30, 1968, **158** (13) 23.

[28]The first and second most important sources were city taxes and state grants.

[29]W. S. Sayre, "The Mayor," p. 589.

the control over cities is taken from the states, it will be taken by the federal government, not the cities."[30]

This need for federal money leads the city into political complications. While the two levels of government have no constitutional relationship, the financial dependence on the national government causes political issues in the city to become linked with the larger issues of national politics. City issues thus become infinitely more complicated and less easily controlled by the city government.

The complications that ensue from the city's relationship with the national government suggest a further dimension to the problems facing blacks. On the one hand, the national government provides the major hope for blacks. On the other hand, it can be the source of the black population's greatest dangers.

The clearest example of this danger is the current emphasis on the metropolitan-area concept. Under this plan, urban areas would be united with the surrounding suburbs to form one large metropolitan area. These areas would be administered by area-wide planning bureaucracies, which would be responsible for channeling grants to various localities and in the process would be able to impose federal policy on these localities.[31] Piven and Cloward point out that if blacks achieve majority control of the cities, they stand a far greater chance of blocking such things as urban renewal programs which turn out to be "Negro removal." Even more important, blacks would at least have a chance to become a powerful bloc in national politics. Faced with this possibility, the national government is most likely to see the appeal of the metropolitan-area concept because it would provide a greater opportunity for government to control the black community.[32] The formation of metropolitan-area governments would tend to nullify any political potential that blacks might have as a city majority. If the city does in fact become part of a metropolitan area, then even an all-black city will leave blacks in the same position in which they presently find themselves, that is, as one more group in a larger structure. The possibility of meaningful black political power in that context is certainly no greater than it is now; it may even be less

[30]E. C. Banfield and J. Q. Wilson, *City Politics,* p. 343.

[31]F. F. Piven and R. A. Cloward, "What Chance for Black Power?" p. 23. For another discussion of the metropolitan area concept, see E. Sofen, *The Miami Metropolitan Experiment: A Metropolitan Action Study.* (2nd ed., enlarged) Garden City: Anchor Books, Doubleday and Co., 1966.

[32]F. F. Piven and R. A. Cloward, "Black Control of Cities," in A. Shank (ed.), *Political Power and the Urban Crisis.* Boston: Holbrook Press, 1969, p. 325.

because of the financial power of the federally controlled metropolitan bureaucracy, and because the national government will most likely be more concerned with pleasing the majority of whites in the outlying areas than the black minority in the central cities.[33]

The political rationale of metropolitan government as an instrument of diffusing the political leverage that blacks might acquire is complicated by the fact that most suburban units do not want to lose their "autonomy" to metropolitan-based government. Thus, it is unlikely that the growth of metropolitan government will take place faster than black political control of our major central cities.

The potential danger to blacks from the national government can also be seen by examining the current trend toward the abolition of the Electoral College in favor of direct election of the President. Such a plan, by decreasing the political importance of urban areas, would also decrease the potential political power of blacks.

The double-edged sword of national power thus leads us to the real question that blacks must face. Any realistic discussion of ghetto problems must focus less on how to change city government (though this is still important) and more on how to influence the national government. The crucial question, therefore, is how much scope is there in the American political system for blacks to influence national policy? To answer this question we must briefly analyze the theory of pluralism in relation to national sources of power.

The basic outlines of the pluralist model of national politics are not unlike the outlines of the local model (though not all theorists who accept pluralism as a description of local politics also accept it at the national level).[34] America is said to be composed of a number of competing groups which represent the general interests of various segments of

---

[33]As Robert L. Allen points out, "This 'metropolitanism' will also serve to cushion the impact of urban black voting majorities on American politics and political priorities." *Black Awakening in Capitalist America: An Analytical History*. Garden City: Doubleday and Co., 1970, p. 188.

[34]The descriptions of both pluralism and elitism presented in this chapter do not reflect the specific approach of a particular pluralist or elitist theorist. Further, we have not attempted to discuss every aspect of pluralist and elitist theory. Instead, we have chosen those aspects of pluralism and elitism that are most pertinent to the concerns of this book. We have also abstracted from the whole body of pluralist and elitist theory a general view of the underlying principles of each theory. The reader should be aware, however, that the terms "pluralism" and "elitism" each include a number of theories which differ on specific issues.

society (labor unions, farmers, business, and so on), and the more specific interests of various ethnic organizations and religious associations. Power is thus fragmented. Because it is divided among a number of competing groups, no single group is able to dominate. No group will therefore be excluded from the decision-making process and every group will have at least the potential for effective political power. David Riesman offers one typical formulation of this position. He posits the existence of a number of interest or veto groups which arise because of the differing interests of political parties, business groups, labor organizations, farm blocs, and so on. Each group is concerned mainly with protecting its own interests by preventing the action of any other group that it sees as threatening its own sphere. Instead of a single ruling group, power resides in the constant give and take among groups. The unorganized public, rather than being dominated by these groups, is sought as an ally in the struggle of each against encroachment by others.[35]

Even though the pluralists believe that there is no single ruling group in the United States, they do concede that "the key political, economic and social decisions" are made by small minorities.[36] The pluralists label such minorities "competing elites." Interest groups function by exerting pressure on these various elites, who form a kind of intervening structure through which the masses are able to influence government. According to the pluralists, these competing elites are not able to function as a stable ruling group. Their power is limited by the necessity to compete with other elites and by the resulting need to appeal to the masses for support.

Even such a brief overview makes it clear why the pluralist framework lends itself to the belief that there is a great deal of maneuverability, a large, relatively open area within which blacks can exert power

[35]D. Riesman in collaboration with R. Denney and N. Glazer, *The Lonely Crowd: A Study of the Changing American Character*. New York: Doubleday and Company, 1953. For a full discussion of this position, see W. Kornhauser, " 'Power Elite' or 'Veto Groups'?" in G. W. Domhoff and H. B. Ballard (eds.), *C. Wright Mills and the Power Elite*. Boston: Beacon Press, 1968, pp. 37–59.

[36]R. A. Dahl, "Power, Pluralism and Democracy: A Modest Proposal." Paper delivered at the annual meeting of the American Political Science Association, Chicago, 1964, p. 3. According to Dahl, "It is difficult—nay impossible—to see how it could be otherwise in large political systems" (p. 3). He justifies elite decision-making on the grounds that "prevailing norms are subtle matters better obtained by negotiations than by the crudities and over-simplification of public debate." (R. A. Dahl, *Who Governs? Democracy and Power in an American City*. New Haven: Yale University Press, 1961, p. 321.)

as a group. If America is, in fact, "fractured into a congeries of hundreds of small 'special interest' groups,"[37] then blacks at least have the potential for power by virtue of their number and their potential unity. Since, as Robert Dahl claims, "all the active and legitimate groups in the population can make themselves heard at some crucial stage in the process of decision,"[38] then whatever power blacks can mobilize should be able to be used to effect crucial decisions. Because of the competition among elites, the elites are invariably forced to bid for support among the electorate, and a large black voting bloc could be of crucial importance. Since no one interest group is homogeneous for all purposes (being strong in some areas and weak in others) and since groups are not unified into long-lasting, stable coalitions, power is fluid and changing; a group may be powerful at one time or in regard to one issue, but weak at another time or in relation to another issue.

Elitism

In our view, power in the United States is not distributed as equally as the pluralist model suggests, nor is the political system as open as the pluralists imply. The critical areas with which we are concerned are the distribution of power, the openness of the system, and the role of elites. In regard to elites, the major issue is whether they are significantly more powerful than other groups. If they in fact have a disproportionate amount of power that is not significantly restrained, then the scope of maneuverability available to blacks is greatly limited.

The Corporate Elite

The weakness of the pluralist "competing elites" theory can be seen if we examine an alternative approach, put forth by such theorists as

[37]N. W. Polsby, "How to Study Community Power," in E. C. Banfield (ed.), Urban Government, p. 450. Dahl's claim is that most groups have more power to veto undesirable alternatives than to determine a decision directly. (R. A. Dahl, M. Haire, and P. F. Lazarsfeld, Social Science Research on Business: Product and Potential. New York: Columbia University Press, 1959. Cited by R. Miliband, The State in Capitalist Society. New York: Basic Books, 1969, p. 3.)

[38]R. A. Dahl, A Preface to Democratic Theory. Chicago: The University of Chicago Press, 1965, p. 137.

C. Wright Mills, G. William Domhoff, and Ralph Miliband, whose description of the United States fits within the terms of what might be called the "elitist" approach. According to this approach, the United States is ruled by a group that is relatively stable over long periods of time. The discussion among these elitist theorists has tended to center around the precise nature of this ruling group. Much debate has gone on as to whether the ruling group is a "power elite," a "ruling class," a "ruling elite," and so on. Unfortunately, in the heat of the debate a most crucial point is often obscured. Despite important theoretical differences, most of these formulations point to exactly the same thing: the dominant role of elites in general and of the corporate elite in particular.[39] Theorists differ as to whether the corporate elite is part of a ruling class, identical to that class, or part of a power elite, but they all seem to agree that various elites, and especially the corporate elite, exert a disproportionate amount of political power which is not significantly restrained in the way the pluralists suggest. Marxist theory is based precisely on the fact that the owners of the means of production (the corporate rich) constitute a "ruling class." While C. Wright Mills rejected the Marxist formulation of a ruling class, the "power elite" concept that he substituted still assigns a crucial role to the corporate elite.[40] G. William Domhoff's claim is that the corporate elite forms "the controlling core of the power elite" and that the interests of the corporate rich are the prime determinants of both the interests and unity of the power elite, with the other two groups playing a secondary role.[41] Finally, Ralph Miliband argues that the most crucial fact about advanced capitalist societies is precisely the existence

[39]Different elitist theorists have defined the term "corporate elite" differently. We are using the term as roughly analagous to the owners of the means of production in the Marxist sense, differentiated from the managerial or technical-intellectual elite of corporations, though for some the managerial elite has become co-opted by the owners of the means of production.

[40]Mills' power elite is composed of the heads of institutional structures rather than the owners of the means of production. But within this group he identifies three major components: the military, political, and corporate elites. While the corporate elite is no longer seen as the only ruling group, it nevertheless exerts considerable power, and this power is augmented by the coincidence of interests among the three groups. See C. W. Mills, *The Power Elite.* New York: Oxford University Press, 1956.

[41]Domhoff goes on to say that his formulation is "a modification and extension of the concept of a 'ruling class.' " ("The Power Elite and Its Critics.," in G. W. Domhoff and H. B. Ballard (eds.), *C. Wright Mills and the Power Elite,* p. 276.) Despite the subtle distinctions between a ruling class and a power elite, Domhoff still sees the corporate elite as playing the most important and pivotal role in American government.

of private and concentrated economic power, which enables the corporate elite to enjoy great power in the political sphere in determining the actions and policies of government.[42]

In their discussion of the corporate elite, these elitist theorists present evidence that shows clearly that the corporate elite in fact has and exercises a disproportionate amount of political power. Studies have shown that the top 1 percent of the population owns 25–30 percent of the nation's privately held wealth and owns 75–80 percent of privately held corporate stock. Moreover, studies have shown that these distributions have changed little over the years.[43]

This economic power is then translated into political power. The corporate elite not only uses privately owned wealth for its own purposes and interests, but also mobilizes the state to cooperate with and support the desires of private business interests. In addition to the direct exercise of political power, the corporate elite is able to exert political power in the form of what Bachrach and Baratz have called "non-decision-making." The point to be understood here is that the political decision-making process is not a completely open one; certain issues and possible solutions are never even considered. The reason for this is that the corporate elite is instrumental in developing and reinforcing the values which govern the decision-making process. As Bachrach and Baratz point out:

> *power is also exercised when A devotes his energies to creating or reinforcing social and political values and institutional practices that limit the scope of the political process to public considerations of only those issues which are comparatively innocuous to A. To the extent that A succeeds in doing this, B is prevented, for all practical purposes, from bringing to the fore any issues*

[42]R. Miliband, *The State in Capitalist Society*, p. 265. One other example of this emphasis on the corporate elite is Peter Bachrach's concept of a "decision-making elite." Bachrach urges political theorists to recognize "that the giants among these institutions are in fact political elites—political elites accountable only to themselves." (*The Theory of Democratic Elitism: A Critique*. Boston: Little, Brown and Co., 1967, p. 82.)

[43]R. Lampman, *The Share of Top Wealth-Holders in National Wealth*. Princeton: Princeton University Press, 1962. Other studies indicate that rising executives—the new technocrats—are assimilated both socially and economically into the same strata inhabited by the corporate elite. (C. W. Domhoff, "The Power Elite and Its Critics," p. 270.)

> *that might in their resolution be seriously detrimental to A's set of preferences.*[44]

This non-decision-making power has been defined elsewhere by E. E. Schattschneider in terms of the concept of mobilization of bias:

> *All forms of political organization have a bias in favor of the exploitation of some kinds of conflict and the suppression of others because* organization is the mobilization of bias. *Some issues are organized into politics while others are organized out.*[45]

In more concrete terms, while the members of the corporate elite may argue about the desired degree of government intervention in the economy, they all agree that their suggestions have the same basic goal—to strengthen and enhance capitalism (or to weaken its opposition). As a result, they use their non-decision-making power to eliminate from the decision-making process any possible solution that would not further this common goal. As Miliband points out:

> *The general commitment deeply colours the specific response and affects not only the solution envisaged for the particular problem perceived, but the mode of perception itself; indeed ideological commitment may and often does prevent perception at all, and makes impossible not only prescriptions for the disease, but its location.*[46]

This seems to be a more concrete statement of the theoretical concepts of Schattschneider and Bachrach and Baratz. The "mobilization of bias" thus begins to be clarified; it is at least in part an overwhelming bias in favor of private property, free enterprise, and all the basic tenets of corporate capitalism. The non-decision-making power of the elite will

[44]P. Bachrach and M. S. Baratz, "Power as Non-decision-making," in E. C. Banfield (ed.), *Urban Government,* p. 457.

[45]E. E. Schattschneider, *The Semi-sovereign People: A Realist's View of Democracy in America.* New York: Holt, Rinehart and Winston, Inc., 1961, p. 71. Emphasis original.

[46]R. Miliband, p. 72.

thus be used both to strengthen the prevailing emphasis on these capitalist tenets and to ensure that all solutions considered are within this framework.

In sum, if we use the concept of mobilization of bias to clarify the role of the corporate elite, it becomes clear that corporate power is manifested in several ways: (1) The corporate elite is able to make independent decisions which affect the country as a whole; (2) Given the inherent bias of capitalism, it is able to manipulate and exert a strong influence on decisions made by the government; and (3) In line with the concept of non-decision-making, it has the power to influence public values so that certain issues never become part of the decision-making process; it is strengthened in turn by the existing mobilization of bias. In other words, the corporate elite is able to set boundaries that narrow the possibilities of government action. In addition, its power is not significantly restrained. Unlike the politicians, members of the corporate elite cannot be voted out of office; they are not responsible to the electorate. In our view, this combination of a concentration of economic power, the ability to translate that economic power into political power, and the lack of significant restraints on the corporate elite, all conclusively refute the pluralist view of an open society in which blacks have a great deal of maneuverability.

The concept of mobilization of bias leads to still another factor which limits the apparent openness of American society—the role of the state in the political process. Since adherence to the tenets of private enterprise is basic to the governmental structure, the state regards it as its obligation to defend those tenets. It considers any action it takes in this direction not as the abandonment of neutrality vis-à-vis competing interest groups, but simply as a necessary step to maintain the continuity of the system. For example, Miliband argues that the state is inevitably the protector of the predominant economic interests within the system. What he calls its "real purpose" is to insure the continued predominance of those interests. As a result, according to Miliband, government intervention in the economic sphere will almost invariably be identical with, and serve the interests of, the corporation. The welfare state thus turns out to be the corporate elite's greatest ally:

> *In no field has the notion of the "welfare state" had a more precise and apposite meaning than here: There are*

*no more persistent and successful applicants for public
assistance than the proud giants of the private enterprise system.*[47]

If the values implicit in the private allocation of goods and people have
racist dimensions, then the government, in its reflection of the interests
of the corporate elite (rhetoric notwithstanding) tends to avoid pressing
for policies that would radically upset the private arrangements made
in the marketplace.[48]

Put in other terms, the corporate elite and the state are clearly
extremely powerful interest groups, hierarchically arranged. Pluralism thus
fails in its inability to realize that various interests enter the competition
of the pluralist model with an unfair advantage. Kornhauser, in a critique
of Riesman's *The Lonely Crowd,* charges him with presenting a distorted
picture by failing to give enough attention to "power differentials" among
the different groups. Riesman's conclusion that power is relatively equal
among groups is thus unwarranted.[49] This critique also applies to much
of pluralist theory. In the spirit of George Orwell, all interests are equal,
but some are more equal than others.

The pluralists' failure to recognize the lack of openness in the political

[47]R. Miliband, p. 72.

[48]Many theorists argue that the neutrality of the state is a product of the inherent nature
of bureaucracy. Following the interpretation of bureaucracy developed by Max Weber, they
have claimed that our national bureaucracy tends to be nonpolitical, and therefore not readily
manipulated by the corporate elite. Since the federal bureaucracy is growing in strength
and importance, they argue, this bureaucracy will prevent the interests of any one group
from becoming dominant. However, studies have shown that while public bureaucracies in
societies dominated by private propertied interests appear to be neutral, they actually have
a large degree of freedom in the proposal and promotion of public policies. Those occupying
bureaucratic positions tend to favor the interests of one group to the detriment of others.
In essence, the bureaucracy utilizes the language and modes of behavior of neutrality to
hide the essentially political nature of its activities. Because of the existing mobilization of
bias, the bureaucracy often interacts with various business interests (for example, the Pentagon
bureaucracy and its intimate connection to the 100 largest corporations, which receive most
of the military contracts). Instead of the neutral role attributed to it, it takes on a political
role which favors those interests. While in theory, for example, the federal regulatory agencies
are set up to regulate business activities, they are, in fact, more likely to serve those interests.
The effect of the political bias of the bureaucracy is to further the interests of the corporate
elite and to buttress the latter's stability.

[49]W. Kornhauser, " 'Power Elite' or 'Veto Groups'?" p. 55.

system stems from several sources. Their failure to recognize the political power of the corporate elite has its roots, first, in their view of the relationship between ownership and control of corporations, and second, in their definition of political power. The pluralists argue that because of the managerial revolution and the rise of the new "technocrats," there is a divorce between ownership and control. While the owners still have certain privileges, they do not control the corporation; the technical-intellectual elite (including corporate managers) does that.[50] While pluralists sometimes admit that a relatively small group in the United States owns disproportionately large amounts of property, the importance of this, they claim, is offset by the increasingly dispersed nature of stock ownership and the actual controlling role of various middle-management technocrats. But as we have shown, this is not the case.

The other source of the pluralists' failure to recognize the importance of the corporate elite stems from their definition of political power. The pluralists are unwilling to admit that corporate power can be considered as political power. Dahl, for example, uses the term "economic notables" to describe the corporate elite. While Dahl admits that these economic notables can also belong to a "political" elite, he claims that the only basis on which they can be included in that elite is in their exercise of influence on concrete "key political decisions." He seems to limit these decisions strictly to include only decisions regarding control of political parties or governmental decisions on various issues.[51] But, as we have shown, such a definition ignores the great political power that is implicit in the concept of non-decision-making put forth by the elitist theorists.

[50]D. Bell, *The End of Ideology.* New York: The Free Press, 1960, p. 42. See also A. A. Berle and G. C. Means, *The Modern Corporation and Private Property.* (rev. ed.) New York: Harcourt Brace Jovanovich, 1969; A. A. Berle and C. G. Means, *Power without Property: A New Development in American Political Economy.* New York: Harcourt Brace Jovanovich, 1959; A. A. Berle and G. C. Means, *The Twentieth Century Capitalist Revolution.* New York: Harcourt Brace Jovanovich, 1954; J. K. Galbraith, *The New Industrial State.* Boston: Houghton Mifflin, 1967; C. Reich, *The Greening of America: The Coming of New Consciousness and the Rebirth of a Future.* New York: Random House, 1970.

[51]See P. Bachrach, *The Theory of Democratic Elitism,* p. 73, for a full discussion of this issue. Dahl's major criticism of the ruling elite model seems completely inadequate. His claim was that the United States does not have a "ruling elite" because the governmental structure can be voted out of office by the electorate at any point. [(See R. A. Dahl, "A Critique of the Ruling Elite Model," in G. W. Domhoff and H. B. Ballard (eds.), *C. Wright Mills and the Power Elite.*] Dahl's definition of political power precludes a consideration of the corporate elite that, in our argument, does exert political power but cannot be voted out of office.

In addition to their failure to recognize the political power of the corporate elite, the pluralists fail in their definition of the role of the state in the political process. According to pluralist theory, the state plays a neutral role in the competition among interest groups. Pluralist formulations of its exact role vary, but basically the state is confined to the role of an impartial mediator or to that of being the instrument through which various conflicting pressures are balanced. As such, it serves as a guarantee that power will never be too heavily balanced in favor of one side or the other. But, as we have indicated, the concept of mobilization of bias makes this assertion rather dubious. A more valid way to study power thus would be to examine first the mobilization of bias in a particular community by examining "the dominant values, the myths, and the established political procedures and rules of the game,"[52] and then to determine which persons or groups are helped by the existing bias and which are hurt by it. The researcher would then have to investigate the degree and way in which persons and groups who favor the status quo can exert influence on the values and institutions of the community in order to limit the scope of decision-making to "safe" issues. Finally, the concept of non-decision-making would have to be used to ascertain which issues are significant enough to yield realistic conclusions regarding the exercise of power. The pluralist criterion for these "key" decisions, formulated by Dahl, was that a key issue must "involve actual disagreement in preferences among two or more groups."[53] But to this must be added an analysis of the mobilization of bias; the result would be that the only issues that can be considered "important" are those that present a threat to the predominant values or to the established "rules of the game." Any others would have to be regarded as unimportant.

The final cause of the pluralist failure is the fact that pluralist assertions about the composition of interest groups simply do not reflect reality. As Bachrach has pointed out, even in America, which is the very model of a pressure-group society, less than a majority of the people are effectively organized into pressure groups. According to data presented by Schattschneider, a relatively small number of laborers, farmers, women, Negroes, and other lower- and lower-middle-class people belong to any organized interest group.[54] Schattschneider sums the situation up:

---

[52]P. Bachrach and M. S. Baratz, "Power as Non-decision-making," p. 463.

[53]R. A. Dahl, "A Critique of the Ruling Elite Model," p. 33.

[54]E. E. Schattschneider, pp. 20–41.

The flaw in the pluralist heaven is that the heavenly chorus sings with a strong upper class accent. Probably about 90% of the people cannot get into the pressure system.[55]

Implications for Black Political Power

The combined effect of all of these factors is seriously to narrow the flexibility of the system with respect to bringing blacks into the mainstream of our society. Even the existence of veto groups in Riesman's sense, or of groups that have more power to prevent alternatives than to implement them, in Dahl's terminology, would seem to lead to pessimism: Since such groups have more power to stop other groups from infringing on their sphere than to implement their own desired programs, the best possibility available would seem to be gradual, incremental change. The pluralist implications of fluidity and openness thus give way to greater rigidity and restrictions in the area in which blacks must operate to achieve equality. What is most important is that certain groups exercise a great deal of power that is largely unchecked. The weakness of pluralism lies in its failure to see the full implications of this.

For blacks, the major implications should be evident. Any solution they put forth which is outside the existing mobilization of bias of the system will have no chance of serious consideration. Programs and actions by blacks that threaten the basic tenets of capitalism or the traditional political framework of the system are destined to fail as long as the system remains intact. This will hold true despite the unity of blacks as an interest group and despite their increasing predominance and possible control of American cities. The hard truth of the matter is that, short of fundamental changes in the American social order initiated by groups in addition to blacks, space for blacks to maneuver is greatly limited. If blacks who enter politics are forced to abide by the rules of the game at the local level, as Banfield and Wilson assert, it is even more true at the national level.

The above conclusions, bleak as they are, should not be taken to mean that blacks have *no* capacity to affect their destiny. Even the elitists would agree that there is still some room for blacks to maneuver.

[55]E. E. Schattschneider, p. 35.

The major source of their ability to maneuver lies in the fact that none of the factors discussed here operates in an absolute way. Miliband argues, for example, that while corporate interests will usually prevail, this does not mean that they will automatically be able to achieve their goals and influence the state in every one of their demands.[56] Similarly, Sweezy argues that the belief that "the state always and everywhere and automatically serves the interests of the ruling class is invalid."[57]

Several factors mitigate against the complete power of the elite. While elites all share a bias in favor of private enterprise, they have very serious differences regarding the desired nature and amount of state intervention in the economy. Although the scope of debate is narrowed mainly to include alternatives that would strengthen or fit within the capitalist framework, the area of disagreement is still large enough to allow for some maneuverability. There is also significant disagreement among elites regarding the extent of the state's responsibility for social reform and the relative merits of various possible alternatives. As Sweezy points out, "In any given situation the range of alternatives is wide and the course to be followed by the state is far from mechanically predetermined."[58] Insofar as the "correct" path is not clear-cut, blacks will be able to exert *some* pressure in the process of choosing among alternatives. A further factor operating in favor of black pressure is the real conflict between the long-term interests of the elite and their short-term needs. Finally, the interests of various segments of the elite are not always identical with the needs of the elite as a whole.

The net result, as elitist theorists seem to agree, is that even within the confines of elite rule, there is some opportunity for other groups to influence governmental action. Under certain circumstances, other classes and segments of classes are able both to wrest concessions from the state[59] and at times to play a role of some real importance.[60]

The picture that emerges from all this is still not an optimistic one.

[56]R. Miliband, pp. 164–165.

[57]P. M. Sweezy, "Has Capitalism Changed?" Cited by G. W. Domhoff, *The Power Elite and Its Critics,* p. 262.

[58]P. M. Sweezy, p. 263.

[59]R. Miliband, p. 164.

[60]G. W. Domhoff, "The Power Elite and Its Critics," p. 277; see also M. E. Sharpe, "Squares in the Higher Circles," and G. W. Domhoff, "A Review of the Higher Circles," *Social Policy,* 1971, **2** (1), pp. 65–67.

To the extent that blacks can maneuver, their maneuvering must be done in the interstices of structured power. These interstices would include those generated by a disagreement among elites or by a misperception of elite interests; it would include areas that result when the interests of the elite can be served in several ways, or when there is a conflict between their long- and short-term goals or between the interests of different segments of the elite.

Given the dominance of corporate capitalist interests in the economic sphere, the only possibility for blacks seems to lie in the political sphere proper. Various activities in the past, such as demonstrations, boycotts, sit-ins, and threatened and actual violence, have all been possible ways for blacks to bring pressure outside accepted channels. But all these activities have built-in dangers. They can work either for or against blacks; they all suffer from the law of diminishing returns. Repetition often leads to the realization that tactics that once seemed dangerous are really harmless and uninfluential; blacks are then forced either to escalate or to concede defeat.

The Democratic Party and the War on Poverty

The possibilities for black political action can be clarified somewhat if we consider the history of the War on Poverty. The traditional view of the War on Poverty is that it was created in response to the existence of various "urban problems." But Cloward and Piven argue very convincingly that this simply is not a sufficient answer. Many of these so-called urban problems were just as widespread in rural areas, yet Office of Economic Opportunity funds were concentrated heavily in the large urban centers of the nation.[61] Furthermore, there were already in existence various programs that could easily have been reformed and enlarged to implement the goals of the War on Poverty. Despite this, a whole new bureaucracy was set up.

The real nature and genesis of the War on Poverty were political. They stemmed from the needs of the National Democratic Party. The Democratic Party during the 1960s was faced with a turbulent, dissatisfied black constituency, concentrated in urban areas that were crucial for a democratic victory. If the Democrats were to retain the allegiance of

[61]F. F. Piven and R. A. Cloward, *Regulating the Poor: The Functions of Public Welfare.* New York: Pantheon Books, 1971, pp. 258–259.

this constituency, something would have to be done. This need, Cloward and Piven argue, was the real stimulus for the War on Poverty. In order to accomplish this goal, the federal government was willing to intervene and set up a whole new bureaucracy which bypassed both state and local governments. In doing so, they were able to establish a direct relationship between blacks and the national government. The result, in effect, was a new alignment; the national government, acting in its own interests, united with and helped blacks, both by direct material aid and by helping them to wrest more money and services from local government. A crucial part of the Democratic Party's strategy was the attempt to stimulate black demands for services through the various agencies that had been set up. Black pressure was thus redirected against local government and served to increase the amount of money that flowed through local agencies. In short, local government was used to advance the interests of the National Democratic Party, a use which possibly backfired against both blacks and the Party.

The political origin of the War on Poverty has been confirmed by several other writers.[62] The same can be said for the ultimate demise of the community action programs. As we have indicated, the War on Poverty undercut local political organizations by its tendency to channel funds to newly created agencies rather than to city government. The result was the creation of another competing power structure within the city, and the local machines inevitably fought back. This possibility was foreshadowed to some degree as early as the original drafting of the legislation. Several congressmen were upset by the possibility that community action grants might go to newly formed organizations that would stimulate action among the poor.[63] However, none envisioned the full dimensions of the problem. As Adam Yarmolinsky points out, "In a community as sensitive to the problems of the distribution and transmission of power as Washington, the power potential—constructive and destructive—of the poor themselves was largely overlooked."[64]

[62]For example, A. Yarmolinsky, "The Beginnings of OEO," in J. L. Sundquist (ed.), *On Fighting Poverty: Perspectives from Experience*. New York: Basic Books, 1969, pp. 34–51. See also J. C. Donovan, *The Politics of Poverty*. New York: Pegasus, 1967; and S. A. Levitan, *The Great Society's Poor Law: A New Approach to Poverty*. Baltimore: Johns Hopkins Press, 1969. Both Donovan and Levitan discuss the political development of the War on Poverty but from a slightly different point of view.

[63]A. Yarmolinsky, p. 46.

[64]A. Yarmolinsky, p. 50.

The compromises that were finally made in the War on Poverty were responses to precisely the political dissatisfaction that the local city machines indicated. Kenneth Clark's and Jeannette Hopkin's study of the community action programs concludes that "as soon as such programs came in conflict with local political and civic leadership, the local and federal governments began to show strong signs of a strategic retreat and began to mollify local Establishment leadership while nevertheless pushing verbally participation of the poor."[65] In this light, Moynihan's contention that these compromises were the result of an attempt to put into practice unclear and not fully thought-out concepts of the social sciences is dubious.[66] In the end, the War on Poverty became more of a liability than a help to the National Democratic Party because of the local political backlash; this was its downfall.

The War on Poverty experience has several implications. First, to the degree that blacks were able to wrest any concessions in their favor, they were able to do so because of pressure on the national, rather than on the local, government. Where pressure on local government was effective, it was in large part because of the federal role in stimulating and aiding such protest. Second, the system was able to formulate these goals largely because various expressions of black discontent led to an identification of interests between the Democratic Party (which wanted black support) and blacks themselves (who wanted increased federal aid). Third, black interests were advanced in this case only because they did not go against the existing mobilization of bias and they did not threaten basic elite interests. Fourth, because of the dependence of the Democratic Party on the black vote, it seems probable that it was the major vehicle for black pressure. Fifth, the negative response of local officials indicates that in the future such funds will have to be channeled through existing political structures. Of all the arguments for black control of cities, this is probably the most convincing one. While black control of the cities cannot, by itself, lead to any solutions, there is at least the possibility that national programs that channel money through a black political structure will not be hindered by the kind of

[65]K. B. Clark and J. Hopkins. *A Relevant War against Poverty: A Study of Community Action Programs and Observable Social Change.* New York: Harper Torchbooks, 1970, p. 156.

[66]D. P. Moynihan, *Maximum Feasible Misunderstanding: Community Action in the War on Poverty.* New York: The Free Press, 1970.

local political pressure that helped to destroy the community action programs.

This is not to say that the War on Poverty provided a basic solution to the problems of blacks or that the Democratic Party is a significant source of hope for them. But if we accept the existence of a mobilization of bias, of the non-decision-making power of both corporate and state elites, of inequalities among interest groups, then the range of possibilities left to blacks is limited. Such a diagnosis may be dismal, but it reflects a more accurate view than the relative optimism of the pluralists.

The possibilities for blacks to overcome some of the basic economic barriers confronting them are also not too hopeful when we consider black needs in relation to broad national economic policy considerations. Some of these considerations are examined in the following chapter.

CHAPTER 13

Race and Broad Economic Policy Considerations

The solutions that are generally suggested to alter the conditions that blacks face involve ideological predispositions which direct attention to the role of the state in relation to the private market.[1] Broadly speaking, there are three such ideologies: (1) the pure-market view, held by the conservative establishment, (2) the welfare-liberal view, held by the governing establishment, and (3) the anticapitalist view, held by those whose solutions are outside the purview of the prevailing private-market framework.

While we will here be mainly concerned with the views and practices of the welfare-liberal establishment, some brief attention will be given to the position of the conservative establishment. The anticapitalist position is elaborated in the concluding chapter.

[1]H. Wachtel, "Looking at Poverty from a Radical Perspective," unpublished paper, Washington, D.C.: American University, February 1971.

The Conservative View[2]

The major conservative contributions to discussions of the role of the state are its unsympathetic critique of the welfare-liberals' nonmarket edifices that originated in the New Deal days and have grown increasingly powerful, and its assertion of the virtues of the private market's "spontaneous" capacity to deal with black problems. The conservatives believe that if only the market forces were allowed to function effectively and over a sustained period of time, everything would fall into place. In *Capitalism and Freedom,* Friedman lamentingly reflected that the legacy of the 1930s, resulting in significant government intervention, produced attitudes that are still with us:

> There is still a tendency to regard any existing government intervention as desirable, to attribute all evils to the market, and to evaluate new proposals for government control in their ideal form, as they might work if run by able, disinterested men, free from the pressure of special interest groups. The proponents of limited government and free enterprise are still on the defensive.[3]

Further in the book, Friedman goes on to suggest that there is now sufficient evidence to compare the state-interventionist approach to problem solving with the attempts of private enterprise in the same direction. His conclusions about the accomplishments of the interventionist "reforms" are extremely negative. Since they represent a conservative's critique of the welfare-liberal's self-generating myth about its own accomplishments, they are worth noting. Friedman argues that the regulation of industries by government agencies on behalf of the public has proved to be a fiasco. Regulation of industries such as the railroads, for example, becomes "an instrument whereby the railroads could protect

[2]In this section we shall present the conservative view as expounded by Milton Friedman, an economist, and Edward Banfield, whom we discussed at considerable length in another context (see Chapter 10). Since their positions overlap, we shall view them together, selecting those parts of their respective views that apply to the areas of our own concern.

[3]M. Friedman, *Capitalism and Freedom.* Chicago: University of Chicago Press, 1963, p. 197.

themselves from the competition of newly emerging rivals—at the expense of ... the consumer" (p. 197).[4] Friedman's view of the income tax laws allegedly enacted to redistribute income from the rich to the poor is equally negative. According to Friedman, the income tax:

> *has become a facade, covering loopholes and special provisions, that renders rates that are highly graduated on paper largely ineffective. . . . An income tax intended to reduce inequality and promote the diffusion of wealth has in practice fostered reinvestment of corporate earnings, thereby favoring the growth of large corporations, inhibiting the operation of the capital market, and discouraging the establishment of new enterprises (p. 198).*

Friedman finds that the agricultural program, purportedly designed to help poor farmers (many of whom are black) and to improve the use of resources in the agricultural sector, has become a "national scandal." "[It has] wasted public funds, distorted the use of resources, riveted increasingly heavy and detailed controls on farmers, . . . and withal has done little to help the impecunious [farmer]" (p. 198).

Even fair-employment-practice acts are negatively viewed by Friedman, though not on the empirical grounds that he used to indict the lack of accomplishments associated with other realms of intervention in the economy (p. 113).

Finally, Friedman argues that the housing programs aimed at improving the conditions of the poor have in fact "worsened . . . conditions . . . contributed to juvenile delinquency, and spread urban blight" (p. 198).

What does this negative critique of the welfare-liberals' governmental "meddling" in the market mean in view of the relatively remarkable accomplishments of America's private enterprise system since World War II? For Friedman it means:

> *The United States has continued to progress; its citizens have become better fed, better clothed, better housed, and better*

---

[4]In our view, "public" regulation without public ownership has given rise to the buck-passing process in which government blames industry and industry blames government at hearings which periodically become source material for scholarly endeavors. It has led to what C. Wright Mills called "organized irresponsibility."

transported; class and social distinctions have narrowed; minority groups have become less disadvantaged; popular culture has advanced by leaps and bounds. All this has been the product of the initiative and drive of individuals co-operating through the free market. Government measures have hampered not helped this development. We have been able to afford and surmount these measures only because of the extraordinary fecundity of the market. This invisible hand has been more potent for progress than the visible hand (government intervention for retrogression) (pp. 199–200).

Edward Banfield comes to similar conclusions from a similar mode of reasoning. He criticizes the welfare-liberal state-interventionists' policies that are specific to the black population. For example:

[subsidies to] induce employers to hire "hard-core" workers achieve very little because the employers tend to make adjustments (which may be perfectly legitimate) that enable them to take the subsidies while employing workers who are not significantly different from those whom they would have employed anyway. Similarly, efforts to reduce unemployment, poverty, or slum housing in a particular city may be counterproductive in that they attract more poor workers to the city. Essentially the same problem will exist with any welfare program that offers generous support to all who can be considered poor. Such a program will encourage people to adapt either by reducing their incomes (the wife leaving her job, for example) or by lying, thus increasing the number of the "poor" and, if the inducement is strong enough, eventually swamping the system.[5]

With regard to the value of training programs, an area in which there is considerable consensus in principle, Banfield further argues that such programs:

[5]E. C. Banfield, *The Unheavenly City: The Nature and Future of Our Urban Crisis.* Boston: Little Brown & Co., 1970, pp. 241–242.

> *do not as a rule offer any solution to the problem of hard-core unemployment because the same qualities that make a worker hard-core also make him unable or unwilling to accept training. More generally, giving lower-class persons "really good" jobs is not a feasible way of inducing them to change their style of life, because that very style of life makes it impossible to give them "really good" jobs (p. 242).*

Moreover, Banfield goes on to point out that even if such training programs could succeed, they would not be worth undertaking, since their cost would far outweigh their benefit (p. 243).

While most of the above interventionist measures are seen as merely ineffective, some are actually seen as worsening the condition of blacks. For example, Banfield quotes a study which concludes that "the principal effect of the minimum wage is to 'injure' some of the lowest-paid workers by forcing them into even lower-paid occupations exempt from the act, one of which is unemployment."[6] Banfield goes on to elaborate a study conducted by the Bureau of Labor Statistics in 1956 which was concerned with the impact of an increase in the minimum wage (from 75 cents to $1.00) on low-wage industries. According to the study's findings:

> *A majority of plants reported doing one or more of the following: increasing expenditures for machinery and equipment, changing plant layout or procedures, discharging some employees or changing product line. After an increase in the minimum, the unemployment rate among the workers least attractive to the employers—Negro teen-agers—jumps. The only people who gain . . . are the relatively skilled and well-paid workers who make and sell the machines or do other things to replace the low-productivity worker who has been priced out of the market by the law-makers (pp. 96–97).*

It is not surprising that Banfield comes to conclusions very close to Milton Friedman's:

> *Government seems to have a perverse tendency to choose measures that are the very opposite of those* [*that are needed*].

[6]G. J. Stigler, "The Unjoined Debate," *Chicago Today,* Winter 1966, p. 5. Cited by E. C. Banfield, p. 96.

> *The reasons for this perversity may be found in the nature of American political institutions and, especially, in the influence . . . of the upper-class cultural ideal of "service" and "responsibility to the community" (p. 239).*

It is not that nothing can be done. The problem, according to Banfield, is that the things that need doing will not be acceptable to the American public, and the policies that might be acceptable will not achieve their goals. If our very institutions and the upper-class attitudes that shape them are sustaining the black malaise, it is not surprising that Banfield should conclude on a note of pessimism: "It is impossible to avoid the conclusion that the serious problems of the cities will continue to exist" for a fairly long time (p. 255).

The only major factor, Banfield suggests, that might change this otherwise dismal prospect is the *accidental*, that is, unplanned or spontaneous, force of economic growth. Thus, like Friedman, faith in the invisible hand of the market marks the positive contribution of those who make up the intellectual vanguard of the conservative establishment.

The Welfare-Liberal View

The views of the welfare-liberals—which are the views of the governing establishment—are difficult to organize into a coherent pattern. The main reason for this difficulty is that welfare-liberal policies, taken as a whole, are derived from roots that are more varied than those shaping the conservative establishment. Whereas the conservative establishment's views are related to a "pure" laissez-faire tradition with axiomatic biases against state intervention, the welfare-liberal policies are tied to three traditions: "pure" laissez-faire, state interventionism that is not unduly competitive with the private sector, and state interventionism as a last resort, that is, when the private sector has failed and is unable to cope with chronic failures of the system.[7] For the most part, welfare-liberal policies legitimize

---

[7]It should be pointed out that use of the government as the agency of last resort is really a variation of the noncompetitive interventionist tradition, since the government rarely organizes and accomplishes anything in the system that would serve as a "demonstration" of what a "purely" nonprofit styled solution would accomplish. Therefore, the last resort efforts that are undertaken are not competitive or threatening to the private sector, nor are they threatening to the ideologies which justify private "solutions" to black problems.

state interventionism by means and forms that are compatible with the functioning of the private sector. Even when they are in the nature of reforms, these policies operate on the assumption that state intervention is supportive of private enterprise. Government and business are seen as potential, if not always *de facto*, partners. The important fact to be understood in examining all welfare-liberal policies is that the policies (both means and ends) are limited by the boundaries established by the distribution of power and interests. These, however, emanate from the private sector. The welfare-liberal establishment cannot pursue policies for the solution of black problems that are too unsettling to the private sector, shake the private sector's investment confidence, or make it unwilling to cooperate with the government. Any tendency in these directions would lessen the capacity of the welfare establishment to govern and maintain its power. In essence, the private sector softens the welfare-liberal's commitment to any scheme that tends to prove incompatible with or threatening to private business interests.

Most black improvement schemes which originate in the welfare-liberal establishment center around jobs and employment opportunities. They are, therefore, aimed not at the whole black population, but at those lower-income portions of it whose members are unemployed, underemployed, or earning insufficient incomes. Moreover, welfare-liberal schemes tend to concern themselves with equality in *opportunity* rather than equality in *outcome*. The reasons for differentiating these two equalities need elaboration if we are to search out and understand the different kinds of welfare-liberal policies and their limitations.

Equal Opportunity versus Equal Outcome

Should *outcomes* be equal or should *opportunities* to achieve unequal outcomes be equal? American society is strongly predisposed in principle to the opportunity process. A schematic analysis of how black-white income differences are related to outcomes and opportunities will suffice to illustrate our point (see Figure 13.1).[8]

An analysis of income differences is an analysis of the factors or variables that "cause" such differences. Black-white income differences

[8]The distinction being made and its organizational scheme were developed by Stephen Michelson, "On Income Differentials by Race: An Analysis and a Suggestion," *Conference Papers of the Union for Radical Political Economics*, December 1968, pp. 86–88.

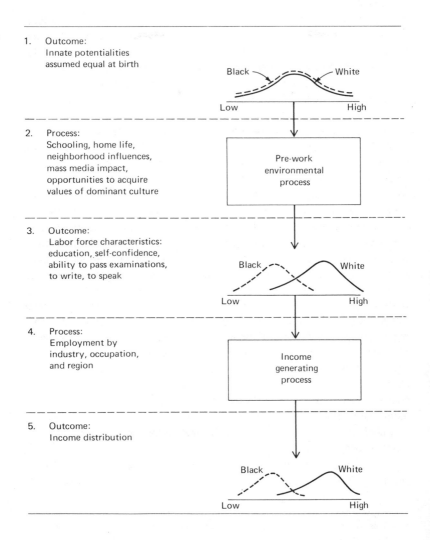

1. Outcome:
   Innate potentialities
   assumed equal at birth

   Black — White
   Low   High

2. Process:
   Schooling, home life,
   neighborhood influences,
   mass media impact,
   opportunities to acquire
   values of dominant culture

   Pre-work
   environmental
   process

3. Outcome:
   Labor force characteristics:
   education, self-confidence,
   ability to pass examinations,
   to write, to speak

   Black   White
   Low   High

4. Process:
   Employment by
   industry, occupation,
   and region

   Income
   generating
   process

5. Outcome:
   Income distribution

   Black   White
   Low   High

FIGURE 13.1   Schematic Outline of the Relationship between Equality
of Opportunity and Equality of Outcome.

are the result of previous outcomes and processes which take place over the life-cycle and within a specified institutional context. More specifically, we can identify in sequence a number of intermediate processes and outcomes which lead to this "final" black-white income difference (Figure 13.1, 5). The first outcome is at birth. Individuals, black and white, are born with a range of potential abilities. Let us assume that the range of potential abilities is normally distributed for both races (Figure 13.1, 1). This initial distribution of "innate" potentialities is injected into a processing box which consists of schooling, home life, neighborhood influences, mass media impact, and opportunities to assimilate the dominant cultural values of the society (Figure 13.1, 2). This first processing machine produces an outcome which, for our purposes, we call labor-force characteristics (Figure 13.1, 3). These characteristics are education, self-confidence, ability to pass examinations, to speak well, to write, to acquire favorable recommendations from prestigious persons, and so on. If potential abilities at birth were equally distributed, and the first processing machine treated both races randomly, the labor-market characteristics for the two races would be identical. The labor-force characteristics are now injected into an income-generating process (Figure 13.1, 4). This machine consists of various industries and all kinds of occupations. The income-generating machine recruits people with various labor-force characteristics and rewards and promotes them differentially in terms of the relative value placed on the characteristics. The reward is income—the "final" outcome over the life cycle (Figure 13.1, 5).[9] If the income-generating machine absorbed people randomly with respect to race because it did not consider race a labor-force characteristic, then black-white incomes would approach equality. As we have argued and demonstrated in previous chapters, race *is* an important negative factor at every stage in the life-cycle; therefore, black-white incomes are not equal.

   In principle, it is possible to formulate policies that ignore the processes that generate the characteristics and concentrate solely on the results

[9]It may well be that innate potentialities at birth are affected by the relative level of incomes insofar as incomes affect health, prenatal medical care of mothers, sanitary conditions of early infant environment, and so on. The relatively lower level of black income may therefore be generationally reinforcing. This implies the need to bring about income equality for several generations. H. G. Birch and J. D. Gussow, *Disadvantaged Children: Health, Nutrition and School Failures.* New York: Harcourt, Brace and Jovanovich, 1970.

or outcomes by working out preferential employment and promotion schemes or by income redistribution schemes. The late Whitney Young, Jr. of the Urban League, for example, was a strong advocate of preferential hiring. This is like supplementing the black population's labor-force characteristics to compensate for unequal "processing." Efforts to supplement black income in order to narrow black-white differences—such as food stamps and rent subsidies—are more common than preferential-hiring policies.

In a predominantly private enterprise economy like our own, work discipline and motivation are assumed to be maintained and stimulated by income differences, and therefore, the radical alteration of these differences in the direction of equality is greatly limited. It is feared that any significant redistribution would break up the organizational capacity of the market to allocate people between industries and among various kinds of work. Supplemental-income schemes, whatever their form, can purchase at best social peace among those who receive the supplements; they cannot achieve social and economic equality.[10]

Put more positively, American capitalism, in theory, believes in the equality of opportunity but not in the equality of outcome. Every man, including black men, should have an equal chance to make it; but the system cannot guarantee that everyone should "make it" equally. Inequality of outcome is viewed as positive and necessary if resource allocation is to be efficient and work efforts are to be at their maximum. In principle, government intervention is viewed as legitimate when it is concerned with equality in opportunity; this type of intervention falls within the established ideological goals of the system. It is equivalent to the government's legal antitrust stand aimed at maintaining the conditions of competition.

With the arrival of the welfare-liberal state, a more formal commitment to the prevention of an increase in inequality has developed. In principle, fiscal measures like the progressive income tax are designed to bring about modest changes in the direction of income equality. In practice, they work, at best, to prevent inequality from increasing; at worst, they foster inequality of income. Herein lies one of the main differences, albeit very narrow, between the conservative establishment and the welfare-

[10]One reason why supplemental-income schemes are currently losing favor among members of the welfare-liberal establishment is that they are not doing well as social sedatives of the black under-class. The price for social peace may be rising too fast even for some welfare liberals.

liberal governing establishment: The former is not interested in tampering with the unequal outcomes; the latter seeks interventionist measures to prevent them from increasing. It is not an important difference, and therefore permits welfare-liberals and conservativesto coexist in comfort and rely on each other's talents when necessary. The conservative is a constant reminder to the welfare-liberal that the market is more important than the welfare-liberal assumes; the welfare-liberal is a reminder to the conservative that the market might not function as perfectly and equitably as the conservative assumes. Mainstream economists have fought major policy battles around these narrow differences. Welfare-liberals and conservatives do not always argue along the same theoretical lines, but they belong to the same political clubs and pursue similar policies as a matter of practice.

Aggregate versus Structural Schools

Welfare-liberal economic policies are derived from two positions which delineate a quasi-split in the welfare-liberal camp. For lack of better categories, we divide the two welfare-liberal camps into the aggregate school and the structural school. The aggregate school places a great deal of emphasis on interventionist policies aimed at ahcieving full employment. A very tight labor market is seen as a necessary prerequisite for equal job opportunities for blacks. The emphasis is primarily economic, focusing on jobs and the development of equal chances to acquire jobs. The essential prerequisite for job opportunities in a tight labor market is associated with the maintenance of a high level of aggregate demand. If there are enough unfilled positions for a long period, employers will eventually be induced to employ, train, and open opportunities to blacks in areas where they have been excluded. It is costly to allow jobs to go begging. Also, tight labor markets lessen the competitive struggle for jobs between black and white workers and, therefore, dull the edge of working-class racism. If antidiscrimination pressure is added to this market pressure, businessmen will be further induced to bring blacks into America's mainstream. All this is assumed to be possible without any anticipated changes in the basic characteristics of the American system as it presently exists. A succinct summary of this position was articulated by James Tobin, a prominent Yale economist who served on the Council of Economic Advisors under John F. Kennedy:

> *I start from the presumption that the integration of Negroes into the American society and economy can be accomplished within existing political and economic institutions. . . . I see nothing incompatible between our peculiar mixture of private enterprise and government, on the one hand, and the liberation and integration of the Negro, on the other. . . . National prosperity and economic growth are* [the main] *engines for improving the economic status of Negroes. . . . The most important dimension of the overall economic climate is the tightness of the labor market. In a tight labor market unemployment is low and short in duration, and job vacancies are plentiful. People who stand at the end of the hiring line and the top of the layoff list have the most to gain from a tight labor market.*[11]

At another point Tobin expounds further:

> *In a slack labor market, employers can pick and choose, both in recruiting and in promoting. They exaggerate the skill, education, and experience requirements of their jobs. They use diplomas, or color, or personal histories as convenient screening devices. In a tight market, they are forced to be realistic, to tailor job specifications to the available supply, and to give on-the-job training.*[12]

Tobin realizes, of course, that the kind of labor market that he envisions as necessary for accelerating black employment opportunities is not a common experience for the U.S. economy. He admits that our main periods of full employment have taken place during war time. Having said this, he proceeds to argue that it is not the *kind* of spending that matters but the *amount*. What the government spends for war to reduce

[11]J. Tobin, "On Improving the Economic Status of the Negro," *Daedalus,* Fall, 1965. Reprinted in L. A. Ferman, J. L. Kornbluh, and J. A. Miller (eds.), *Negroes and Jobs.* Ann Arbor: University of Michigan Press, 1968, pp. 550, 551, 552.

[12]J. Tobin, "On Improving the Economic Status of the Negro," in T. C. Parsons and K. Clark (eds.), *The Negro American.* Boston: The Beacon Press, 1967. Cited by W. Tabb, *Political Economy of the Ghetto.* New York: W. W. Norton & Co., 1970, p. 111. See also article by H. P. Minsky, "The Role of Employment Policy," in M. S. Gordon (ed.), *Poverty in America.* San Francisco: Chandler Publishing Co., 1965, pp. 175–200.

unemployment and create jobs, it can spend for nonmilitary goods to accomplish the same ends. Although "there may be more political constraints and ideological inhibitions in peacetime . . . the same techniques of economic policy are available if we want badly enough to use them. The . . . main reasons we do not take this relatively simple way out are [due to] inflation and balance of payment deficits."[13] This leads Tobin to discuss America's preoccupation with the two global policy questions which prevent the country from coping with the problems faced by the black population. Tobin concludes here somewhat more pessimistically than he began:

> This has been an excursion into general economic policy. But the connection between gold and the plight of the Negro is no less real for creeping inflation and for protecting our gold stock and "the dollar." But it will not be easy to alter these national priorities. The interests of the unemployed, the poor, and the Negroes are under-represented in the comfortable consensus which supports and confines current policy.

The second standard welfare-liberal solution centering around job opportunities for blacks is derived from a structural analysis of the economy. Changes in the composition of demand, associated with technological changes, have altered the manpower requirements of the economy from a need for a less skilled, less educated labor-force to a need for a more skilled, and more educated labor-force. But the supply of workers with the right skill-education characteristics has lagged behind the relatively recent changes in the composition of the demand for labor. This view was articulated with considerable force by Charles Killingsworth before a Senate Subcommittee in 1963. Killingsworth summarizes his view from the unemployment data examined, as follows:

> The fundamental effect of automation on the labor market is to "twist" the pattern of demand—that is, it pushes down the demand for workers with little training while pushing up the demand for workers with large amounts of training. The shift from goods to services is a second major factor which twists the labor market in the same way. There are some low-skilled, blue collar jobs

*in service-producing industries; but the most rapidly growing
parts of the service sector are health care and education, both
of which require a heavy preponderance of highly trained people. . . . These changing patterns of demand would not create
labor market imbalance, however, unless changes in the supply
of labor lagged behind.*[14]

Since blacks are over-represented in the lower-skilled, less educated categories, more blacks have become superfluous to the whole
economy. Black unemployment rates are not only two to three times
greater than white rates in the lower-skilled occupations, but numerous
blacks, despairing at not finding a job, have dropped out of the labor
force. This has led to the creation of a permanent black lumpen-
proletariat. Thus, even when aggregate demand increases and thereby
tightens the labor market, a condition viewed as a prerequisite to the
generation of black employment opportunities, black unemployment is
not affected as might be expected. This was evidenced by the growing
tendency for black unemployment rates to remain increasingly unaffected
as the economy recovered from the trough periods of its major business
recessions in the postwar period. For example, in the business recessions
from 1953 to 1961, black male unemployment rates did not decrease
in the recovery part of the recession. For white males, recovery meant
a decrease in unemployment rates.[15] Black unemployment rates, in other
words, unlike those for whites, had become increasingly less responsive
to upward changes in business activity over the whole period. These
kinds of data are consistent with the structuralist view of the economy.

Given the evidence for the structuralist view, segments of the
welfare-liberal establishment turned their focus to the individual characteristics of the black labor force. Black workers do not have the "right"
skills, they are not in the "right" location to acquire jobs, and they do
not have the "right" information to acquire jobs that might, in fact, be
available. While the welfare-liberal's analysis, unlike the conservative
one, recognizes that some aspects of black problems are related to institutions, their interventionist solutions are not aimed at changing the institu-

[14]C. Killingsworth, "Hearings before Subcommittee on Employment and Manpower." U.S.
Senate, 88th Congress, 1st Session, September 20, 1963, Part 5, pp. 1475–1479.

[15]E. J. Burtt, Jr., *Labor Markets, Unions, and Government Policies.* New York: St. Martin's
Press, 1963, p. 390.

tions (as James Tobin clearly indicated), but at using government power to reshape the black labor force to fit the existing institutions. There are three welfare-liberal solutions to the structural definition of black problems: information, retraining, and reallocation.

Information

The information gap suffered by blacks has led to outreach programs to find hard-to-employ blacks who are not accessible by normal means such as newspaper advertisements and standard employment agencies. Employers must go to black churches, street corners, and organizations, and they must advertise in black newspapers in order to reach those blacks who have dropped out of the labor force. A similar effort must be made to get job information to those blacks who are underemployed. This effort to bring information to underemployed workers will improve the allocation of black labor among industries and occupations.

Retraining

Blacks lack specific skills as well as general education. Subsidies must be provided to black employees and trainees while they are in retraining programs. Since the drop-out rate in such programs has been high, numerous studies have been made to assess the programs' effectiveness. Most manpower experts agree that on-the-job training in a congenial, sympathetic and well-structured context is best. Training without the assurance of a job is undesirable. Of course, higher subsidies are preferred to lower ones.

Reallocation

The growing distance between the location of new jobs and the place of residence of unemployed blacks has led to efforts (not too successful) to devise low-cost transportation to the new jobs, or to push for the construction of low-cost housing in the suburban areas where the job market is allegedly tighter.

Since the aggregate tight-labor market view, expounded by Tobin, and the structuralist thesis, articulated by Killingsworth, are not mutually exclusive, policies derived from both could be pursued simultaneously.

The beginnings of this occurred in the Kennedy years and were further developed in the Johnson years.

As we have indicated in Chapter 7, the sluggishness in the economy's growth observed in the latter part of the fifties required an increase in overall aggregate demand, and the particular pattern of structural unemployment required more specific retraining of workers to meet the structural changes in the market. Kennedy sought to meet the problems associated with these two welfare-liberal economic interpretations by proposing a tax-cut without decreasing the level of government spending, and by devising various kinds of retraining acts to meet the implications of the structuralist school.[16]

The recommended tax cut and the implementation of the retraining acts became a reality in the Johnson years. They represented the best of the state interventionist policies characteristic of welfare-liberal efforts to solve the nation's economic problems in relation to black ones. One leftist welfare-liberal offshoot to these policies was the Community Participation Act. The act was designed to create a program:

> *which mobilized and utilized resources, public and private . . . in an attack on poverty; which provided services, assistance and other activities . . . to give promise of progress toward elimination of poverty or a cause or causes of poverty through developing employment opportunities, improving human performance, motivation, and productivity, or bettering the conditions under which people live, learn, and work; which is developed, continued, and administered with the maximum feasible participation of residents of the areas and members of the groups served; which is conducted, administered, or coordinated by a public or private nonprofit agency. . . .*[17]

An act that called for the participation of the black poor implied, however indirectly, that changing institutions, not only changing the

---

[16]Economic Opportunity Act of 1964; Manpower, Development and Training Act; Area Development Act, and Vocational Training Act of 1963.

[17]Section 202A, Title II, Economic Opportunity Act of 1964.

characteristics of poor blacks, had to be part of the solution. The concept of local planning boards involving maximum feasible participation of blacks in their own poverty-ridden communities represented the limit beyond which welfare-liberal reforms would not extend. It was not long before black participation was greeted with backlash reactions from segments of the white population. Once the dust from the summer riots of 1966 and 1967 had settled, it became increasingly clear that a "maximum feasible misunderstanding" had developed.[18]

Businessmen, perhaps sooner than some politicians and academicians, saw the issue of local participation with instinctive clarity. They began with the time-honored assumption that the resources at hand to eliminate poverty were limited, and therefore had to be used efficiently. This, of course, meant that local participation might not be too efficient if the "people" deliberated about where and how to allocate resources. The argument against local participation was developed with unmistakable clarity at a National Industrial Conference Board gathering of "concerned" businessmen. They addressed themselves to the whole range of problems faced by the hard-core unemployed. Following a number of negative comments on job creation *via* business location in ghetto areas, and after the suggestion that "business involvement in the ghettos [should be] a one-time, short-term, effort," one panel chairman addressed himself to the matter of local participation:

> *How valid is the argument that local participation in planning and organization of business employment programs for ghetto residents is essential to their success? We believe that the need for local participation by ghetto residents in business plans and decisions associated with providing them jobs is much overrated. While there is some "confidence" factor in this approach, the fact remains that the hard core unemployed are the least qualified to understand, manage, or judge programs to help them. If employment opportunities are accessible and sufficiently attractive financially, . . . and this can be brought to the attention of the resident, those able and willing to work will do so. Those not willing to work won't work whether or not they are invited*

[18]D. P. Moynihan, *Maximum Feasible Misunderstanding: Community Action in the War on Poverty.* Glencoe, Ill.: The Free Press, 1970.

to participate in planning and management of the program. Organized ghetto groups demanding involvement are doing so less to help find employment for their constituents than to enhance their own local power and prestige and, as such, are more a hindrance than a help in efforts to develop job opportunities.[19]

The "pushing" of reform from above by encouraging it from below reached its limitations in the form of severe contradictions. A government that represents the existing distribution of political power cannot finance the creation of alternative centers of power, at least not on any important scale. Moreover, the new "participants" representing the black poor often possessed class characteristics that differed greatly from those that local government officials were accustomed to confronting. In addition, corruption, inefficiency, nepotism, internecine fights among the organized fragments in the black community itself, and confrontation politics over meagre resources all converged to discredit local participation. These problems stimulated an active hostility to the concept of black poor participation itself among some of the same welfare-liberals who originally supported the idea.

As disillusionment with the participation of the black poor accelerated among those at the top, and as the "experiment" by the welfare-liberal governing establishment proved more problematic than the society was willing to accept, a new chord was struck among welfare-liberals. This culminated in the benign neglect statement of Daniel Patrick Moynihan. Moreover, the benign neglect theme emerged (almost as if the system were ideologically preparing itself for the implication of failure) in a macroeconomic context in which many establishment economists were beginning to realize that the economy could not achieve full employment without excessive inflation. Since fighting inflation loomed higher on the priority list than fighting black unemployment, government opted for fighting inflation by creating unemployment.[20] The effort to cope with inflation involved the creation of an unemployment rate (6 to 8 percent) which was not conducive to bringing black workers into the industrial mainstream. The ideological

[19]Basic Education and Industrial Employment of Hard Core Unemployed," *Proceedings,* National Industrial Conference Board, June 1968.

[20]The reason most commonly offered for U.S. preoccupation with inflation is our concern with the deterioration of our position in foreign markets.

disillusionment with the Kennedy-Johnson welfare-liberal solution to black problems and the inability of the American economy to provide a sustained tight labor market go to the root of the quandary that characterizes the white society's benign neglect reaction to black protests.

Moynihan's February 1970 memorandum to President Nixon on the status of Negroes is relevant not because he occupied a position in the Department of Urban Affairs, but because it reflected a mood among the "enlightened" white middle class (a mood that has shown its face in previous historical periods). Moynihan underscored the income and occupational breakthrough that had allegedly been experienced by many blacks in the 1960s. He also injected a number of distortions into his description of various trends. For example, he exaggerated the progress blacks have made in the sphere of education, the increase in the number of female-headed black families and welfare recipients, the rising incidence of black criminal and quasi-criminal pathology, and the general development of social alienation among lower-class and prospering middle-class blacks. Moynihan finally raised the question of what should be done. He acknowledged the possibility of "perhaps nothing" and then went on to outline his thesis:

> The time may have come when the issue of race could benefit from a period of benign neglect. The subject has been too much talked about. The forum has been too much taken over to hysterics, paranoids, and boodlers. . . . We may need a period . . . [in which] extremists are [denied] opportunities for martyrdom, heroics, histrionics or whatever. . . . A tendency to ignore provocations from groups such as the Black Panthers might also be useful. [It should be remembered that] there is a silent black majority as well as a white one. It is mostly working class, as against lower middle class. It is politically moderate . . . and shares most of the concerns of its white counterpart. This group has been generally ignored by government and the media. The more recognition we can give to it the better off we shall be. (I would take it, for example, that Ambassador Jerome H. Holland is a natural leader of this segment of the black community. There are others like him.) [21]

[21]D. P. Moynihan, "Memo to. Nixon on the Status of Negroes, January 16, 1970," *New York Times,* March 1, 1970, p. 69.

Translated into language that has appeared before as part of an "enlightened" white backlash, Moynihan's message would read as follows: We enlightened whites tried to do something *for* you, but it was met with an over-reaction that has weakened the authority structure. Now is the time to slow down "reconstruction." Our comfortable position does not require that we remain continuously involved, since we have the capacity to govern "by relationships based on power" if necessary. Moreover, we can afford to wait for a quiet respite. You must not take this position as racist, since I, Moynihan, know that the majority of blacks are not only silent but are "good niggers." In fact, I even have my own natural black leader selected for the majority of the "good" working-class "niggers." I can tell you that he is well educated and a good race symbol.

The meaning of the Moynihan message is the retrenchment of the white liberal whose feelings have been hurt by "ungrateful" blacks who have not fully "appreciated" all that the white liberal has done for him. This retrenchment is politically realistic in view of the fact that the fully employed war economy between 1965–1968 did not bring the kind of employment opportunities deemed necessary for blacks to make significant gains.

In our discussion of the aggregate school of welfare-liberal thinking, it should be recalled that its exponents forcefully argued that a secure black position in the economy could not be achieved without first achieving a sustained period of full employment. It was further argued that the only thing preventing us from achieving full employment was our preoccupation with the balance of payments and inflation. The period from 1965 to Nixon's tight money policy in 1970 displayed the kind of overheating of the economy that the aggregate school required if black progress were to occur. The overheated economy was terminated by Nixon's tight money policy in order to bring down the rate of inflation which would, at the same time, help our balance of payments deficit. For political reasons, however, Nixon had to shift to an expansionary monetary and fiscal policy prior to achieving a sufficiently significant slowdown in the economy to ward off the inflationary process. Thus, the period between 1965 and the present represents a brief "laboratory" experiment. The results do not offer much hope to the welfare-liberal's aggregate high-level employment position. It now appears that an overall unemployment rate of 3½ percent for white workers, which means about a 6 percent unemployment rate for black workers and about a 20 percent unemployment rate for black youth, is the best we can achieve *if* we could learn to live with a 5 to 7 percent rate of inflation. This rate, however, is unacceptable to government—that is, business. It has been estimated by some economists that a white unemployment rate of about 6 to 8 percent is necessary in order to contain inflation to about 2 to 3 percent. This suggests that a successful anti-inflationary effort would bring the black unemployment rate to about 12 percent and the black youth unemployment rate to about 35 percent. The combination of this degree of black and white unemployment is not conducive to creating job opportunities for blacks on any terms, equal or preferential.

Added to both the backlash mood of the benign-neglect welfare-liberals and the unresolved unemployment-inflation trade-off, one must include the growing recognition that the American majority dislikes blacks and is, for the most part, unaffected by the acuteness of the daily miseries of blacks. No politician can ignore this so long as he wishes to remain "practical" and achieve political success. The full implications of this were spelled out by Herbert J. Gans, a socially concerned, welfare-liberal, urban sociologist. Gans argues that the real nature of the urban crisis stems:

> in large part from shortcomings in American democracy, particularly the dependence on majority rule. . . . Most voters—and the politicians that represent them—are not inclined to give the cities the funds and powers to deal with poverty, or segregation. This disinclination is by no means as arbitrary as it may seem, for the plight of the urban poor, the anger of the rebellious, and the bankruptcy of the municipal treasury have not yet hurt or even seriously inconvenienced the vast majority of Americans. . . . Many Americans . . . are opposed to significant governmental activity on behalf of the poor and black. . . . Not only do they consider taxes an imposition on their ability to spend their earnings, but they view governmental expenditure as economic waste. . . . In effect, then, the cities and the poor and the blacks are politically outnumbered. This state of affairs suggests the . . . most important reason for the national failure to act: the structure of American democracy and majority rule.[22]

[22]H. Gans, "We Won't End the Urban Crisis until We End Majority Rule," *New York Times Magazine,* August 3, 1969, pp. 13–14.

Disillusionment with the welfare-liberal state has revitalized a new interest in income-maintenance schemes, an interest held by none other than Richard M. Nixon.

In some sense, Nixon's income-maintenance reform bill represents a bridge between disheartened welfare-liberal state interventionists on the one hand, and the free market conservatives on the other. They have come together to declare a need, in the absence of alternatives, to maintain the welfare system as a permanent feature of American life. The need is now seen as a matter of principle rather than one of expedience. But since the welfare system has become almost synonomous with black laziness, inefficiency, obtrusive meddling in the individual's right to privacy, and high administrative costs, it must be streamlined into an institution that is universal with respect to whom it serves. It must be made more efficient by the elimination of the welfare bureaucracy and must force (or encourage) people (mainly blacks) to undertake menial jobs if no others are available. Thus, the welfare system is now being redesigned: The conservatives are to get a work-incentive device built into the system, and welfare-liberals are to get their guaranteed annual income, however small relative to needs.

The welfare-liberal state, whatever its capacity to stay afloat in the rough waters ahead, is basically drifting aimlessly and is bankrupt with respect to generating any viable solutions. Kenneth Clark, Negro psychologist, integrationist, and welfare-liberal activist, expressed his disillusionment with the welfare-liberal state by taking a mild turn to the right: "Business and industry are our last hope. They are the most realistic elements of our society. Other areas in our society—government, education, churches, labor—have defaulted in dealing with Negro problems."[23]

The welfare-liberal's war on black poverty and related matters has failed. It failed not because social scientists played an improper role, not because issues got intertwined with party politics, not because insufficient money was devoted to programs—even though each of these was operative. The welfare-liberal state has failed because the private market still dominates the society to which the welfare-liberal state is wedded. Our basic social and political institutions are, as we have already argued on a different level, at the mercy of profit-driven capitalists, and therefore the welfare-liberal government:

[23]K. Clark, "Business—The Last Hope," *The Bell System and the City,* 1968, **1** (4), p. 6.

> can at times influence and rechannel economic forces, but only
> marginally and only within the limits defined by the dominant
> business culture. The basic power to initiate economic activity—its
> volume, rate, direction and composition—rests solidly in private
> hands, in fact in fewer hands all the time as manufacturing, trans-
> port, banking and finance become more concentrated. [The wel-
> fare state] can do little but react to the use or misuse of such
> private power after the key decisions have been made in areas
> of technology, investment, labor skill requirements, industrial
> location, prices, foreign trade and investments.[24]

The evolving high-level stagnation of the American economy with
its accompanying features—unemployment problems, the paradox of public squalor and private affluence, the counterrevolutionary stance toward
Third World nations, the vast employment of resources to develop an
overkill war capacity—has come to the forefront after the private calculus
has done its work, and after the "fury of private interests" has staked
out its claim on the nation's wealth and resources. Therein lie the basic
reasons for the welfare-liberal's failure to generate any solutions to black
problems that are worthy of the common meaning imputed to the term
"welfare."

[24]R. B. DuBuff, "Western Economic Development: A Radical Synthesis," unpublished man-
uscript, 1971, pp. 10–11. Emphasis original.

14

The Political Economy of Reconstruction

In the area of "What Is To Be Done?" to achieve the basic structural changes in society that will lead to black-white equality, there is no monopoly on truth. Our aim in this chapter is to present and discuss the political tactics and strategies that are capable of fundamentally redirecting the present drift of American society.

Our approach is not programmatic. We are not concerned with devising a shopping list of things that the black community needs. We are also not concerned with devising new tax schemes to finance ghetto projects; nor are we interested in examining the costs and benefits of proposals aimed at "helping" the black community in this or that endeavor. In our opinion, there is already a surplus of programs and studies. What is needed is the political and social determination to implement any one of several comprehensive programs that already exist in blueprint form. That is to say, we need new social and political energies to direct resources away from their existing uses (for example, the military-industrial sector, or superhighways), as well as to prevent new increases in productive capacity from being wasted on trivia. We need the determination to modify some institutions and replace others. We need to develop a commitment to the goal of redistribution of income and wealth, since the black population's deprivation and alienation are primarily relative in nature.

It is evident that the kind of changes that we consider necessary will meet resistance from many sources in American society. While efforts to achieve change need to be waged on many levels, the political struggle is the most crucial to the black community. It is not without reason, therefore, that there is a growing awareness that the black population's ability to acquire the economic resources needed to forge large-scale programs depends heavily on the acquisition of political power. In the words of Robert Browne, in a speech delivered at the 1969 National Black Economic Development Conference:

> [A]ny significant economic development we achieve will come about largely through political maneuvering, and we must therefore be very together and know exactly what we are doing. . . . Black economic development is not economic at all, but political. There is no question of "pulling ourselves up by our bootstraps." We have no bootstraps. We are starting with so few economic resources of our own that our tactic must be to utilize cleverly what strength we do have, namely, the political force of 25 million potentially united black minds, for extracting some economic resources from those who do have them.[1]

Beyond this general formulation of the need for black political power, black consensus as to the political tactics, strategies and forms to be adopted are practically nil. Programmatic rhetoric is saturated with words and ideas that are not carefully linked to sound tactics and strategies. It is not uncommon to find revolutionary tactics aimed at achieving goals that are relatively modest and well established as legitimate by the larger society. There are moderate, political establishment-oriented men like the late Whitney Young, Jr. who, after the 1966 and 1967 riots, remarked quite often that "we are all revolutionaries now." This merely reflected

---

[1]R. Browne, "Toward an Overall Assessment of Our Alternatives," *The Review of Black Political Economy,* 1970, (1), pp. 24–25.

a rhetorical shift, from integrationist slogans to those more congruent with black power. On the practical level, Young acted (characteristically) in the direction of finding more jobs for blacks within the boundaries of the system. Finally, there are extreme separatist goals which are devoid of any identifiable means of achievement.

A critical cause of the gross discrepancy between black rhetoric and practice is the absence of a coherent ideology. If an ideology is to serve a revolutionary purpose capable of cultivating a sustained commitment, it must incorporate a vision beyond the existing societal structure, and simultaneously be able to interpret the negative and alienating experiences of the moment. The ideology must be buttressed by tactics and strategies embedded in the American experience, and it must be capable of enlarging the capacity for collective action within the vacillating currents of American society. The cultivation of an ideology must be grounded in the realities of American society in general, and in the nature of the black experience and predicament specifically. Thus, an analysis of the political economy of reconstruction must begin with a number of realistic assumptions and observations which, if not considered, will inevitably lead to the failure of any projected salvation scheme.

Underlying Realities

We begin with the observation that the black ghetto is a *permanent* cluster which is not going to be readily dispersed by piecemeal open housing programs or by a black exodus into the suburbs.

Second, the black population, in our view, is caught in a serious dilemma. It is seen as too large to be integrated into the American mainstream because that would involve unacceptable costs to the dominant white majority, and too small to achieve power by its own effort. The main political implication of this predicament is that both integrationist and separatist tactics and strategies are incapable of achieving their respective goals. In this sense, both orientations are utopian, since neither adequately deals with the problem of cultivating collective means to realize their social ends.

Third, the over-representation of blacks in the lower and lumpen-proletariat classes is intimately associated with race. The ghettos, there-fore, are concentrations of people marked both by their color and by their lower-class position. The middle layers of white America cannot readily dissociate these two phenomena, and therefore they strenuously resist the entry of middle-class blacks or working-class blacks into "their" communities, "their" schools, and "their" places of work. The Great White Fear is that middle-class blacks (who are "good types") will be followed by lower-class blacks (who are "bad types"). The possibility of racial integration with blacks of comparable class positions easily degenerates into race exclusion, even when there are no class differences. Race, therefore, becomes an independent force in the determination of the black man's status. "Pure" racism is probably experienced more acutely by middle-class than by lower-class blacks. While the inferior status of the whole black population is determined by race factors, class factors, and their interaction, race alone, because of the perennial existence of a large black lower class, has proved to be virtually ineradicable from the American mind. The factor of race puts all blacks into an inferior status group, even those blacks whose education and income are equal or superior to some segments of the white population's. This is why blacks who "make it" retain a preoccupation with race; their new class position in the larger American society is no guarantee that they can enter that society.[2] Since race tends to be an independent determinant of black status, class interests and struggles alone are insufficient for the development of a salvation scheme for blacks. That is to say, it is not enough to view the black problem as a low-income problem. The varied nationalist groups (as we have shown in Chapter 8) are in many respects confused and inconsistent, but in one major sense they are right: the race emphasis, though overworked, must be added to the class emphasis simply because whites differentiate on the basis of color as well as class.

Fourth, in a capitalist society, discrimination against blacks takes place under the banner of freedom to choose. The freedom of choice for a white consumer means the freedom to avoid living next door to blacks. Freedom to organize an association around your job or trade means freedom to dissociate from blacks by keeping them out of your trade or industry or keeping them from competing with you within your

[2]In one sense, the black middle-class leadership is split with respect to the importance of race versus class. Black integrationists are saying to whites: think of me in terms of my class position and ignore my color. The black race advocates, in contrast, argue that whites will not let blacks into their world on the basis of class, and therefore blacks should get together on the basis of race. All blacks, whatever their class, are first persons of color before they are designated by their class characteristics (for example, income or education).

trade or industry. The employer's freedom to combine labor and capital in production means freedom not to hire or promote black labor in relation to white labor, or freedom to avoid the social costs of technological unemployment, or costs connected with the movement of a plant from the central city.

To the black man, these white market freedoms and the privacy of wealth have meant the negation of his own freedom—if not to exist, at least to live. Thus, salvation to the Negro, employed or unemployed, has too often existed outside the private market, either in the form of secure but low-paying civil service jobs or in the form of dependence on doles from the government in the welfare state.

Hence, it requires no great powers of reason to understand why the Negro is not a natural ally of the capitalist system. This is not to say that capitalism cannot *logically* incorporate him into the market system. But it is not a question of logic alone. Given the values of the decision makers in the market, the objectives of the dominant whites are in fact realized by their freedom to exclude blacks from jobs, industries, neighborhoods, and from integrated educational opportunities. The black militant's castigation in racial terms of the white power structure in general, rather than in some specific Marxist or socialist terms like "the ruling class" or "vested interest groups," is not a vagary obscuring reality. Nor is it a sign, as some white liberals and black moderates have maintained, of racism in reverse. The simple truth is that many white discriminatory interests tend to coalesce in the market.

Because the Negro's fate now is basically at the mercy of the private sector, in which persons whose freedom to discriminate in the use of their wealth and income is viewed by them as an inalienable market right, the Negro can hardly expect the spontaneous forces of the market to function on his behalf. But once the solution to the black condition is viewed as existing outside the market, it is automatically seen to fall inside the domain of political action. Because of the particular looseness that prevails between our political institutions and our economic ones, white political responses to black pressures tend to take the form of an appeal to the merciful "instincts" of private decision makers to be fair-minded against, perhaps, their own interests. This means that the realistic enforcement of antidiscriminatory decrees and the development of serious programs, even under the dubious assumption of good intentions on the part of welfare state administrators and politicians, are extremely difficult if not impossible.

Fifth, the migration pattern between regions and within metropolitan areas is leading to concentrations of blacks in our major central cities. As blacks become numerical majorities in the central cities in the decade ahead, they will naturally seek, and probably acquire, control of the central city governments. The more speculative implications of this process will be examined later. One outcome of black political control of central cities that is less speculative is the likelihood that the many more persons supplying services for city governments (such as education, social work, sanitation, fire and police protection) will be black as whites continue to depart from the central cities, and as those whites who presently supply city services are replaced by blacks because of retirement or voluntary changes in job location.[3]

Sixth, accompanying the exodus of whites from the central cities is the exodus of wealth, which has meant the deterioration of the central city's social capital, as well as a decline in its spirit of enterprise. Schools, streets, transit systems, water supply sources, sewage, and terminals are overworked or not properly maintaned to meet the kinds of demands placed on them. The correction of this relative deterioration by raising local revenues is unlikely, since the central city's tax base is shrinking rapidly relative to needed expenditures. What blacks, therefore, are inheriting is the management of local governments that are on the verge of bankruptcy. The process is not new in the history of the black populations' relative deprivation; the poor tend to inherit poverty. Just as blacks have often attained entry into industries as they were declining (too little, too late), they now appear to be in sight of political control of a level of government that is on its last legs.

Seventh, the national economy is going through one of its slow growth phases again (the last major one was from 1955–1961) in the context of corporate-administered prices that have been rising simultaneously with growing unemployment (white collar as well as blue collar). The soft labor market has not only sharply undercut, for all practical purposes, those short-lived efforts on the part of corporate businesses to recruit hard-to-employ blacks, but it has also invoked a squeeze on all levels of government employment—the one area in which blacks have made some inroads. It is evident at this juncture that the welfare state

[3]We do not mean to suggest that this process will be without its difficulties. As we have suggested in Chapter 12, white-dominated unions, for example, may and can act as a barrier to this process.

is far from being able to achieve the kind of tight labor market that is a necessary condition for sustained black employment gains and the struggle against discrimination within the context of a capitalist labor market.

The Radical Scenario

Our concerns in Chapters 7, 12, and 13 should be viewed as laying the groundwork for our final scenario of the political economy of reconstruction. In our view, "new politics" and new centers of political power, capable of stimulating and organizing new social energies, are the precondition to the successful implementation of any kind of large scale black program. New political forces emerge only in the context of a crisis society in which many problems converge. In the decade ahead, we expect such problems to converge in a way that will play havoc with the institutions of the welfare state, which are increasingly taking on the appearance of organized chaos.

Welfare-Liberalism

The welfare-liberal's rhetoric about integration and his efforts to develop job-training programs to help black males find employment have both fallen by the wayside. Integration is not a sensible preoccupation when it is divorced from other kinds of supporting policies. The achievement of meaningful integration through the enforcement of antidiscriminatory laws cannot take place at a sufficiently rapid rate for two reasons: (1) the existence of latent and manifest racism which is nurtured by the forces that maintain the permanent ghetto, and (2) the tenuous relationship between the private decision makers, who exclude blacks, and the public policy makers in charge of enforcing the antidiscrimination laws; this dichotomy makes enforcement procedures cumbersome and piecemeal.

The success of job-training programs, especially for the hard-to-employ black male workers, requires the kind of tight labor market conditions that the welfare state has been unable to achieve for any sustained period. Periodic unemployment rates in the range of 5 to 7 percent for white workers act as a strong conservatizing force on the issues concerned with special programs devoted to employing and promoting blacks. White unemployment abets rather than discourages racist behavior.

One could identify additional dilemmas facing welfare-liberals, for example, urging middle-class blacks out of the ghetto into integrated or white neighborhoods and simultaneously exhorting black ghetto residents to follow "responsible" middle-class ghetto leadership; or, the sponsoring of ghetto projects that implicitly assume the permanence of the ghetto, coupled with the pursuit of integrationist policies aimed at dispersing the ghetto. Since these dilemmas have come to a head and cannot be readily resolved within the welfare-liberal framework, the welfare state appears to have grown into an impotent giant.

Welfare-liberal institutions have developed into a structure which is neither pluralistic nor completely monopolistic and in which neither effective competition for power nor complete collusion exist. These institutions, moreover, are part of a larger terrain of unsettled regional, intergovernmental, and interdepartmental contradictions—all of which are related to the race question that is seething under the political roofs of entangled municipal bureaucracies. As a result, the welfare state finds itself with leaders whose vision—if it ever existed—has outlived its usefulness.

Democratic Party

More concretely, the *strategic* deformity of welfare-liberalism is traceable to the incomplete transformation of the Democratic Party (the welfare state's main architect) in the 1930s. This was due to the fact that the New Deal, in the words of Harvey Wheeler, undertook:

> the minimum amount of innovation which could keep the American social system intact under the crisis conditions. . . . Although the New Deal never resolved the depression crisis, it none-the-less did hold the American social system together in the sense implied by the term conservative.[4]

Paradoxically, the New Deal saved capitalism because it failed. Were it to have succeeded, the New Deal would have had to alter the system

[4]H. Wheeler. Cited by C. McWilliams, "Time for a New Politics," *The Nation*, May 26, 1962.

in more fundamental ways and not merely salvage it. On the one hand, the measures that were undertaken were deficient in both quantity and quality. On the other hand, the New Deal gave unions, professionals, and intellectuals a sense of importance in the Democratic Party that made them more tolerant of the unemployment and structural weaknesses of the system. In choosing to live in the same house with a southern minority, the new welfare-liberals were eventually sterilized, especially with respect to coping with the general conditions in which the black population lives.

From the point of view of the growing inability of the Democratic chieftains to hold together the Party's variegated elements, the black activists inside the Democratic Party and the black independent advocates outside it jointly operate to pull the Party in opposing directions. On the one hand, there is a pull in the direction of token reformism, and on the other hand, the Party is thrust in the direction of cryptically conservative assurances about maintaining law and order to its white supporters preparing to bolt the Party. As these inconsistent tendencies gain momentum in a situation in which even the radical right is learning the art of moderate rhetoric, the Democratic apparatus may become unable to satisfy its constituencies. As this process accelerates, the Party's resolve to solve any major problem may be almost worthless. The Party may eventually disintegrate or become permanently crippled from loss of support by all parts of the loose mosaic that presently constitutes its political surface.[5]

In our view, the historical default of the Democratic Party is only beginning to reveal itself. The Party's failure may mean that the long overdue political and administrative changes needed to cope with the possible convergence of serious economic, organizational, and race tensions in the midst of a technological revolution may not be forthcoming, for lack of political volition, at the proper time or in sufficient magnitude. We believe this to be the case even if the Cold War and our over-preoccupation with policing the Third World should abate somewhat and thereby release more resources for nonmilitary uses.

[5]The strains that the Negro struggle is putting on the Democratic Party's capacity to maintain national consensus have been recognized in somewhat different terms by Samuel Lubell: "For the Democratic coalition the political danger posed by the swelling Negro vote is not that the Negroes will bolt to the Republicans, but rather that the Negro demands may drive white Democratic voters out." "The Negro and the Democratic Coalition," *Commentary,* August 1964, **38**, p. 23.

The immediate result of any cut in military spending will probably be more unemployment in an economy already experiencing creeping stagnation. But even if this were not the case, it must be noted that changing the composition of our Gross National Product and equalizing its distribution involve the matter of forging new priorities that can only be implemented and decided upon in the political arena. There is nothing automatic about this process. Moreover, it is unlikely that the Democratic Party, given its present state of impotence, will find the political determination to exploit the potential peace dividend even if it should occur. The result is the possibility of a political vacuum which may be filled by a Bismarkian right-wing coalition of conservative politicians financed and joined by the major representatives of the corporate estate.

The Black Population

From the point of view of the black population, the system's tendency to exclude blacks on the basis of race has pushed them into a state of relative isolation in a context of urban decay. This new state of affairs is fraught with considerable danger because it provides the emerging Bismarkian right-wing coalition with a sizeable social scapegoat as a rationale to justify its regressive regimentation.

When the black majority was rural, it was basically impossible for the black middle class to interlock politically with the black lower class. There were, of course, isolated cries from lonely members of the black intelligentsia, but the black middle class, however small, was isolated from the black population as a whole. The reaching upward on the part of the middle-class Negro for a higher station in life necessarily required that he look to the white establishment for political favors, patronage, approval, or economic opportunity. This was accomplished, in general, by demonstrations of "worthiness," by "proving" that he was not like the rest of his race, or by denying blackness and "appearing" white. Acquiescence was rationalized as a belief that the whole race would be helped if a small upper crust "made it" and "proved" to whites that not all blacks were "bad." It was hoped that the benefits would trickle down to the black majority in the lower class. The ensuing ridicule which E. Franklin Frazier directed at the black bourgeoisie was not without cause nor is it presently without relevance.

However, as the black middle and lower class increasingly became part of the urban matrix, as the black middle class enlarged and became more educated, as the fact of race stubbornly prevailed over the fact of class, the grosser illusions of the black middle class faded, or at least changed their complexion. Moreover, a segment has separated from the growing layer of educated middle-class blacks to adopt the traditional role of a revolutionary intelligentsia. For the Negro, revolutionary expressions have tended to manifest themselves in nationalist terms.

From the inferior status position determined by the interaction of race and class, black nationalism, in its variety of expressions, periodically emerged as an instrument of black salvation. While Theodore Draper, as we have noted in Chapter 8, appeared to take great delight in his clever ridicule of the bizarre and totally unrealistic forms that black nationalism has taken from the earliest periods of American history to the present,[6] there is one fundamental question he did not raise and could not have answered had he raised it: Why has the nationalist theme occurred and recurred, however absurdly, in the American society over the years? The answer to that question would have changed Draper's cynical arrogance to an examination of the depths of America's racist culture, and perhaps would have led him to write with more humility, or at least, more sympathy about the black man's search for a cultural homeland in the only society that he has historical memory of—the United States.

The black population, however indigenous to the American system, has no homeland. Its African heritage has been destroyed by force and ridicule. Its resurrection is impossible. It is not without reason that Harold Cruse commented wryly that it will take more than a dashiki to forge a black revolution.[7]

[6]T. Draper, "The Fantasy of Black Nationalism." *Commentary,* September 1969.

[7]In a more serious vein, Harold Cruse has argued:

"The American Negro cannot be understood culturally unless he is seen as a member of a detached ethnic of people of African descent reared for three hundred years in the unmotherly bosom of Western civilization. With regards to the African motherland, the American Negro is not an African, not even remotely. Not only have three hundred years separated him culturally from Africa; so have several thousand miles of geographical distance cut him off from any kind of real communication with Africa. As a detached offshoot of African peoples he is isolated, cut off, and has been subjected to racial intermingling in the process."

Rebellion or Revolution? New York: William Morrow & Company, 1968, pp. 49–50.

Search for Identity

The cultural destruction of the black population's preslave past, without the creation of a serious avenue of re-entry into a larger community *ideal,* has produced a culturally homeless people. This cultural vacuum is the main source of the black population's need for a *social* identity, which nationalism has periodically sought to fill. Unfortunately, black nationalism in the context of American society has no fertile soil in which to take root, and, therefore, it comes and goes; it flares and burns out. It has moments of poetic truth only to become absurd when elaborated into a real program capable of guiding political action. In the end, black nationalism appeals to a small minority. It becomes the intimate ideology of sectarians rather than the secular ideology of the masses.

What is needed is a nationalist surrogate that is rooted in the reality of the black predicament and can be struggled for within the rhythm of the general problems and crises of American society, problems and crises that affect the white population as well. It is precisely because of the need for a nationalist surrogate, as opposed to nationalism in the sense of nationhood, that the black advocates of nationalist roads to salvation seem unrelated to American realities. Black nationalism sometimes appears "foreign," and therefore appears to need a great deal of elaboration and explication before it can be understood. A nationalism that needs so much cerebration and attention is suspect; it lacks the objective conditions for sustained growth, assimilation, and fruition. This makes black nationalism different from the nationalism brewing among Third World peoples, with whom black revolutionaries frequently identify. It makes tactics, strategies and policies derived from the neocolonial paradigm inapplicable, a lesson that many nationalists have not learned. Because of the objective circumstances of life, black nationalism will either become transformed to mean the political determination of blacks to take over central-city governments, or it will become more sectarian than it is at present. The only real surrogate for nationalism that is objectively possible is the "self"-determination of communities within the framework of black politically controlled cities. But this self-determination, in city and neighborhood, must be *selective* and *limited* in nature for a fundamental reason: Central cities, and therefore black communities, can never be financially independent of the American system, whatever its nature. To foster the illusion in rhetoric that it can is a disservice to the process of achieving black economic and social equality. While there is an objective possibility of blacks achieving control of localities where they are majorities or near majorities, the national context in which this political process is occurring needs consideration.

Rightward Bound

The national economic picture is riddled with great uncertainties that have, in our view, a new dimension. The national economy, in the midst of a new international situation of intense competition from Europe, is again experiencing, as we have noted, the twin tendencies of rising prices and decreasing employment opportunities. While this process has occurred before to stimulate a preoccupation with wage-price guidelines, the context of the present revival of these twin tendencies has led to a more permanent dislodging of standard welfare state Keynesian policies. The combined monetary and fiscal tinkering processes that traditional Keynesians have used in the past are not operating well. Policies aimed at stimulating the economy may affect the unemployment rate only to add fuel to the inflationary problem. Policies aimed at modifying the latter worsen the employment picture. This contradiction came to a head in Richard Nixon's rapid evolution from a free market-oriented conservative, to his declaration that he was now a Keynesian, to his final adoption of a state-managed capitalism known in the present context as an incomes policy involving governmentally controlled wages and prices. The incomes policy was buttressed by additional policies aimed at stimulating more private investment (when 25 percent of our existing plant capacity is idle), stimulating the automobile industry (when the last thing we need in this country today is more cars and highway construction to keep them moving), and reducing government spending and employment (when the public sector is in dire need of services and resources).[8]

Juxtaposed with the domestic economic situation are the national and international noneconomic forces that were identified and discussed in Chapter 7. These forces are impinging upon the agencies of the welfare state and affect the general "climate of opinion" in which the specific black-white drama is being played out. The Cold War, if not over, has

[8]P. Sweezy and H. Magdoff, "The End of U.S. Hegemony," *Monthly Review,* 1971, **23** (5), p. 16.

certainly moved into more temperate zones. Our outreaches into the Third World are increasingly costly and incapable of ideological justification. Anticommunism no longer serves as an internally binding ideology. The Common Market is becoming better integrated, capable of competing even more effectively than it has already done. The administrative errors (military and industrial) of the whole post-World War II period are now sufficiently obvious to serve as political ammunition for critics of the system.

Each of these problems, by itself, is not of sufficient magnitude to break up today's political balance and coalitions. But as the total set of problems grows in size, as tensions accumulate to challenge a divided public and an inert political center, a predatory competitive struggle for political power at all levels may be in the making in the not too distant future. In a situation without a Left of any consequence, the amorphous welfare-liberal center may make a poor showing against an articulate political Right composed of conservative and extreme right-wing Republicans, Southern Democrats, and a loose assortment of political hacks from the "provinces" and lily-white suburbs, whose main preoccupation with the race question takes the form of keeping "their" neighborhoods and schools reserved for "their" kind. This "new" coalition will have scope as well as depth, since national positions of power will be supported by all kinds of "upstate-type" representatives who are entrenching themselves for a fight against the big metropolitan areas in which the black central cities are still critical.

The ideology of this new coalition manifests itself in an obsession with "law and order." But the "law and order" issue in the contemporary and specific context of a national government controlled by technically competent right-wingers, using the economic tools borrowed from Keynes and buttressed by more direct control of prices and wages, will mean something far different from getting people to abide by the rules of the game as these have been legislated by democratically elected representatives, evaluated by a judicious and sensitive Supreme Court, and enforced by a police force whose stance is officially defined as that of a politically neutral civil service. In the 1970s, "law and order" may well be the ideology of American fascism. Its victims may be numerous, but perhaps not large enough to swing the majority of ordinary citizens in another direction. This is not to argue that an alternative to our perceived dismal future does not exist in some abstract sense. It simply does not exist as a practical matter. Some may argue that we have overdrawn this picture of the future social surface. Perhaps we have. The real world, of course, is much sloppier, more complex, and more uncertain.

In the Long Run

While this new stage of welfare management by a conservative business-dominated Republican Party has implications of gloom that stretch far beyond the technical feasibility and desirability of wage-price controls, the long run may hold more hopeful possibilities. As the black "independent" advocates push to seek control of central city governments in our major metropolitan areas, a consequence by design (or otherwise) could be the breakup of the Democratic Party. This development is a prerequisite to the formation of a new national party (or the complete reconstruction of the Democratic Party) ultimately capable of initiating new programs and reordering our national objectives. In essence, the process envisioned is not the creation of a third party, but the development of a new second party.

The breakup or fundamental alteration of the Democratic Party will free a significant portion of the labor movement (organized and unorganized), professional classes, and other nonpropertied segments of the white population from the Party's patronage system and established routines, and especially, it will free the party from the current hold of the southern white bourbons. As the Party becomes financially bankrupt and politically stunted in dispensing political patronage at the state and local levels, many middle-range Democrats and leaders (for example, teachers, lawyers, union leaders) may be propelled to seek a "radical" departure from the Party's present state of drift. There may also be "new" constituencies ready for a more radical turn.

One probable outcome of Nixon's attempt to regulate income distribution directly by political instruments is the politicizing of organized labor and other nonpropertied and less protected groups in ways that have not occurred since the 1930s. The economic interests of large numbers of people have suddenly become unmistakably linked to conscious political decision making at the national level. In other words, the economics of collective bargaining has now been transformed into the politics of collective bargaining. As Nixon's policies run into difficulties, as we believe they will, their failure may not be totally in vain. Since the race issue and the many international problems that will be encountered are sources of profound instability, extending beyond the control efforts of an incomes policy in the present domestic context, Nixon's new regulatory direction may turn out to be the initial stimulant in the politicization and radicalization of the American labor movement. This could serve as one of the critical new forces in the development of a new national party whose primary objective would be the political overhaul of the prevailing relations between the federal, state, and city governments in general, and the infrastructure of city life and politics specifically.

Such a vast internal development program would have to involve motion in three directions: (1) making housing a public utility and putting land under public domain, (2) socializing the aggregate investment decision, so that both its level and composition are socially conceived and motivated, and (3) opposing our present imperial course which has entered a new and costly stage and is forging a reactionary alliance in domestic politics that cannot but impede a humane solution to the social domestic conflict ahead. The old reactionary alliance of southern Democrats and northern Republicans may be able to impose "order" from above, but it cannot summon the developmental resources (human and nonhuman) that are needed to eliminate the inner-city disorder in which the vast majority of blacks are forced to live. Priority for urban development not only leads to questions about how, and for what purposes, we use our national wealth, but also leads to developmental planning and the question as to who is to sit on the emergent developmental planning boards. Developmental urban planning involves viewing the ghettos as underdeveloped sectors which must undergo a total rebirth in all spheres of life in order to remove their "foreign deficit" in the form of cultural drain, brain drain, political drain, and last but not least, financial drain.

National planning, initially given its official peacetime blessing by Nixon in an increasingly inept welfare state, could be carried much further in a more radical setting. Blacks will have acquired far more political power at the local level. The black middle class will be larger and better educated (given the recent trends of black college enrollment) and will have acquired experience in the management of city governments, however bankrupt.

In a different context, national planning will involve not only the negative components of wage-price constraints, but more positively, it will involve the physical mobilization and allocation of people and resources for the fulfillment of collective needs. The early beginnings of community planning and participation and the new ideas and laws about development corporations that were part of the conception of the Office of Economic Opportunity may get a second thrust.

In this way, the political, social, and economic ideas that emerged in the mid-sixties as a result of black protest in our central cities may evolve, in a different climate of opinion, to have meaning for the whole society. Social planning is not only needed for our inner cities, but is needed to cope with the problems of urban sprawl, public transportation, pollution, overproduction of shoddily-produced goods by our corporate society, and the ugliness of the countryside. It is also needed if we are to achieve a more equal distribution of income and wealth associated with a vast expansion of publicly needed goods. These are concerns that transcend black-white relations, as well as the capacities of our corporate-dominated society.

In sum, the outcome of the black-white struggle, especially in the context of the Democratic Party's faltering welfare state, is fraught with uncertainty. The immediate future, as our analysis has suggested, is not hopeful. Nevertheless, there is little value to be gained by becoming desperate, disillusioned, cynical, or moved by the tactics of rage. Such manifestations neither solve problems nor seriously meet the deeper needs that individuals have in a highly urban society. Thus, it is intellectual and political laziness to yield to the inevitability of taxes and death. Any state of general ferment offers opportunities for great social change and the betterment of the human condition, though nothing, of course, is inevitable. We can do no better than to close with Karl Marx's famous passage:

> *Men make their own history, but they do not make it as they please; they do not make it under circumstances chosen by themselves, but under circumstances directly encountered, given and transmitted from the past. The tradition of all the dead weighs like a nightmare on the brain of the living.*[9]

One important ingredient of America's nightmare is its racist history. The question, therefore, remains: Will our dead racist past that still weighs "on the brain of the living" be overcome in the uncertain and chaotic struggles that lie ahead?

[9]K. Marx, "The Eighteenth Brumaire of Louis Bonaparte," *Karl Marx, Selected Works,* Vol. II. New York: International Publishers, 1933, p. 315.

Index